Windows® CE2 Program[ming] For Dummies®

CW00485578

Essential steps to create a Windows CE application

- ✔ Minimize memory usage
- ✔ Add code to respond to WM_HIBERNATE messages
- ✔ Provide a Windows CE setup program
- ✔ Provide Windows CE help files
- ✔ Provide communication with desktop PCs
- ✔ Test frequently on a real Windows CE device as well as in the emulation environment.

User interface checklist

Use this checklist to ensure that your application conforms to Windows CE standards:

- ✔ The application window is not sizable and doesn't have a caption bar.
- ✔ The application window has a command bar with a menu and toolbar buttons (as appropriate).
- ✔ Dialog boxes have OK and Cancel buttons in the caption bar.
- ✔ The taskbar application button has an icon and a document name.

Windows CE database properties

If you want to do this	Follow this example
Specify a property number	`const WORD HHPR_AUTHOR_ NUMBER=10;`
Specify a property ID with data type	`CEPROPID propAuthorName =MAKELONG(CEVT_ LPWSTR, HHPR_AUTHOR_ NAME);`
Delete a property value in a record	Assign `CEDB_PROPDELETE` to the `wFlags` member of the `CEPROPVAL` variable
Change the sort order	Reopen the database and specify a different index

Solving two common Windows CE programming problems

- ✔ **Displaying an icon in taskbar buttons:** Send a WM_SETICON message to your application window passing the icon handle:
  `SendMessage(hWnd,WM_SETICON, 0, (LPARAM) hIcon);`
- ✔ **Combo boxes with no scrollbars:** A combo box in Windows CE doesn't display the vertical scrollbar in the list box unless the list box is more than 5 lines deep.

...For Dummies: #1 Computer Book Series for Beginners

COMPUTER BOOK SERIES FROM IDG

Windows® CE2 Programming For Dummies®

Cheat Sheet

Using Unicode

Windows CE only supports Unicode and not the ANSI character set. Be sure to:

- ✔ Declare string buffers using the TCHAR data type:
  `TCHAR szBuffer[100];`

- ✔ Use the TEXT or _T macro to convert constants to Unicode:
  `wsprintf(szBuffer, TEXT("my string"));`

- ✔ Keep in mind that Unicode characters take two bytes

- ✔ Use the wide character versions of the standard string library functions — for example, use `wcslen` instead of `strlen`

Indispensable online Windows CE resources

Resource	Description
www.microsoft.com/windowsce	Windows CE news and development tools
microsoft.public.win32. programmer.wince at msnews. microsoft.com.	Windows CE developer newsgroup on news server
www.softpath.ie/windowsce	Windows CE developer information
www.windowsce.com	General Windows CE news and information

...For Dummies: #1 Computer Book Series for Beginners

WINDOWS® CE 2 FOR DUMMIES®

by Nick Grattan

IDG
BOOKS
WORLDWIDE

IDG Books Worldwide, Inc.
An International Data Group Company

Foster City, CA ♦ Chicago, IL ♦ Indianapolis, IN ♦ Southlake, TX

Windows® CE 2 Programming For Dummies®

Published by
IDG Books Worldwide, Inc.
An International Data Group Company
919 E. Hillsdale Blvd.
Suite 400
Foster City, CA 94404
www.idgbooks.com (IDG Books Worldwide Web site)
www.dummies.com (Dummies Press Web site)

Library of Congress Catalog Card No.: 98-70132

ISBN: 0-7645-0304-9

Printed in the United States of America

10 9 8 7 6 5 4 3 2 1

1E/RS/QS/ZY/IN

Distributed in the United States by IDG Books Worldwide, Inc.

Distributed by Macmillan Canada for Canada; by Transworld Publishers Limited in the United Kingdom; by IDG Norge Books for Norway; by IDG Sweden Books for Sweden; by Woodslane Pty. Ltd. for Australia; by Woodslane Enterprises Ltd. for New Zealand; by Longman Singapore Publishers Ltd. for Singapore, Malaysia, Thailand, and Indonesia; by Simron Pty. Ltd. for South Africa; by Toppan Company Ltd. for Japan; by Distribuidora Cuspide for Argentina; by Livraria Cultura for Brazil; by Ediciencia S.A. for Ecuador; by Addison-Wesley Publishing Company for Korea; by Ediciones ZETA S.C.R. Ltda. for Peru; by WS Computer Publishing Corporation, Inc., for the Philippines; by Unalis Corporation for Taiwan; by Contemporanea de Ediciones for Venezuela; by Computer Book & Magazine Store for Puerto Rico; by Express Computer Distributors for the Caribbean and West Indies. Authorized Sales Agent: Anthony Rudkin Associates for the Middle East and North Africa.

For general information on IDG Books Worldwide's books in the U.S., please call our Consumer Customer Service department at 800-762-2974. For reseller information, including discounts and premium sales, please call our Reseller Customer Service department at 800-434-3422.

For information on where to purchase IDG Books Worldwide's books outside the U.S., please contact our International Sales department at 650-655-3200 or fax 650-655-3295.

For information on foreign language translations, please contact our Foreign & Subsidiary Rights department at 650-655-3021 or fax 650-655-3281.

For sales inquiries and special prices for bulk quantities, please contact our Sales department at 650-655-3200 or write to the address above.

For information on using IDG Books Worldwide's books in the classroom or for ordering examination copies, please contact our Educational Sales department at 800-434-2086 or fax 817-251-8174.

For press review copies, author interviews, or other publicity information, please contact our Public Relations department at 650-655-3000 or fax 650-655-3299.

For authorization to photocopy items for corporate, personal, or educational use, please contact Copyright Clearance Center, 222 Rosewood Drive, Danvers, MA 01923, or fax 978-750-4470.

 is a trademark under exclusive license to IDG Books Worldwide, Inc., from International Data Group, Inc.

About the Author

Nick Grattan first became interested in computers while majoring in zoology and entomology at Imperial College, University of London — the move from one type of bug to another seemed natural, although the impression remains that there are more bugs in computing than in zoology.

Nick started developing Windows applications in 1985 with Windows 1.0. He developed a Windows HP2392 terminal emulator over the next four years, working in London, England and Austin, Texas. The product was sold worldwide by Hewlett Packard.

In 1990, Nick moved to Dublin, Ireland, from the USA and joined Software Paths as Technical Director. This leading company specializes in providing training and consultancy in Windows, client server, and Internet development. During his time at Software Paths, Nick has also written numerous articles and given talks throughout Europe. In 1996, Nick was appointed Microsoft Regional Director for Ireland. The Regional Directors are a group of 90 worldwide technology specialists.

Nick started working with the Windows CE version 1.0 beta, and has since developed Windows CE courses and written Windows CE applications.

Nick can be contacted through e-mail at nick@softpath.ie.

ABOUT IDG BOOKS WORLDWIDE

Welcome to the world of IDG Books Worldwide.

IDG Books Worldwide, Inc., is a subsidiary of International Data Group, the world's largest publisher of computer-related information and the leading global provider of information services on information technology. IDG was founded more than 25 years ago and now employs more than 8,500 people worldwide. IDG publishes more than 275 computer publications in over 75 countries (see listing below). More than 60 million people read one or more IDG publications each month.

Launched in 1990, IDG Books Worldwide is today the #1 publisher of best-selling computer books in the United States. We are proud to have received eight awards from the Computer Press Association in recognition of editorial excellence and three from *Computer Currents'* First Annual Readers' Choice Awards. Our best-selling *...For Dummies®* series has more than 30 million copies in print with translations in 30 languages. IDG Books Worldwide, through a joint venture with IDG's Hi-Tech Beijing, became the first U.S. publisher to publish a computer book in the People's Republic of China. In record time, IDG Books Worldwide has become the first choice for millions of readers around the world who want to learn how to better manage their businesses.

Our mission is simple: Every one of our books is designed to bring extra value and skill-building instructions to the reader. Our books are written by experts who understand and care about our readers. The knowledge base of our editorial staff comes from years of experience in publishing, education, and journalism — experience we use to produce books for the '90s. In short, we care about books, so we attract the best people. We devote special attention to details such as audience, interior design, use of icons, and illustrations. And because we use an efficient process of authoring, editing, and desktop publishing our books electronically, we can spend more time ensuring superior content and spend less time on the technicalities of making books.

You can count on our commitment to deliver high-quality books at competitive prices on topics you want to read about. At IDG Books Worldwide, we continue in the IDG tradition of delivering quality for more than 25 years. You'll find no better book on a subject than one from IDG Books Worldwide.

John Kilcullen
CEO
IDG Books Worldwide, Inc.

Steven Berkowitz
President and Publisher
IDG Books Worldwide, Inc.

Eighth Annual
Computer Press
Awards ≥1992

Ninth Annual
Computer Press
Awards ≥1993

Tenth Annual
Computer Press
Awards ≥1994

Eleventh Annual
Computer Press
Awards ≥1995

IDG Books Worldwide, Inc., is a subsidiary of International Data Group, the world's largest publisher of computer-related information and the leading global provider of information services on information technology. International Data Group publishes over 275 computer publications in over 75 countries. Sixty million people read one or more International Data Group publications each month. International Data Group's publications include: **ARGENTINA:** Buyer's Guide, Computerworld Argentina, PC World Argentina; **AUSTRALIA:** Australian Macworld, Australian PC World, Australian Reseller News, Computerworld, IT Casebook, Network World, Publish, Webmaster; **AUSTRIA:** Computerwelt Osterreich, Networks Austria, PC Tip Austria; **BANGLADESH:** PC World Bangladesh; **BELARUS:** PC World Belarus; **BELGIUM:** Data News; **BRAZIL:** Annuário de Informática, Computerworld, Connections, Macworld, PC Player, PC World, Publish, Reseller News, Supergamepower; **BULGARIA:** Computerworld Bulgaria, Network World Bulgaria, PC & MacWorld Bulgaria; **CANADA:** CIO Canada, Client/Server World, ComputerWorld Canada, InfoWorld Canada, NetworkWorld Canada, WebWorld; **CHILE:** Computerworld Chile, PC World Chile; **COLOMBIA:** Computerworld Colombia, PC World Colombia; **COSTA RICA:** PC World Centro America; **THE CZECH AND SLOVAK REPUBLICS:** Computerworld Czechoslovakia, Macworld Czech Republic, PC World Czechoslovakia; **DENMARK:** Communications World Danmark, Computerworld Danmark, Macworld Danmark, PC World Danmark, Techworld Denmark; **DOMINICAN REPUBLIC:** PC World Republica Dominicana; **ECUADOR:** PC World Ecuador; **EGYPT:** Computerworld Middle East, PC World Middle East; **EL SALVADOR:** PC World Centro America; **FINLAND:** MikroPC, Tietoverkko, Tietoviikko; **FRANCE:** Distributique, Hebdo, Info PC, Le Monde Informatique, Macworld, Reseaux & Telecoms, WebMaster France; **GERMANY:** Computer Partner, Computerwoche, Computerwoche Extra, Computerwoche FOCUS, Global Online, Macwelt, PC Welt; **GREECE:** Amiga Computing, GamePro Greece, Multimedia World; **GUATEMALA:** PC World Centro America; **HONDURAS:** PC World Centro America; **HONG KONG:** Computerworld Hong Kong, PC World Hong Kong, Publish in Asia; **HUNGARY:** ABCD CD-ROM, Computerworld Szamitastechnika, Internetto online Magazine, PC World Hungary, PC-X Magazin Hungary; **ICELAND:** Tolvuheimur PC World Island; **INDIA:** Information Communications World, Information Systems Computerworld, PC World India, Publish in Asia; **INDONESIA:** InfoKomputer PC World, Komputek Computerworld, Publish in Asia; **IRELAND:** ComputerScope, PC Live!; **ISRAEL:** Macworld Israel, People & Computers/Computerworld; **ITALY:** Computerworld Italia, Macworld Italia, Networking Italia, PC World Italia; **JAPAN:** DTP World, Macworld Japan, Nikkei Personal Computing, OS/2 World Japan, SunWorld Japan, Windows NT World, Windows World Japan; **KENYA:** PC World East African; **KOREA:** Hi-Tech Information, Macworld Korea, PC World Korea; **MACEDONIA:** PC World Macedonia; **MALAYSIA:** Computerworld Malaysia, PC World Malaysia, Publish in Asia; **MALTA:** PC World Malta; **MEXICO:** Computerworld Mexico, PC World Mexico; **MYANMAR:** PC World Myanmar; **NETHERLANDS:** Computer! Totaal, LAN Internetworking Magazine, LAN World Buyers Guide, Macworld Netherlands, Net, WebWereld; **NEW ZEALAND:** Absolute Beginners Guide and Plain & Simple Series, Computer Buyer, Computer Industry Directory, Computerworld New Zealand, MTB, Network World, PC World New Zealand; **NICARAGUA:** PC World Centro America; **NORWAY:** Computerworld Norge, CW Rapport, Datamagasinet, Financial Rapport, Kursguide Norge, Macworld Norge, Multimediaworld Norge, PC World Ekspress Norge, PC World Nettverk, PC World Norge, PC World ProduktGuide Norge; **PAKISTAN:** Computerworld Pakistan; **PANAMA:** PC World Panama; **PEOPLE'S REPUBLIC OF CHINA:** China Computer Users, China Computerworld, China InfoWorld, China Telecom World Weekly, Computer & Communication, Electronic Design China, Electronics Today, Electronics Weekly, Game Software, PC World China, Popular Computer Week, Software Weekly, Software World, Telecom World; **PERU:** Computerworld Peru, PC World Profesional Peru, PC World SoHo Peru; **PHILIPPINES:** Click!, Computerworld Philippines, PC World Philippines, Publish in Asia; **POLAND:** Computerworld Poland, Computerworld Special Report Poland, Cyber, Macworld Poland, Networld Poland, PC World Komputer; **PORTUGAL:** Cerebro/PC World, Computerworld/Correio Informático, Dealer World Portugal, Mac*In/PC*In Portugal, Multimedia World; **PUERTO RICO:** PC World Puerto Rico; **ROMANIA:** Computerworld Romania, PC World Romania, Telecom Romania; **RUSSIA:** Computerworld Russia, Mir PK, Publish, Seti; **SINGAPORE:** Computerworld Singapore, PC World Singapore, Publish in Asia; **SLOVENIA:** Monitor; **SOUTH AFRICA:** Computing SA, Network World SA, Software World SA; **SPAIN:** Communicaciones World España, Computerworld España, Dealer World España, Macworld España, PC World España; **SRI LANKA:** Infolink PC World; **SWEDEN:** CAP&Design, Computer Sweden, Corporate Computing Sweden, Internetworld Sweden, it.branschen, Macworld Sweden, MaxiData Sweden, MikroDatorn, Nätverk & Kommunikation, PC World Sweden, PCAktiv, Windows World Sweden; **SWITZERLAND:** Computerworld Schweiz, Macworld Schweiz, PCtip; **TAIWAN:** Computerworld Taiwan, Macworld Taiwan, NEW ViSiON/Publish, PC World Taiwan, Windows World Taiwan; **THAILAND:** Publish in Asia, Thai Computerworld; **TURKEY:** Computerworld Turkiye, Macworld Turkiye, Network World Turkiye, PC World Turkiye; **UKRAINE:** Computerworld Kiev, Multimedia World Ukraine, PC World Ukraine; **UNITED KINGDOM:** Acorn User UK, Amiga Action UK, Amiga Computing UK, Apple Talk UK, Computng, Macworld, Parents and Computers UK, PC Advisor, PC Home, PSA Pro, The WEB; **UNITED STATES:** Cable in the Classroom, CIO Magazine, Computerworld, DOS World, Federal Computer Week, GamePro Magazine, InfoWorld, I-Way, Macworld, Network World, PC Games, PC World, Publish, Video Event, THE WEB Magazine, and WebMaster; online webzines: JavaWorld, NetscapeWorld, and SunWorld Online; **URUGUAY:** InfoWorld Uruguay; **VENEZUELA:** Computerworld Venezuela, PC World Venezuela; and **VIETNAM:** PC World Vietnam.   3/24/97

Dedication

To Therese and Hannah — the best girls in the world! Thanks for your never-ending patience and understanding.

Author's Acknowledgments

Many thanks to Jill Pisoni, who gave me the opportunity to write this book, and to the other members of IDG Books who contributed so much to making this book happen: Tere Drenth, Ryan Rader, and Joe Jansen. I'm especially indebted to Tere for helping to get this book finished — I hope your Christmas was not too disturbed. Special thanks also to the technical editors, Mike Frey and Chris Heitmann.

I would like to thank Mike Hegeman of Hewlett Packard, who supplied an HP 320LX with Windows CE 2.0 ROMS for testing these samples, and to Microsoft for supplying early versions of the Windows CE development tools and for answering my questions.

I'd also like to thank my colleagues at Software Paths, Dublin, who listened to my ramblings about Windows CE and provided valuable feedback.

Publisher's Acknowledgments

We're proud of this book; please register your comments through our IDG Books Worldwide Online Registration Form located at http://my2cents.dummies.com.

Some of the people who helped bring this book to market include the following:

Acquisitions, Development, and Editorial

Project Editor: Tere Drenth

Senior Acquisitions Editor: Jill Pisoni

Copy Editors: William A. Barton, Andrea C. Boucher, John Edwards, Brian Kramer, Joe Jansen, Rowena Rappaport, Tina Sims

Technical Reviewers: Mike Frey, Chris Heitmann

CD Reviewer: Chris Heitmann of Digital Marketing Concepts (CAH@dmc networks.com)

Media Development Manager: Joyce Pepple

Permissions Editor: Heather H. Dismore

Editorial Manager: Elaine Brush

Editorial Assistant: Paul E. Kuzmic

Production

Associate Project Coordinator: Karen York

Layout and Graphics: Steve Arany, Cameron Booker, Lou Boudreau, Maridee V. Ennis, Angela F. Hunckler, Jane E. Martin, Drew R. Moore, Heather Pearson, Brent Savage, Deirdre Smith

Proofreaders: Christine Berman, Chris Collins, Michelle Croninger, Nancy L. Reinhardt, Rebecca Senninger, Janet M. Withers

Indexer: Liz Cunningham

Special Help

Kathleen Dobie, Copy Editor; Ryan Rader, Project Editor; Joell Smith, Associate Technical Editor

General and Administrative

IDG Books Worldwide, Inc.: John Kilcullen, CEO; Steven Berkowitz, President and Publisher

IDG Books Technology Publishing: Brenda McLaughlin, Senior Vice President and Group Publisher

Dummies Technology Press and Dummies Editorial: Diane Graves Steele, Vice President and Associate Publisher; Mary Bednarek, Acquisitions and Product Development Director; Kristin A. Cocks, Editorial Director

Dummies Trade Press: Kathleen A. Welton, Vice President and Publisher; Kevin Thornton, Acquisitions Manager

IDG Books Production for Dummies Press: Beth Jenkins Roberts, Production Director; Cindy L. Phipps, Manager of Project Coordination, Production Proofreading, and Indexing; Kathie S. Schutte, Supervisor of Page Layout; Shelley Lea, Supervisor of Graphics and Design; Debbie J. Gates, Production Systems Specialist; Robert Springer, Supervisor of Proofreading; Debbie Stailey, Special Projects Coordinator; Tony Augsburger, Supervisor of Reprints and Bluelines; Leslie Popplewell, Media Archive Coordinator

Dummies Packaging and Book Design: Patti Crane, Packaging Specialist; Kavish + Kavish, Cover Design

◆

The publisher would like to give special thanks to Patrick J. McGovern, without whom this book would not have been possible.

◆

Contents at a Glance

Cartoons at a Glance

By Rich Tennant

"ONE OF THEIR BLIMPS BROKE ITS MOORING AND FLOATED IN HERE ABOUT TWO HOURS AGO. THEY HAVEN'T BEEN ABLE TO LOCATE IT YET."

page 335

page 221

"OKAY, SO MAYBE COMDEX WASN'T READY FOR OUR MICROWAVE SLOW-COOKER THIS YEAR, BUT I STILL THINK WE SHOULD GO AHEAD WITH THE TRACKBALL GARAGE DOOR OPENER."

page 7

page 127

"YOU KNOW, IF WE CAN ALL KEEP THE TITTERING DOWN, I, FOR ONE, WOULD LIKE TO HEAR MORE ABOUT KEN'S NEW POINTING DEVICE FOR HANDHELD PCs."

page 281

IN A STROKE OF SELF-RELIANCE, RAY EXTENDS THE POWER OF HIS H/PC BY TAPPING INTO THE BATTERY OF HIS SLEEPING NEIGHBOR'S HEARING AID.

page 179

Fax: 978-546-7747 • E-mail: the5wave@tiac.net

Table of Contents

Introduction

· ·

*W*indows CE represents the latest direction Microsoft has taken in moving the Windows family of operating systems out to new platforms and computers. While Windows NT moves into the territory occupied by the largest computers, Windows CE moves to the very smallest devices, and is aimed at mass markets with huge potential.

Windows CE is an *embedded operating system* or *EOS*. An EOS is an operating system that is built into a device, and typically runs a single application that runs the device. This means that Windows CE is working its way into non-computer devices as well as palmtop and handheld PCs (H/PCs). Windows CE has a modular structure, which allows designers to pick and choose the facilities and features they require, such as communication options, the types of user interfaces, and hardware support. However, the application programming techniques remain the same, regardless of the device that Windows CE is used in.

Windows CE offers an elegance and simplicity that isn't found in Windows NT and Windows 95. It is a pure, 32-bit operating system that supports dynamic memory management and true multiprocessing with threads, but without the baggage that Windows NT and Windows 95 has, such as 16-bit and MS-DOS application support. This simplicity makes Windows CE fun and enjoyable to program.

About This Book

In this book, I cover the essential programming techniques that you need in order to write Windows CE applications. I try to keep the text as simple as possible, avoiding complex, irrelevant detail.

You can get a solid understanding of how to program Windows CE by reading this book from cover to cover. However, if you already have ideas on the techniques that your Windows CE application requires, you can jump straight in at the chapters you need — flip from Chapter 14 to Chapter 5 — and apply the techniques I describe.

Of course, I'm not able to cover absolutely everything that every person could possibly want to know about Windows CE programming. So, if you can't find your once-in-a-blue-moon questions answered here, I encourage you to read the relevant online help descriptions of functions used in this book, and to use the resources listed in Chapter 24.

System Requirements

To make full use of Windows CE 2 programming (and this book, as well), you need to have:

- ✔ A Pentium PC with a CD-ROM and at least 24MB of memory.
- ✔ Windows NT 4.0 for testing Windows CE 2.0 applications on your PC.
- ✔ Microsoft Visual C++, Version 5.0.
- ✔ Windows CE Toolkit for Visual C++.

If you aim to distribute Windows CE applications, you also need at least one Windows CE device for testing. You don't want to rely entirely on testing applications on your PC.

And What About You?

I can think of plenty of reasons why you're reading this book. You may be:

- ✔ An experienced Visual C++ programmer and want to find out what's different about Windows CE programming.
- ✔ An embedded systems developer encountering Windows development in any shape or form for the first time.
- ✔ A system designer or project manager wanting to find out what's involved in developing.
- ✔ A person who picked up this book by mistake while really looking for *Beer For Dummies* (now *that's* a book I would like to have written!).

Here are my assumptions about you:

- ✔ You have worked with the C and C++ languages. Several C and C++ features show up in chapters without much explanation, and a solid understanding of those two languages is essential for understanding this book.
- ✔ You have used a Windows CE device, such as a handheld PC (H/PC).

If this doesn't sound like you, run to the nearest bookstore for *C For Dummies,* by Dan Gookin, or *C++ For Dummies,* 2nd Edition, by Steven R. Davis (both by IDG Books Worldwide, Inc.). And if you need help working your H/PC, check out *Windows CE 2 For Dummies,* by Jinjer L. Simon (IDG Books Worldwide, Inc.).

You will be at an advantage if you've already done some programming using the Microsoft Foundation Classes (MFC) or the Windows Application Programming Interface (API, which is also known as Win32).

How to Use This Book

The rules for using this book are pretty simple. All code appears in a special font, like this:

```
#include <windows.h>
```

Some code will contain text in *italics*. This text is a place holder, and you can substitute other values. For example:

```
wsprintf(szBuffer, "An output string");
```

Be sure to follow the examples' syntax exactly. Always remember that C and C++ are *case sensitive languages*. You need to follow the mix of upper- and lowercase exactly.

This book contains code fragments that illustrate the points that I make. You may find it easier to see the whole picture if you look at the code samples on the CD-ROM.

You will also see text like wsprintf in the book. This shows a function, variable, or value from a code sample that I describe.

Finally, In some of the steps, I show bold code to highlight one or more lines of code that should be added to existing code (such as the following):

```
LRESULT CALLBACK WndProc(HWND, UINT, WPARAM, LPARAM);
HINSTANCE  hInst = NULL;
```

How This Book Is Organized

This book consists of six major segments, or *parts*. Each part contains several chapters, and each chapter contains several sections. You can read the book start-to-finish if you like, or you can dive in wherever you need help on a particular topic. The sections that follow provide a breakdown of what you find in each of the six parts.

Part I: Building a Windows CE Application

In this part, I help you gather the tools required to build Windows CE applications. Also in this part, I tell you about command bars, dialog boxes, and drawings. Finally, I describe some of the other development environments (such as the Microsoft Windows CE Toolkit for Visual Basic 5.0 and Microsoft Windows CE 2.0 Toolkit for Visual J++) that you can use to build Windows CE applications.

Part II: Discovering the Unique Features of Windows CE

Creating a setup program, building help files, using Windows CE databases and accessing the contacts database — these topics are all specific to Windows CE applications and may be new to you. Nearly all Windows CE applications use these features, and Part II covers them in detail.

Part III: Peeking Behind the Scenes

Windows CE devices are small and compact — this means that you need to be careful of the amount of memory and other resources that your application uses. In Part III, I explain memory management, processes and threads, power management, and dynamic link libraries (DLLs).

Part IV: Working with the Shell and the Object Store

In Part IV, I describe how to make use of user interface shell features such as shortcuts and notifications (so you can respond run an application in response to an event or at a given time). I also tell you how to add icons to the taskbar status area. Finally, I describe accessing the registry and how file input/output (I/O) works in Windows CE.

Part V: Improving Desktop Connectivity and Communications

Windows CE supports a wide range of different communications options, so in Part V, I describe how to choose the communication technique that is appropriate for your application. I explain serial communications and Windows sockets in detail, as these are two of the most popular techniques.

Part VI: The Part of Tens

Use the chapters in Part VI as a checklist to ensure that your Windows CE applications are up to scratch and to follow the requirements and recommendations of the Windows CE logo program. I also list ten or so useful sources of information about Windows CE programming.

About the CD Appendix

After the Part of Tens, you find an appendix that describes the two cool software demos and the sample applications and code on the CD-ROM. The About the CD Appendix also provides instructions for building and running these applications.

Icons Used in This Book

I use lots of little icons throughout this book to highlight information that is worth a second look:

 This icon identifies cool code samples — located on the CD-ROM — that illustrate how to implement the feature I'm discussing at that point. You can locate the code, and in most cases, copy the appropriate code directly into your own application.

 This icon flags time-saving, practical suggestions or easy ways to solve particular problems.

 Watch out for these icons! If you have time, read every warning carefully — think of them as a help desk that keeps a list of common mistakes made when writing Windows CE applications. You can save hours of development effort by heeding these warnings.

I use this icon to highlight information that is often forgotten, but is very important. Take note of these and commit them to memory, if possible.

This icon identifies information that you can safely skip over — but may not want to because the information is so darned interesting! Sometimes this technical stuff describes *why* something works the way it does, or shows how a Windows NT or Windows 95 feature is implemented (or not implemented) in Windows CE. Regardless, it's a good one to watch for.

I use this icon to direct you to other ...*For Dummies* books — such as *C For Dummies, C++ For Dummies,* or *TCP/IP For Dummies* — that contain all the details that my editor wouldn't let me put in this book (or it would have been over 2,000 pages!).

So, Now What?

Enough chat — time to get started — pick a page and dive right in.

Be sure to break open the seal on the CD, load it into your CD-ROM and open up the sample code for each chapter as you read it. The best way to figure out Windows CE 2 programming is to experiment, so try making changes to the sample code and seeing what happens.

Most of all, I hope you enjoy Windows CE programming. *Go naighre an bothair lait* (don't forget — I live in Ireland!). And here's to you writing great Windows CE applications.

Part I

Building a Windows CE Application

In this part . . .

Windows CE represents one of the most exciting new developments in the Windows family of operating systems in many years, including a new operating system that doesn't need to support MS-DOS or other legacy operating systems. However, because Windows CE uses much of the same Applications Programming Interface (API) as Windows 95 and Windows NT programming, Windows CE has a familiar feel to Windows programmers.

In this part, I introduce you to the Windows CE development environment (which is built around Visual C++ Version 5.0) and step you through compiling and running an application on a Windows CE device. Then, I show you how to build an API application and an MFC application. Finally, I describe the user interface components that are specific to Windows CE.

Ready to get going? Great — time for you to write a Windows CE application!

Chapter 1

Selecting and Testing Windows CE Development Tools

. . . .

In This Chapter

▶ Meeting the three different types of Windows CE devices

▶ Choosing which version of Windows CE to use

▶ Installing your development tools for Windows CE

▶ Building and running an application

. . . .

*I*nstalling and setting up the Windows CE development environment correctly are essential for reliable development. This is especially the case with Windows CE, because development and debugging rely on the communications link between your desktop PC and the Windows CE device. In this chapter, I describe the development tools that you need and then take you through the process of building and running an application — it should be fairly simple because the source code is on the enclosed CD-ROM!

To help you understand some of the terminology used in this chapter (and throughout the book), refer to Table 1-1.

Table 1-1	Definition of Terms
Term	*Explanation*
Installing	This is the process by which the development tools (such as Visual C++ and the Windows CE Toolkit for Visual C++) are copied onto your PC's hard disk and setup options are configured.
Developer Studio	This is the application that you use to develop your application. Developer Studio is supplied as part of Microsoft Visual C++.
Building	An application must be built from the code you write. Building the application results in an executable (.exe) file. This .exe file can then be run.

(continued)

Table 1-1 *(continued)*

Term	Explanation
Running	After you have an executable (.exe) file, your application can be run. Running an application results in the application being loaded into memory and the application window appearing.
Emulation	You can use emulation to run your Windows CE application on your desktop PC, as long as your PC is running Windows NT 4.0.
Testing	You need to run your application so that you can test that the application functions properly.
Debugging	If your application doesn't run correctly, you need to identify where the error is. The debugging process allows you to step through each line of code as the line of code is executed.

The Three Configurations of Windows CE

Windows CE is a compact operating system that can run on a wide variety of devices, ranging from handheld PCs (H/PCs) to the sub-H/PC format and through to video players, automobile information systems, entertainment systems, and computer terminals. (Some people refer to Windows CE as Windows for Washing Machines.) Windows CE is an *embedded operating system* (EOS), which is an operating system that is built into a device, typically runs a single application that controls the device, and can be incorporated into a wide range of household and industrial devices.

Windows CE functions are grouped into building blocks called *modules.* Device manufacturers can build a customized operating system by selecting only those Windows CE modules they require. As you probably expect, you can find a core set of modules that all Windows CE implementations require — these core modules provide fundamental capabilities, such as memory management and the ability to run applications.

Because there are thousands of different combinations of modules and components, it is very difficult to write a single application that can run on all the different combinations. Therefore, Windows CE recognizes three distinct configurations that can be targeted by developers.

To write a Windows CE application, you must first decide what type of configuration to target. Each configuration has its own special characteristics, so supporting all three in one application is very difficult. The three configurations are known as *H/PC (Mercury), Apollo,* and *Gryphon.*

To make developing applications easier, Microsoft provides _emulation_ for all three standard configurations. An emulation is a program which runs on a PC and looks and works like a real Windows CE device. You can run and test your application under emulation, but you eventually need to run your application on a real Windows CE device because the emulation is not perfect.

Handheld PC (H/PC or Mercury)

The H/PC is currently the most familiar configuration, and it's the only configuration that is supported by Windows CE 1.0. The H/PC configuration is also known as Mercury. Figure 1-1 shows a typical emulation screen from an H/PC.

H/PCs have either monochrome or color displays and a keyboard. As with all Windows CE devices, memory is limited (between 2 and 16MB is common for both storing data and running programs). You can add memory by using flash cards, and PCMCIA devices (such as modems and network cards) can also be added.

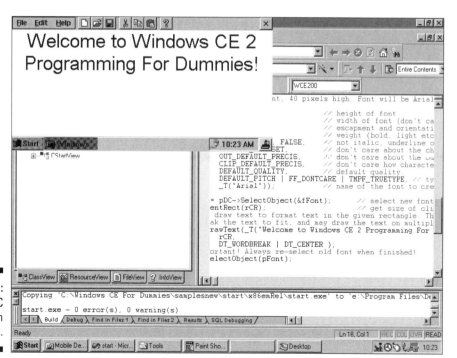

Figure 1-1:
An H/PC
emulation
screen.

The user interface (provided by the Windows CE shell) is similar to that found in Windows 95 and Windows NT. However, note the following distinct differences:

  ✔ **Applications don't have separate menus and toolbars:** These items are combined in a command bar.

  ✔ **Application windows can't be resized:** Application windows in Windows CE don't have sizeable borders — they always occupy the entire area above the taskbar.

The sample applications in this book are designed to run on the HP/C format, but the principles and techniques apply to all types of Windows CE devices.

Gryphon

This Windows CE configuration is even smaller than that of the H/PC — it doesn't even have a physical keyboard! The Gryphon shell (which implements the user interface) is simpler than that found in the H/PC, and the whole device is focused on providing Personal Information Management (PIM)–type features, including address and contact information, calendars and appointments, and task lists. Figure 1-2 shows the Apollo user interface, as displayed in emulation, with the *soft keyboard.* The soft keyboard allows text to be entered as if the device had a real keyboard.

Figure 1-2:
An Apollo user interface, as displayed in emulation, with the soft keyboard displayed.

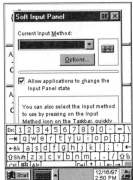

Apollo

Apollo is designed to provide multimedia information, control, and entertainment systems for use in automobiles. The user interface is different both to look at and to program than that for the H/PC. You don't use the standard techniques for creating and controlling windows — instead, Windows CE provides Component Object Model (COM) interfaces.

COM is a programming technique that allows objects to present a programmable interface through which other applications can make use of the object's functionality. COM interfaces consist of functions that return values and take arguments, and can be called from almost any language, including C and C++. COM is now available on Windows CE 2.

Apollo supports a number of interfaces that are not generally found on other Windows CE devices, such as voice recognition and navigation through Global Positioning Satellite (GPS) systems. These devices do not have a keyboard (which is a bonus for road safety). Figure 1-3 shows the user interface as displayed in emulation while running on a PC.

Figure 1-3: A Gryphon user interface as displayed in emulation running on a PC.

The Microsoft Foundation Classes (MFC) that are part of Microsoft Visual C++ for Windows CE 2.0 are designed to work with the H/PC format. You should use the Windows CE 2.0 Software Development Kit (SDK) to develop applications for Gryphon or Apollo. This kit provides emulation environments for all three configurations.

You will probably find it easier to learn to program H/PCs first and then move on to the other configurations (Gryphon or Apollo). Of all three configurations, the H/PC is closest to Windows 95 and Windows NT in the way the user interface looks and is programmed.

Windows CE Version 2.0, 1.01, or 1.0?

This book is about writing Windows CE 2.0 applications. So, it should come as no surprise to you that there was a Windows CE 1.0 (although, in today's mad world of version numbering, it's not always a safe assumption!), and thousands of Windows CE 1.0 devices were sold and are still in use. Applications that were written specifically for Windows CE 2.0 do not run on Windows CE 1.0 devices. You must decide whether to write an application that is compatible with Windows CE 1.0 or to go entirely for Windows CE 2.0.

TIP

All Windows CE 1.0 devices use the Mercury Handheld PC format. Most of these devices can be upgraded to Windows CE 2.0 by simply swapping a small ROM board. Most Windows CE 1.0 users are likely to upgrade, so it's probably safe to go straight for Windows CE 2.0. (Windows CE also offered a version 1.01 as well, but most H/PCs continued to use Windows CE 1.0 even after the release of version 1.01.)

Developer Studio displays an additional toolbar when building Windows CE applications. This toolbar allows you to specify the version of Windows CE (see Figure 1-4). Each version of Windows CE has its own header (a file with an *h* suffix) and library files that define the available functions, and these items are in separate directories. You can view and set the directories for the different Windows CE versions by choosing Tools⇨Options in Developer Studio and then clicking the Directories tab (see Figure 1-5). Each version of Windows CE (1.0, 1.01, and 2.0) has different header and library files, and these files are stored in separate directories. (Fortunately, you generally don't need to change these settings unless the compiler or linker produces errors reporting that header or library files could not be found.)

Figure 1-4:
Specify the
Windows
CE version.

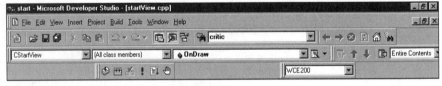

Figure 1-5:
Setting
directories
for header
and library
files.

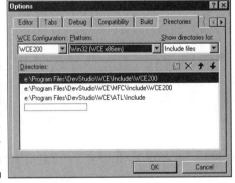

Tooling Up

Getting the right tools together is important for any job. You need to be especially careful when developing with Windows CE, because different tools are available, and some are easier to use than others. For example, you need to know whether you should use The Windows CE Toolkit for Visual C++ or the Windows CE Software Development Kit (SDK). You can also refer to Chapter 8, which looks at some development tools that don't use C or C++.

I recommend that you use the following tools:

- ✔ **Microsoft Visual C++ Version 5.0 Professional or Enterprise Edition:** You can buy this either as a stand-alone package or as part of Microsoft Visual Studio. When using Visual C++, you actually use the Developer Studio to edit, compile, and link your applications — Developer Studio is part of all Visual C++ editions. Developer Studio allows you to develop applications using Java (with Microsoft Visual J++) and Microsoft Visual Interdev (for building Internet applications), as well as Visual C++.

- ✔ **The Windows CE Toolkit for Visual C++:** This is an add-in for Visual C++ that provides all the libraries, compilers, and tools that are required to build Windows CE applications.

Preparing for the differences between Windows 95/NT and Windows CE

Windows CE has a much smaller API than either Windows NT or Windows 95, due to the small devices that it's expected to run on. Many of the differences that you may notice are functions that are either not present or have limited capabilities. The user interface is optimized for the smaller size of display, and the interface uses different controls. (Some Windows CE devices don't have a user interface at all!)

The following are the main differences that you see when comparing Windows CE and Windows 95/NT programming:

- ✔ **Windows CE is missing whole groups of functions that are found in Windows 95/NT.** Windows CE does not support many of the subsystems that you find in Windows NT and Windows 95. For example, Open Database Connectivity (ODBC, which is used for connecting to databases from Windows NT and Windows 95 applications) is not supported.

- ✔ **Windows CE may not have a certain function, but it gives you a better alternative function.** For example, you can use the `TextOut` function to draw text in Windows 95 and Windows NT, but this isn't present in Windows CE. Instead, you should use the much more powerful `DrawText` function that I describe in Chapter 7.

- ✔ **Windows CE ignores the parameters of many functions.** These parameters are generally passed as 0 or `NULL` as appropriate.

- ✔ **Windows CE doesn't use menus and toolbars.** Instead, it uses the command bar, described in Chapter 5.

- ✔ **All strings in Windows CE are Unicode, not ANSI.** Each Unicode character takes *two* bytes to store a single character. The "Unicode" section in Chapter 3 describes how to use Unicode strings.

You *must* have both Visual C++ 5.0 *and* the Windows CE Toolkit for Visual C++ to build Windows CE applications. Windows CE Toolkit for Visual C++ is an add-in and cannot be used without Visual C++ 5.0. You can perform default installations of both packages.

You can install Visual C++ for Windows CE 2.0 under Windows 95 and build Windows CE applications, but you cannot test your applications in *emulation* (that is, run your Windows CE applications on your desktop PC), debug, or use the remote tools. I therefore recommend that you use Windows NT 4.0 for developing Windows CE applications.

The Windows CE Toolkit for Visual C++ provides all the additional tools required to develop Windows CE applications. The following tools are included:

- ✔ Header and library files that define the Windows CE Application Programming Interface (API).

- ✔ Compilers for each of the microprocessors supported by Windows CE (such as the Hitachi SH3 and NEC VR4100 chips or the Philips PR3910 MIPS chip).

- ✔ The Microsoft Foundation Classes (MFC) for Windows CE. These classes are a subset of the MFC used in Windows 95/NT development.

- ✔ Emulations that allow you to run and test your Windows CE applications on your desktop PC.

- ✔ Debuggers that permit debugging of Windows CE applications on the desktop PC under emulation or on the Windows CE devices.

- ✔ Tools, such as remote tools that allow you to monitor what's happening on a Windows CE device, and tools for downloading files.

Some, but not all, of these tools are available in the Microsoft Windows CE 2.0 Software Development Kit (SDK). However, you still need a development environment, such as Microsoft Visual C++ 5.0, to use the SDK. The SDK is a separate package available from Microsoft. I recommend that you use the Microsoft Visual C++ for Windows CE package for programming handheld PCs (H/PCs). You should use the SDK when you're developing for one of the other Windows CE configurations that I describe earlier in this chapter.

Testing Your Installation

You need to test your installation of Visual C++ 5.0 and Windows CE Toolkit for Visual C++. The best way to do this is to build an application that's already been tested. Then, if you get error messages, you know that they are related to how your tools are installed and are not connected with the application itself.

The enclosed CD-ROM contains a completed project that you can use to test your development environment. The project is located in the \samples\start directory and is designed to be built using Visual C++ 5.0 and Windows CE Toolkit for Visual C++. This application was built using the Microsoft Foundation Classes — Chapter 4 explains how to build such an application.

Follow these steps to test your installation:

1. **Copy the files from the CD's \samples\start directory into a directory called \samples\start on your local hard disk.**

   You need to copy the entire contents of the directory \samples\start and the contents of subdirectory \samples\start\res.

2. **Run Visual C++ 5.0 from the Start menu.**

   Choose Start⇨Programs⇨Microsoft Visual C++ 5.0⇨ Microsoft Visual C++5.0 from the Windows NT Start button on the taskbar.

3. **Choose File⇨Open Workspace.**

   This displays the Open Workspace dialog box. You can use this dialog box to choose the workspace you want to open.

4. **Choose the \samples\start\start.dsw file and choose OK.**

   The Open Workspace dialog box that appears works just like a standard File Open dialog box.

Figure 1-6 shows the workspace open in the Developer Studio with the following three main windows, which you use to edit and build your application:

- The Workspace window, which displays the classes, resources, files, or online help pages, depending on which tab is selected

- The Code Edit window, which is used to edit the code that's associated with your applications

- The Output windows, where the compiler, linker, and other tools write information, including errors

Running Applications in Emulation or on Windows CE Devices

Before building your Windows CE application, you need to decide where you want to run it — the so-called *target* device. You do this by selecting the active configuration in Developer Studio after opening the workspace by choosing Build⇨Set Active Configuration. You have the following choices:

- ✔ **Emulation:** Your application is compiled to be run on your desktop PC under Windows NT using a special application that emulates a Windows CE device.

- ✔ **Windows CE Device:** Your application is compiled to be run on a Windows CE device that is attached to your desktop PC. You need to specify the type of chip the Windows CE Device has (such as the SH3 and MIPS chips) as part of the active configuration. If your application is built successfully, Developer Studio copies your application to the Windows CE device and runs it automatically.

- ✔ **Debug/Release:** You need to decide whether you want to produce a *debug* or *release* version of your application. You would generally produce debug versions while developing your application and then produce a release version to deliver to your users.

Debug versions allow you to use the Visual C++ Windows CE remote debugger to execute your application and then trace the execution of each line of code. Debug versions are larger and slower to execute as the applications contain a lot of extra information. You should not distribute a debug version of your application to users.

Workspace   Code Edit window

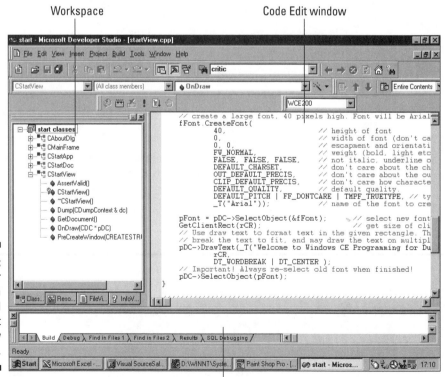

Figure 1-6:
Developer
Studio with
the Visual
C++ project
start.dsw
open.

Output window

If you intend to run your application on a Windows CE device, you must ensure that the communication between the Windows CE device and your desktop PC is working correctly. You can verify this communication by running the Windows CE Mobile Devices application, selecting the application, and ensuring that you can explore the folders and files.

Setting up communications for Windows CE is described in *Windows CE For Dummies* and *Windows CE 2 For Dummies,* both by Jinjer L. Simon (IDG Books Worldwide, Inc.).

Different Windows CE devices use different microprocessor chips (such as the SH3 and MIPS chips), so it's important that you select the correct chip for the Windows CE device that you're using when setting the active configuration. You cannot run a MIPS-compiled application on an SH3 Windows CE device.

To select the active configuration in Developer Studio, follow these steps:

1. **Choose Build⇨Set Active Configuration to display the Set Active Project Configuration dialog box.**

2. **Select the appropriate configuration from the Project Configurations list and choose OK.**

Figure 1-7 shows the Set Active Configuration dialog box with the SH3 Release configuration selected. To build for emulation, select one of the x86em configurations.

Figure 1-7:
Selecting
the Active
Configuration
to set the
target
Windows
CE device.

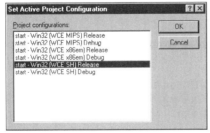

Building Your Application

Building your first application is simple — especially because the code has been written for you. You should have already copied the code for the start workspace from the CD, opened the workspace, and set the active configuration. This workspace contains all the code necessary to build the application. Use the following steps to build your application:

1. Choose Build⇨Build start.exe, or press F7.

After you have built the application, the Remote Executable Path and File Name dialog box appears, as shown in Figure 1-8. This dialog box asks you to confirm the downloading of start.exe to the Windows CE device or emulation location. By default, start.exe is copied to the root folder on the Windows CE device. You can change the location if you like. (For example, choosing windows\start.exe places the file in the windows folder.)

Figure 1-8:
Developer
Studio
prompts you
to download
start.exe
and allows
you to
specify the
location.

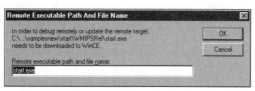

2. Click OK.

The output window in Developer Studio shows you the progress of the download and then displays start.exe - 0 error(s), 0 warning(s), indicating that all is well.

Running Your Application

After you build an application, you can run the application under emulation or on a Windows CE device, depending on the settings that you select for the active configuration. When the application is run, the main application window appears and you can then use the application. To do this, choose Build⇨Execute start.exe from the Developer Studio menu, or press Ctrl+F5.

The start.exe application shows a welcome message like the one shown in Figure 1-9. This welcome message indicates that the application is running correctly. The formatting of the text may be different for you, because formatting depends on the resolution of the Windows CE device. Your application may not run correctly because:

✔ The communications link between your desktop PC and the Windows CE device is not working correctly. You see this message in the Developer Studio output window:

```
Failed to connect with device within 30 seconds, abort-
    ing...
Make sure that repllog.exe ('PC Link') is running on the
    device and try again
```

✔ You selected the incorrect chip for your Windows CE Device (for example, if you select MIPS when your Windows CE device has an SH3 chip). In this case, the application downloads correctly, but fails to run (the application window does not appear).

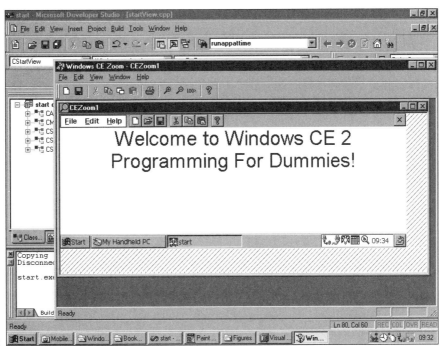

Figure 1-9:
The welcome message from start.exe.

Programming with the API or MFC

When writing a Windows CE application, you can choose from one of the following programming techniques:

Programming using the Application Programming Interface (API). You can use C or C++ to write your applications by calling the Windows CE API directly. (Flip to Chapter 3 for more of the Windows CE API.) The advantages of using the API are as follows:

- ✔ You can use C or C++ as the programming language.

- ✔ It generates the smallest, fastest-executing applications.

- ✔ There is less to learn.

- ✔ You can write applications for any type of Windows CE device, not just the H/PC.

Programming using the Microsoft Foundation Classes (MFC), using only C++. You can create an application using the AppWizard in the Developer Studio. This writes much of the standard code that's required by applications, and you use the MFC classes to add new functionality. The advantages of using the MFC are as follows:

- ✔ Much of the tedious code that's required by all applications is written for you.

- ✔ The application architecture that is provided by MFC makes programs better structured and easier to maintain.

- ✔ You can generally develop applications faster.

Note that each technique has its merits, and the best choice depends mainly on the type of application that you want to write and on your skills and knowledge. Keep in mind these additional pointers:

- ✔ If you're starting from scratch with Windows and know C++, you're better off using the MFC. It takes a little longer to learn, but after you're over the initial hump in the learning curve, you can write applications faster and provide more functionality for your users.

- ✔ If you need to produce applications that are very small and fast or you only want to program using C, then use the API. Using the MFC makes your applications larger and run a bit slower.

The MFC doesn't support all Windows CE API functions, because not all Windows CE functions are included in MFC classes. If you need to add functionality that does not have an MFC class, you must call API functions in an MFC application.

In this book, I describe many different Windows CE programming techniques, mainly using API function techniques. Where appropriate, I show you MFC code as well.

Chapter 2

Understanding Emulation

- -

In This Chapter

▶ Using emulation

▶ Setting the emulation screen size

▶ Using the object store

- -

*E*mulation creates an environment under Windows NT (called, obviously enough, the emulation environment) that is as close as possible to an actual Windows CE device. You can run your Windows CE applications in this emulation environment, testing your applications without downloading them to a Windows CE device. Emulation is provided for the H/PC environment with Visual C++ for Windows CE 2.0 and for the Apollo and Gryphon environments in the SDK.

Emulation is useful for the following reasons:

✔ You don't have to download each newly compiled .exe file to the Windows CE device; this can save a great deal of development time.

✔ Debugging an application that's running under emulation is generally faster than debugging it on a Windows CE device.

Starting and Stopping

The emulation environment automatically starts when you attempt to run your Windows CE application with the active configuration set to x86em release or x86em debug. You can leave the emulation environment running, but close your application before recompiling. Close the emulation environment by selecting the start button *on the emulator* (this is very important!) and then choosing the Suspend menu command.

You can also start the emulation environment using the program empfile.exe — this is described in the section "Storing in the Object Store," later in this chapter.

Substituting Emulation for Testing

Emulation is no substitute for testing on Windows CE devices! You can encounter the following differences:

- ✔ **Emulation has buckets more memory:** You may find yourself using far too much memory for a typical Windows CE device.

- ✔ **Certain API functions support features and options under emulation that are not supported in Windows CE:** This means that you can successfully call one of these functions in emulation from your Windows CE application, but the same function call fails when the application is run on a Windows CE device.

- ✔ **Performance is almost always better under emulation:** Screen redrawing can be much slower on Windows CE devices.

- ✔ **Some user interface and other features don't work:** For example, tooltips for command bar buttons don't work under emulation.

Resolving Screen Resolution

You won't find a standard screen resolution for H/PCs. Many of the original devices provide 480 x 240 pixels of resolution, with some supporting 640 x 200. It's very important to test your application on different resolutions to ensure that all data is viewable at lower resolutions and that you make use of the extra space on higher resolutions. You can change the resolution that's used by emulation through the desktop PC's Registry. First, run the Registry editor and locate the keys, as follows:

1. **Choose Start⇨Run on your desktop PC.**

2. **Enter** regedit **into the** Open **edit box, and choose OK.**

   This runs the Registry editor and opens the Registry for your desktop PC.

3. **Expand the** HKEY_LOCAL_MACHINE **key from the list of keys.**

   This displays a list of keys, including the Software key.

4. **Expand the** Software **key and locate the** Windows CE SDK **under the** Software **key.**

   This key is where the Registry values for the emulation environment are located.

5. Expand the `Emulation,` `Mercury,` **and** `Screen Settings` **keys**.

You're now navigating down through the keys to the screen settings for the Mercury emulation environment. The complete keys are shown in Code Listing 2-1.

Code Listing 2-1

```
HKEY_LOCAL_MACHINE\Software\Microsoft\
    Windows CE Platform SDK\
    Emulation\Mercury\Screen Settings\SM_CXSCREEN
HKEY_LOCAL_MACHINE\Software\Microsoft\
    Windows CE Platform SDK\
    Emulation\Mercury\Screen Settings\SM_CYSCREEN
```

6. Double click the `SM_CXSCREEN` **or** `SM_CYSCREEN` **key to display the Edit DWORD Value dialog box**.

The values for these keys are in hexadecimal or decimal units and represent the width and height of the emulation display in pixels. Double clicking the key displays a dialog box that you can use to edit the key values. Figure 2-1 shows the Edit DWORD Value dialog box in the Registry editor.

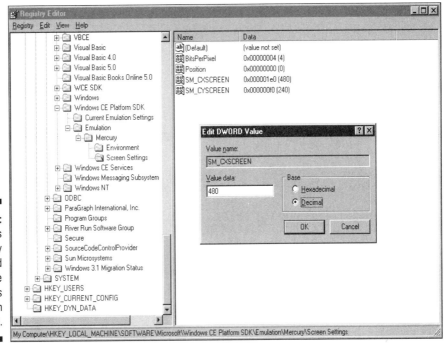

Figure 2-1:
Windows
NT Registry
Editor used
to edit the
emulator's
screen
width.

Storing in the Object Store

The object store is your storage place for all the files and folders that are used in the emulation. For H/PC emulation, the object store file is mercury.obs in the \program files\DevStudio\wce\emul\mercury folder.

You need to copy your application .exe file into this object store (that is, into the file mercury.obs) before you can run the .exe file. Developer Studio automatically copies your .exe file into mercury.obs for you.

You may need to copy other files (such as data files) into the object store. This can be done manually using the desktop PC application empfile.exe, which is located in the \program files\DevStudio\wce\emul\ mercury\windows folder.

The \program files\DevStudio\wce\emul\mercury folder and its subfolders are actually a mirror of the contents of the emulation object store in mercury.obs. You can type **EMFILE -s** to synchronize all the files in the program files\DevStudio\wce\emul\mercury folder and the Object Store.

You can copy individual files using empfile.exe by executing the following command:

```
EMPFILE -c <desktop PC filename and path>
        wce:<wce file filename and path>
```

For example, to copy the file document.txt from the c:\temp directory on your desktop PC into the Windows folder in the emulation object store, enter the following command:

```
EMPFILE -c c:\temp\document.txt wce:\windows\document.txt
```

The application empfile.exe starts the H/PC emulation and also moves files into and out of the object store.

To see information on all the supported options, type **EMPFILE /?**. Notice that you can delete and run files in the object store.

Chapter 3

Building Your First
API Application

In This Chapter

▶ Creating a workspace and project

▶ Writing source code for the application

▶ Building and testing the application

▶ Understanding the code

You can write Windows CE applications using either the Windows CE API with C or C++ or the Microsoft Foundation Classes (MFC) with C++ only. The API allows you to build the fastest and smallest application that can run on a wide range of Windows CE devices. MFC applications tend to be larger, but more functionality is provided, and you are generally required to write less code. MFC applications currently run only on handheld PC (H/PC) devices.

In this chapter, I go through the steps that are required to build an API application. You can follow the steps and build and test the application using the Developer Studio. I suggest that you read this chapter even if you only intend to write MFC applications — the information here can help you understand MFC programming better.

Creating a Developer Studio Workspace and Project

Developer Studio does not provide a Wizard that allows you to build an API application, so you must create a workspace, project files, and source files by yourself. When you first create a workspace and project for the application, the project is contained in the workspace.

TIP

You may not finish developing this application in one session. When you rerun Developer Studio to continue working on your application, you open the *workspace* by selecting File➪Open Workspace. Don't try to open the individual files.

First, create the workspace:

1. **Run Visual C++ 5.0 from the Start menu.**

   Choose Start➪Programs➪Microsoft Visual C++ 5.0➪Microsoft Visual C++5.0 from the Windows NT Start button on the taskbar.

2. **Choose File➪New.**

   The New dialog box appears.

3. **Select the Projects tab of the New dialog box, and click Win32 Application.**

   The Projects tab contains a list of all the different types of projects you can create. You can find Win32 Application in this list.

4. **Enter \samples in the Location text box.**

5. **Enter FirstApp in the Project name text box.**

   Note that the project name is automatically appended to the path you entered in the Location text box.

6. **Uncheck Win32 in the Platforms list box, and ensure that all the other platforms are checked (WCE MIPS, WCE SH, and WCE x86em).**

   The dialog box should now have the same options set as shown in Figure 3-1.

7. **Click the OK button to create the project.**

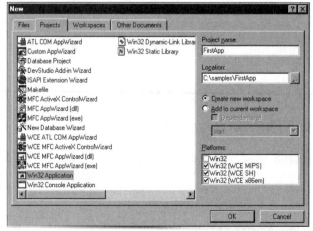

Figure 3-1:
Creating a workspace and project for an API application.

Making a C/C++ Source File

First, I discuss how to create the minimum code that's required to build a Windows CE application using the API.

Follow these steps to create a source file and add it to the project:

1. **Choose File➪New.**

   The New dialog box appears.

2. **Select the Files tab of the New dialog box.**

   This tab displays a list of the different types of files you can add to the project.

3. **Select C++ Source file.**

   (C++ Source file is one of the file types displayed in the list.)

   You should select the C++ Source file option even if you're writing using C. A C compiler no longer exists. Your code is then compiled with the C++ compiler, enforcing stricter programming standards.

4. **Enter** FirstApp.cpp **in the File name text box.**

   Note that the Add to Project check box is automatically selected (see Figure 3-2). As a result, the new file is automatically added to the project. You can also do this manually by choosing Project➪ Add To Project➪Files. This is useful if the files already exist.

5. **Click the OK button to create the file.**

Figure 3-2:
Adding a
new C++
source file
to the
project.

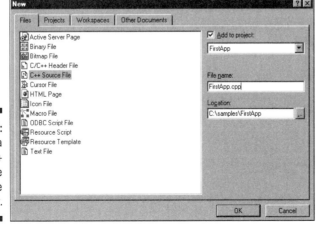

Adding the Code

You must write about 70 lines of code to build the minimum Windows CE application; this code is placed in the FirstApp.cpp file. (See Code Listing 3-1.)

The following code is located on the included CD in the \samples\chapter3\ mincode.txt file. You can open the file with Notepad and copy it into the FirstApp.cpp file. You can use this code as the basis for all your new API applications.

I explain this code after showing you how to build and test the application (see Code Listing 3-1).

Code Listing 3-1

```
#include <windows.h>
#include <commctrl.h>

TCHAR szAppName[ ] = TEXT("Test Windows CE");
TCHAR szTitle[ ]   = TEXT("Test Windows CE Application");

LRESULT CALLBACK WndProc(HWND, UINT, WPARAM, LPARAM);
HINSTANCE  hInst = NULL;

int WINAPI WinMain(HINSTANCE hInstance,
      HINSTANCE hPrevInstance,
      LPTSTR lpCmdLine, int nCmdShow )
{
    HWND           hWnd;
    MSG            msg;
    WNDCLASS       wc;

    memset(&wc, 0, sizeof(wc));
    wc.lpfnWndProc    = (WNDPROC) WndProc;
    wc.hInstance      = hInstance;
    wc.hbrBackground  = (HBRUSH)
          GetStockObject(WHITE_BRUSH);
    wc.lpszClassName  = szAppName;
    RegisterClass(&wc);

    InitCommonControls(); // Initialize common controls
    hInst = hInstance; // Save handle to create command bar

    hWnd = CreateWindow(szAppName,        // Class
                  szTitle,                // Title
                  WS_VISIBLE,             // Style
                  CW_USEDEFAULT,          // x-position
```

```
                        CW_USEDEFAULT,        // y-position
                        CW_USEDEFAULT,        // x size
                        CW_USEDEFAULT,        // y-size
                        NULL,                 // Parent handle
                        NULL,                 // Menu handle
                        hInstance,            // Instance handle
                        NULL);                // Ignored

    ShowWindow(hWnd, nCmdShow);
    UpdateWindow(hWnd);
    while ( GetMessage(&msg, NULL, 0, 0) != FALSE )
        {
        TranslateMessage(&msg);
        DispatchMessage(&msg);
        }
    return(msg.wParam);
}

LRESULT CALLBACK WndProc(HWND hWnd, UINT message,
                    WPARAM uParam, LPARAM lParam )
{
    switch (message)
    {
    case WM_DESTROY:
        PostQuitMessage(0);
        break;
    default:
        return (DefWindowProc(hWnd, message,
            uParam, lParam));
    }
    return (0);
}
```

Building and Testing Your Code

First, be sure that the correct target platform is selected; otherwise, your application may not build correctly. You do this by setting the active configuration.

Flip to Chapter 1 for more detailed information on setting the active configuration.

1. **Select Build⇨Set Active Configuration.**

   The Set Active Project Configuration dialog box appears, containing a list of all the valid project configurations.

2. **For emulation mode, select the WCE x86em Release or Debug project.**

3. **For Hitachi SH3 chips, select the WCE SH Release or Debug project.**

4. **For an NEC, Phillips, or other MIPS processor, select the WCE MIPS Release or Debug project.**

   Choose your project from the project list in the Set Active Project Configuration dialog box. For this sample code, select Release, because you aren't going to debug the code.

5. **Build the application by choosing Build⇨Build FirstApp.exe, or press F7.**

   The Remote Executable and Filename dialog box appears when the build operation is complete. If you don't see this dialog box, your application has errors.

   The most likely reason for errors in building the application is errors in the code you typed. Check carefully that the code matches exactly what's shown in Code Listing 3-1. You can copy this code from the CD to avoid typing errors.

6. **Click Yes in the Remote Executable and Filename dialog box.**

   This dialog box confirms that your application is downloading to the Windows CE device or the emulation environment. After clicking Yes, the application downloads, and the message `FirstApp.exe - 0 error(s), 0 warning(s)` appears in the output window in Developer Studio. The most likely reason for errors at this stage is that the communications link between your PC and Windows CE device is not working correctly.

7. **Execute the application by selecting Build⇨Execute FirstApp.exe.**

   You now see your application running either on the Windows CE device or in the emulation environment, depending on the project you selected in the Set Active Project Configuration dialog box.

Although it is functional, this application is a bit Spartan — I did say this is the *minimum* code required for a Windows CE application! In fact, this code presents you with only a blank window; you see no buttons or other features. How do you close this application? Follow these steps:

1. **Press and hold Alt.**

2. **Tap once (on a Windows CE device) or click once (when running in the emulation environment) on the application's entry in the taskbar.**

   The system menu appears.

3. **Choose Close from the menu choices.**

You can press Ctrl+Alt+Delete on a Windows CE device, and Windows CE displays a list of running tasks. Then select a task and choose End Task to terminate the application.

Changing to Unicode Strings

Before explaining Code Listing 3-1, I have to briefly discuss Unicode characters. Most programmers grew up in a world where the data type *char* was a byte and 8 bits represented all characters. The character set standards set by ANSI define the characters that are used by all 256 codes provided by single-byte characters.

Countries around the world use far more than 256 characters, so a byte is not sufficient to define all of these different characters. To solve this problem, the Unicode standard was proposed, whereby a character is represented by 2 bytes (or 16 bits).

Windows 95 provides some support for Unicode, although most strings are held using 8-bit characters. You can write Windows NT programs to use either ANSI or Unicode strings, but Windows CE *only* supports Unicode. It's time to find out how to program using Unicode characters!

I thought moving to Unicode would be easy — just tell the compiler that I want a character to use 16 bits, and it would perform the conversion. This is, unfortunately, not the case. But as you figure out how to program Unicode character strings, it will become second nature.

Declaring Unicode strings

A char in C or C++ is always a single byte, regardless of whether you're programming for an operating system that supports Unicode. You must use a new data type for declaring variables to hold Unicode characters.

The following code declares a Unicode string buffer that can hold 30 characters:

```
TCHAR szBuffer[30];
```

Windows CE defines various data types for creating pointers to Unicode string buffers. The most useful type is LPWSTR, although you often see LPTSTR used as well.

Unlike Windows 95 and Windows NT, you don't need to worry about whether you're calling an API function that supports Unicode or ANSI strings, because all strings are Unicode!

Replacing standard string functions

You must replace standard string functions (such as `strlen`) with Unicode equivalents (`wcslen`, in the case of `strlen`). The standard string functions all expect a single byte character string, and fail if a Unicode character string is passed to them.

You can find the Unicode version of a string function by searching for the ANSI version (for example, `strlen`) in the C++ online help. The Unicode versions of these functions are documented in the same section.

Converting string constants

You must tell the compiler to convert all string constants (that is, strings enclosed in double quotation marks) to Unicode. By default, string constants are ANSI, with each character taking a single byte.

Windows CE provides the `TEXT` macro for this purpose. In the following code, I create a Unicode string pointer that points at a Unicode string constant:

```
LPWSTR lpMyBuffer = TEXT("This is a Unicode String");
```

The MFC (described in Chapter 4) uses a different macro (one called `_T`), but the effect is the same, as shown in the following example:

```
LPWSTR lpMyBuffer = _T("This is a Unicode String");
```

Understanding How the Code Works

I now describe the source code in FirstApp.cpp and explain how it works. Don't be discouraged — it may be a lot to take in at one time. If, on the first reading, you get a reasonable overall understanding but don't fully appreciate every detail, you're doing well.

You can take much of the code as written and simply use it in your applications. As you become more adventurous, you may explore the code more deeply, especially if you want to use more advanced features.

Starting with the declarations

First, Code Listing 3-2 shows the declarations and related lines that appear at the start of the source file.

Code Listing 3-2

```
#include <windows.h>
#include <commctrl.h>

TCHAR szAppName[ ] = TEXT("Test Windows CE");
TCHAR szTitle[ ]   = TEXT("Test Windows CE Application");

LRESULT CALLBACK WndProc(HWND, UINT, WPARAM, LPARAM);
HINSTANCE  hInst = NULL;
```

Windows.h contains all the data type and structure definitions and proto-types for the Windows CE API functions. Commctrl.h contains similar information for common controls, including the Windows CE command bar.

Next, I declare and initialize two global variables: szAppName and szTitle. These are Unicode strings. Finally, I create a function prototype for the WndProc function (defined in the section "Declaring message-handling functions").

Running applications, windows, and WinMain

Windows CE runs an application by calling a function called WinMain in the application. Typically, applications create a main application window. At some stage, the user closes the main application window, and this window then instructs the application to terminate.

The WinMain function declaration typically looks like Code Listing 3-3.

Code Listing 3-3

```
int WINAPI WinMain(HINSTANCE hInstance,
     HINSTANCE hPrevInstance,
     LPTSTR lpCmdLine, int nCmdShow )
```

Most people think of an application (which executes code and does processing) and the application window (which the user sees and interacts with) as being one and the same. In fact, they are two separate entities. The application does not automatically terminate when the application window is closed. You can have an application running with no windows open.

The WinMain function has the following elements:

- int: This is the function's return type. The value that is returned from this function is the application's exit or return code.

- ✔ WINAPI: This declares that the function uses the typical Windows calling convention.

- ✔ HINSTANCE hInstance: This passes the instance handle to the application. This value is necessary when using resources (such as dialog boxes and bitmaps).

- ✔ HINSTANCE hPrevInstance: You can ignore this. It is no longer used and always has a NULL value.

- ✔ LPTSTR lpCmdLine: This is a pointer to the Unicode command line string that the application was launched with. This typically contains a filename or instructions to be carried out by the application.

- ✔ int nCmdShow: This is a value that indicates how the main application window should appear. This value can specify whether you want the window to be hidden or appear maximized.

In this application, WinMain creates and manages the main application window.

Registering windows

Before you can create a window, you must first register a class. Follow these steps to register a class and then create a window:

1. **Register a window class with a particular name and information on how windows of that class are to appear and behave.**

   You use the RegisterClass function to register a class whose information is provided in a WNDCLASS structure.

2. **Create one or more windows of that class using the** CreateWindow **function.**

   This function returns a *handle* to the window. Every window has a number that uniquely identifies it, and this is called a handle.

Note that the window class that you are registering is *not* a C++ class. It is simply some information that specifies the characteristics of windows that are to be created from that class.

Table 3-1 describes each member of the WNDCLASS structure that is required to define the class for the application window. Code Listing 3-4 shows you how a WNDCLASS structure is initialized to '0's using memset, assigned the necessary values to define the class, and then passed to RegisterClass to register this new class with Windows CE.

Table 3-1	WNDCLASS Members That Are Used to Define a Windows Class	

Member	*Purpose*
`lpfnWndProc`	The name of the function that responds to messages sent to the window by Windows CE. Windows CE sends messages to a window to notify it of events such as a stylus tap or key press. (Don't forget that Windows CE devices don't have mice. Instead, a *stylus* is used to select objects on the screen by tapping.)
`hInstance`	The instance handle that is passed to the application by Windows CE is assigned to this member. The instance handle indicates which application owns the registered window class. Window classes are automatically unregistered when the application terminates.
`hbrBackground`	The "brush" that is used to repaint the background of the window when it needs to be redrawn. In this case, the `GetStockObject` function is used to obtain a handle from Windows CE to the standard white brush.
`lpszClassName`	Each class needs to have name, and this member points to the `szAppName` string buffer that's declared at the start of the source file.

Code Listing 3-4

```
WNDCLASS      wc;

memset(&wc, 0, sizeof(wc));// init. the structure to '0's
wc.lpfnWndProc    = (WNDPROC) WndProc;
wc.hInstance      = hInstance;
wc.hbrBackground  = (HBRUSH) GetStockObject(WHITE_BRUSH);
wc.lpszClassName  = szAppName;
RegisterClass(&wc);
```

Other WNDCLASS members

Additional fields are defined in WNDCLASS but are not used here. Most of these fields are irrelevant in Windows CE programming, but are used when writing Windows NT and Windows 95 applications. For example, the hCursor member is used to set the mouse cursor (whatever pointer, hourglass, or cursor that you design) that appears when the mouse cursor is moved over the window. You cannot set a cursor for a window with Windows CE. The lpszMenuName member points to a string containing the name of a menu to be displayed in the window. Menus are created using command bars in Windows CE, so you cannot use the lpszMenuName member to define the menu for a window.

Creating windows

After a window class has been created, you can call the CreateWindow function to create windows of that class.

Code Listing 3-5 makes a call to CreateWindow and is returned a handle to the newly created window. As you can see, CreateWindow takes one or two arguments, which are described in Table 3-2.

Code Listing 3-5

```
hWnd = CreateWindow(szAppName,    // Class name
            szTitle,              // Title
            WS_VISIBLE,           // Style
            CW_USEDEFAULT,        // x-position
            CW_USEDEFAULT,        // y-position
            CW_USEDEFAULT,        // x-size
            CW_USEDEFAULT,        // y-size
            NULL,                 // Parent handle
            NULL,                 // Menu handle
            hInstance,            // Instance handle
            NULL);                // Ignored
```

Table 3-2   Arguments That Are Passed to CreateWindow for an Application Window

Argument	Purpose
szAppName	The name of a class that was previously registered using RegisterClass.

Argument	Purpose
szTitle	A pointer to a string to be used as the title for the window. This text appears in the taskbar icon for this application.
WS_VISIBLE	The window's *style*. The style allows you to specify the appearance of the window, such as the type of its border. In this case, WS_VISIBLE specifies that the window should be made visible after it's created. You should always specify at least one style in a Windows CE application window; otherwise, the window has a caption bar, which is not standard.
CW_USEDEFAULT	This constant value is passed to four arguments. These arguments specify the upper-left location for the window and its width and height. CW_USEDEFAULT specifies the default location for the window which, in the case of Windows CE, causes the application window to occupy the entire desktop.
Parent Window	The first NULL value specifies the parent of this window. Application windows don't have a parent.
Menu Handle	The second NULL value specifies the menu for this window. Windows CE applications never use this argument to specify a window. Instead, you use the command bar.
hInstance	The instance handle of the application that owns the window.
Ignored	The last NULL value can be used to pass data to the window on creation. You can safely ignore this argument.

The following code shows the next calls that you make. After you create the window, call the ShowWindow function to ensure that the window appears according to the value that's passed to the application in nCmdShow. Next, call UpdateWindow to ensure that you repainted the window and that it's up to date.

```
ShowWindow(hWnd, nCmdShow);
UpdateWindow(hWnd);
```

Notice that the ShowWindow function must specify *which* window to show. The function specifies the window by passing the window handle that returns from calling CreateWindow.

Coding the window message loop

Every windows application that displays a window must have a *message loop.* This code is located at the end of WinMain and consists of a while loop that constantly calls the GetMessage function.

GetMessage returns with the next message for any window in the application and places data about the message in the variable msg (which is a structure of type MSG). Note that this function does not return until there *is* a message for the application.

A message can describe a key press or a stylus tap. Each message is destined for a particular window in the application. For example, in the case of a stylus tap, it is the window that is tapped. For a key press, it is the window with the input focus.

The body of the loop first calls TranslateMessage. This function translates multiple messages into other messages. For example, a key up message and a key down message are translated to a key press message. Next, you call DispatchMessage to send the message on to the appropriate window, as shown in Code Listing 3-6.

Code Listing 3-6

```
while ( GetMessage(&msg, NULL, 0, 0) != FALSE )
      {
      TranslateMessage(&msg);
      DispatchMessage(&msg);
      }
   return(msg.wParam);
```

Note that a message is really only data that is contained in an MSG structure.

Declaring message-handling functions

How does a window handle a message? If you look back to when you registered the window class, you see that the window specified the function name WndProc. This is a special function, called a *message-handling function,* that Windows CE calls whenever a message is destined for a window of that class.

Every window must have a message-handling function that Windows CE calls when a message is destined for that window. Message-handling functions always have the following declaration:

```
LRESULT CALLBACK WndProc(HWND hWnd, UINT message,
                  WPARAM uParam, LPARAM lParam )
```

A message-handling function has the following elements:

- ✔ LRESULT: A long integer. The function returns a value of type LRESULT.
- ✔ CALLBACK: Specifies that this function is to be called by Windows CE.
- ✔ WndProc: The name of the function. You choose what to call the function, and you use the name when registering a window class.
- ✔ HWND: The first argument. This is the window handle where the message goes.
- ✔ UINT: An unsigned integer value that indicates what type of message is being passed. Each message has its own constant value, such as WM_LBUTTONDOWN, which indicates that the pointer is clicked inside a window.
- ✔ WPARAM and LPARAM values: Specify information about the message. For example, in the case of WM_LBUTTONDOWN, these values determine where in the window the mouse click took place.

You may think that WPARAM is a WORD (2-byte) value, given its name. In fact, both WPARAM and LPARAM are LONG (4-byte) values.

A message-handling function usually contains a switch statement that contains case statements for each message that the window needs to handle. In Code Listing 3-7, only the message WM_DESTROY is handled. (This message is described in the next section.) All other messages are handled by the default statement, which passes the message to the DefWindowProc function.

Code Listing 3-7

```
switch (message)
    {
    case WM_DESTROY:
        PostQuitMessage(0);
        break;
    default:
        return (DefWindowProc(hWnd,
                message, uParam, lParam));
    }
return (0);
```

Code Listing 3-7 shows that all unhandled messages should be passed to DefWindowProc. Windows CE has default message processing for many messages, and if the default handler is not called, your application may fail. Also, if the function handles a message, it should return 0.

Quitting the application using WM_DESTROY

The user closes the application window to signify terminating the application — remember that the application window and the application are two separate entities.

When you close the application window, Windows CE sends the message-handling function a WM_DESTROY message. This gives the window an opportunity to perform any last-minute tasks before it is closed.

When the application window receives a WM_DESTROY message, the application must terminate. This means stopping the message processing loop in WinMain. It does this by calling PostQuitMessage. This function causes GetMessage to return FALSE, which terminates the loop and causes WinMain to return. When WinMain returns, the application terminates.

Adding an Application Icon

You may have noticed that the taskbar button for your application does not have an icon. Your application looks less professional next to all those other applications that have icons. In this section, I show you how to design an icon and then add the code that's necessary to display it in the taskbar.

Designing an icon

First, you need to add the icon. I can show you the steps, but I can't give you the artistic skills necessary to develop great icons! Follow these steps:

1. **Click the ResourceView tab in the workspace view.**

2. **Right-click FirstApp resources in the workspace view, and select Insert from the pop-up menu.**

   The Insert Resource dialog box appears. The Resource type list in this dialog box contains a list of all the different types of resources that you can add to your application.

3. **Click Icon, and then select New in the Insert Resource dialog box.**

   Icon is one of the items in the Resource type list.

4. **Right-click IDI_ICON1 in the resource list in the workspace view, and select Properties.**

   The Icon Properties dialog box appears.

5. Change the ID (identifier) to `IDI_FIRSTAPP`**, and press Enter.**

Each icon has an identifier (which is an integer number) that can be used to reference the icon in your application.

6. Design the icon.

The icon design window opens automatically when the icon is created and appears to the right of the ResourceView window. The icon is displayed as a grid where each cell in the grid represents a single pixel in the final icon.

Developer Studio provides icon editor features that are similar to the Paint application in Windows 95.

Each icon that you add to an application can have several different images of different sizes and color resolutions. This allows Windows CE to select the most appropriate icon for display.

By default, a 4-color, 32-x-32-pixel icon is created. However, the icon that is displayed in the taskbar button is only 16 x 16 pixels. If you don't design a 16-x-16-pixel icon, Windows CE scales down the 32-x-32-pixel icon. You should design both a 32 x 32 and 16 x 16 image, because this scaling action does not always produce the best results. You can switch between the different icons by using the Device combo box (drop-down list box) that appears just above the icon design window in Developer Studio (when icons are being edited). Follow these steps to add the 16 x 16 icon:

1. **Choose Image⇨New Device Image.**
2. **Select 4 Color (16 x 16), and select OK.**
3. **Design the icon.**

Displaying an icon in the taskbar

To display your icon in the taskbar when your application runs, follow these steps:

1. **Load the icon from the resources in the application's .exe file using the** `LoadImage` **function.**

2. **Send a message using the** `SendMessage` **function to your main application window telling it to use the icon.**

If you have used icons in Windows 95 or NT, you are used to specifying the icon when the window class is registered. However, it isn't done that way with Windows CE!

A number, not a name

Resources can either be specified by a string name or an integer identifier (ID). These days, it's unusual to use the string name, but all the resource management functions still expect a string name. The MAKEINTRESOURCE macro simply changes the integer identifier into a string that specifies the same resource.

The call to LoadImage requires the following information:

- ✔ The instance handle of the application.
- ✔ The identifier of the icon to load (IDI_FIRSTAPP). Note that you must use the MAKEINTRESOURCE macro to convert this integer value into a string version of the value before it can be passed to LoadImage.

You must specify the following information when calling LoadImage:

- ✔ **The type of image to load:** You need to use IMAGE_ICON because you're loading an icon. This function can also load bitmaps, cursors, and other images.
- ✔ **The width (16 pixels) and height (16 pixels) of the icon to load:** This allows you to specify which image in the icon you want to load.
- ✔ **Information on how to convert colors if the icon does not support the required number of colors:** Simply pass LR_DEFAULTCOLOR for this argument.

Use the code in Code Listing 3-8 to load the icon. Note that the function returns a handle to the icon, which is stored in the hIcon variable.

Code Listing 3-8

```
HICON hIcon = LoadImage(hInstance,
        MAKEINTRESOURCE(IDI_FIRSTAPP),
        IMAGE_ICON, 16, 16, LR_DEFAULTCOLOR);
```

Now that you have loaded the icon, you must send a message to the main application window telling the application to use the icon. So far, you've been handling messages that were generated by Windows CE, and your WndProc function has handled them.

The SendMessage function allows you to send messages to a window (including your own application window) to make the window do something. The SendMessage function requires the following arguments:

✔ **The handle of the window to send the message to** (hWnd).

✔ **The identifier of the message to send:** WM_SETICON is the message that you need to send.

✔ **The** WPARAM **value:** The nature of this value depends on the message that's being sent. In the case of WM_SETICON, WPARAM is set to 0, indicating that the small (that is, 16 x 16) icon is being set.

✔ **The** LPARAM **value:** Again, the value to be passed depends on the message that you are sending. For WM_SETICON, it is the handle of the icon. Note that this must be cast to an LPARAM to remove any compiler errors.

Code Listing 3-9 shows you a call to SendMessage that sends a WM_SETICON message to the main application window.

Code Listing 3-9

```
SendMessage(hWnd,WM_SETICON, 0,
        (LPARAM) hIcon);
```

Just one last thing — where should you put these two lines of code? They need to be executed after the window has been created but before it is displayed to the user. You therefore add the code to WinMain after the call to CreateWindow but before the call to ShowWindow, as follows in Code Listing 3-10.

Code Listing 3-10

```
hWnd = CreateWindow(szAppName,         // Class
                    szTitle,           // Title
                    WS_VISIBLE,        // Style
                    CW_USEDEFAULT,     // x-position
                    CW_USEDEFAULT,     // y-position
                    CW_USEDEFAULT,     // x-size
                    CW_USEDEFAULT,     // y-size
                    NULL,              // Parent handle
                    NULL,              // Menu handle
                    hInstance,         // Instance handle
                    NULL);
HANDLE hIcon = LoadImage(hInstance,
        MAKEINTRESOURCE(IDI_FIRSTAPP),
        IMAGE_ICON, 16, 16, LR_DEFAULTCOLOR);
SendMessage(hWnd,WM_SETICON, 0,
        (LPARAM) hIcon);
ShowWindow(hWnd, nCmdShow);
UpdateWindow(hWnd);
```

Chapter 4

Building Your First MFC Application

· ·

In This Chapter

▶ Understanding the MFC

▶ Creating an MFC application

▶ Using the MFC document and view classes to structure your application

▶ Adding a menu item to your MFC application

· ·

*T*he Microsoft Foundation Classes (MFC) provide the fastest and most productive way to write Windows CE applications for H/PCs. The MFC provides a set of C++ classes that you can use in your applications for tasks such as creating windows, drawing, and handling messages. The Developer Studio further simplifies your programming efforts by providing Wizards that handle some of the more tedious programming tasks. The AppWizard writes much of the standard code that's required by your application, and the Class Wizard makes adding new code fast and easy.

Before you can take full advantage of these time- and effort-saving features, you need to understand how the MFC classes interact, and this can take a fair amount of time. In this chapter, I show you the basics of how to write an MFC application and how to add new menus and message handlers to your application.

You can work through this chapter and build the sample application, MFCFirst, from scratch. However, you can find the source code for MFCFirst in the \samples\MFCFirst folder on the enclosed CD-ROM. If you don't want to build the MFC application as you read through the chapter, you can copy the files from the CD-ROM onto your hard drive and open the workspace MFCFirst.dsw in Developer Studio.

You *must* copy all the subfolders to ensure that all the files are copied.

What Is the MFC?

The Microsoft Foundation Classes (MFC) are a set of C++ classes that provide an application framework that you can use to build Windows CE applications.

Fundamentally, MFC provides you with the following items:

- ✔ An architecture, or framework, through which you can build Windows CE applications. This framework is the *document/view architecture,* and is described in the section "Working with Documents and Views" later in this chapter.

- ✔ A set of classes that provide an alternative mechanism for calling the Windows CE API functions. If you know the Windows CE API, using these classes is straightforward, because the class methods have the same names as the corresponding Windows CE API functions.

If you program Windows 95 or Windows NT with the MFC, all of this is very familiar to you. The major difference is that the MFC for Windows CE is much smaller and has fewer classes. If you haven't programmed using the MFC, don't worry. Programming CE applications with the MFC isn't all that difficult, because Developer Studio helps you along with tools such as the AppWizard and the Class Wizard.

Building an MFC Project with the AppWizard

If you worked through building the API application in Chapter 3, you know that you need to do quite a bit of work just to get the application up and running. With MFC, help is at hand! The *AppWizard* prompts you for information about the type of application that you want to build and then creates the source code for the application.

Creating the project

First, you must create a new project for the MFC application. Follow these steps to do so:

1. **Run Visual C++ 5.0 from the Start menu.**

   Choose Start⊏>Programs⊏>Microsoft Visual C++ 5.0⊏>Microsoft Visual C++5.0 from the Windows NT Start button on the taskbar.

2. **Choose File⇨New.**

   As shown in Figure 4-1, Developer Studio displays the New dialog box.

3. **Click the Projects tab.**

   This displays a list of all the different types of projects you can create.

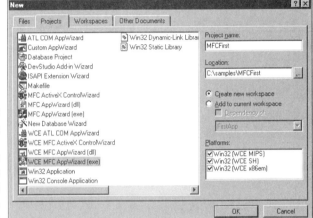

Figure 4-1:
Creating a
new
Windows
CE MFC
application.

4. **Select WCE MFC AppWizard (exe) from the list of project types.**

   Take care to select the correct type of project. Don't select MFC AppWizard (exe), because this type of project is used to create desktop applications for Windows 95 and Windows NT.

5. **Enter a folder name into the Location field, or select a folder by clicking the ... button, next to the Location field.**

   The location field specifies the folder that contains the new folder created for this project. You can decide yourself which folder to use on your hard disk, or you can select `c:\sample`.

6. **Enter a name for the project.**

   For this sample application, enter **MFCFirst** in the Project name field. Notice that the Location field is updated, adding the folder MFCFirst to the folder name you entered. Notice also that the Create new Workspace radio button is selected. Developer Studio creates a workspace for this new project automatically.

7. **Ensure that all the Platforms are selected, as shown in Figure 4-1, by clicking each of the checkboxes in the Platforms list.**

   You can use this project to build versions of your application for each platform you select from this list.

8. **Click OK.**

Developer Studio creates the project and starts the AppWizard, which guides you through the process of building your application.

Using the AppWizard

After you create a new project (as I describe in the preceding section), Developer Studio invokes the AppWizard. The AppWizard displays four dialog boxes that collect information about the type of application you wish to build.

The application that you build in this chapter uses all the default values in the AppWizard, so you can simply click the Next button on each dialog box.

Step 1 — setting the application type

The first dialog box, shown in Figure 4-2, asks you to specify the overall type of application that you want to build. You have the following options:

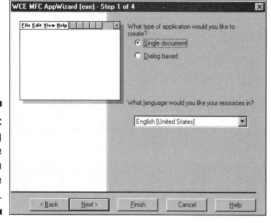

Figure 4-2: Selecting the application type in the AppWizard.

✔ **Single document:** This option creates an application with an application window that occupies the entire Windows CE screen.

✔ **Dialog based:** You can create an application that displays a dialog box rather than an application window. You can then add controls to the dialog box to interact with the user. Use the dialog-based option for applications that are short lived — that is, those in which the user runs the application, supplies some information, and then closes the application.

This dialog box also allows you to specify the language that resources are to be created in (for example, menus and dialog boxes). You usually select English (United States) here.

Step 2 — selecting application options

Clicking the Next button displays the second dialog box, as shown in Figure 4-3. This dialog box enables you to select the following options:

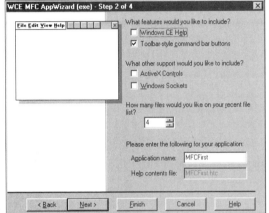

Figure 4-3:
Application
options
in the
AppWizard.

✔ **Windows CE Help:** This option adds a Help menu and question mark (?) icon to the command bar. If you select this option, you must create a Windows CE help file for your application, as I describe in Chapter 10.

✔ **Toolbar-style command bar buttons:** By default, your application has a toolbar with buttons that correspond to the important menu commands (such as File⇨New). You can remove the check mark next to this option if you don't need toolbar buttons.

✔ **ActiveX Controls:** Selecting this option allows you to include ActiveX controls in your application. These controls are written by other companies or yourself, and extend the user interface that's provided by Windows CE. For example, you can use an ActiveX control to add spreadsheet-type functionality to your application.

✔ **Windows Sockets:** You use sockets to allow applications to communicate with each other over TCP/IP networks, including the Internet. Chapter 20 explains how to use Windows sockets for communicating with other applications. If you intend to communicate with other applications using Windows sockets, you should make sure that this option is checked.

✔ **How many files would you like on your recent file list?:** MFC classes automatically maintain the list of files recently used by your application. You use this option to specify the maximum number of files on this list. I recommend leaving this option set at 4.

✔ **Application name:** The internal name for your application. This is the name that Windows CE uses internally to refer to your application. This field defaults to the project name and you shouldn't need to change the application name field.

✔ **Help contents file:** The HTC file that contains your application's help contents. This option is only enabled if you select the Windows CE help check box. Chapter 10 describes how to write help files for Windows CE applications.

Step 3 — selecting miscellaneous options

After you select the desired options, click Next to display the third AppWizard dialog box, as shown in Figure 4-4. This dialog box allows you to choose from the following options:

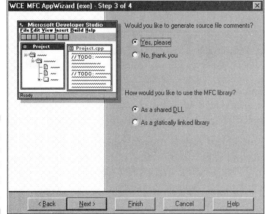

Figure 4-4:
Miscella-
neous
options in
AppWizard.

✔ **Would you like to generate source file comments?** I recommend that you always tell the AppWizard to generate source file comments!

✔ **How would you like to use the MFC Library?** If you specify a statically linked library, all the MFC code that your application requires to run is linked to your application, which can make it quite large. Most MFC applications use the shared library option. The sample application uses the MFC dynamic link libraries (DLLs), which are shared with other applications.

Always select the *As a shared library* option, because this is most efficient and reduces the amount of RAM that your application needs to run and keeps the application smaller.

All the MFC code is stored in the file mfcce20.dll, which is normally located in the windows folder on the Windows CE device. Many H/PCs have mfcce20.dll in ROM, so it doesn't take up valuable RAM.

Step 4 — setting class names

Clicking the Next button takes you to the AppWizard's last dialog box, which is shown in Figure 4-5. This dialog box enables you to change the class names for the code that the AppWizard generates and the filename in which the code is to be stored.

You should not need to change either the class names or the filenames. Changing class names and filenames makes following your code more difficult for other programmers.

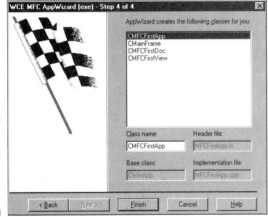

Figure 4-5:
Classes that are created using AppWizard.

The classes listed in Figure 4-5 (such as CMFCFirstApp and CMainFrame) are the classes for which AppWizard generates code. Each of these classes is derived from classes that form part of the MFC library.

For example, the CMFCFirstApp class uses CWinApp as the base class (that is, the class from which it is derived). The code for CMFCFirstApp is in your application, and you can modify it. CWinApp is part of the MFC library, and you don't modify the code in it.

As you select each class in the class list, the dialog box displays the header file, the implementation file, and the base class. The base class is only editable for the CMFCFirstView class.

You may be a bit rusty on the object-oriented and C++ terms (such as *base class, header files, implementation files,* and *deriving classes*). If so, you may want to check *Object-Oriented Programming For Dummies* by Namir C. Shammas, *C++ For Dummies,* 2nd Edition and *MORE C++ For Dummies,* both by Stephen R. Davis (all published by IDG Books Worldwide, Inc.).

The `CMFCFirstView` class is responsible for displaying the data in the application window. You can change the base class to present data in different ways. Table 4-1 lists the different options.

Table 4-1	Selecting a Base View Class
Base View Class	*Purpose*
CView	The default view, which presents a blank window.
CEditView	The application window displays an edit window. You can use this view to create a Notepad-type application.
CFormView	The application window displays a form, which is really a dialog box with controls. This view is useful for creating database-type input forms.
CListView	This view displays a list control in the application window. You can use this view to maintain simple lists of data.
CScrollView	The application window displays a blank view with vertical and horizontal scrollbars. You may want to use this view in a picture editor where the picture is too large to display on one screen.
CTreeView	The application window displays a view with a tree control. You can use this view to create Explorer-type applications.

To change the base class for the view you should:

1. **Select the class CMFCFirstView from the list of classes in the AppWizard.**

   All the classes that the AppWizard creates for your application are listed in the AppWizard creates the following classes for you list.

2. **Select the required base class from the Base class combo box (drop-down list).**

   For example, if you want to base your view class on `CEditView`, select CEditView from the Base class combo box.

For the sample application that you're creating in this chapter, ensure that CView is the base class for CMFCFirstView, and then click the Finish button. The AppWizard then prompts you with a dialog box that confirms the details of the application to be built. Click OK, and the AppWizard creates the source code for your application.

The source code created by the AppWizard is a skeleton that implements the basic functionality required by most Windows CE applications. For example, the application will have a default menu and buttons on the command bar. You need to add your own code to implement your application's functionality.

Building the application

After the AppWizard creates the source code for your application (as I describe in the preceding section), you need to build the application, download the application to the target device, and then run the application.

You many not finish developing this application in one session. When you rerun Developer Studio to continue working on your application, you open the *workspace* by selecting File⇔Open Workspace. Don't try and open the individual files.

You can enter a pathname and different filename for the application in the dialog box that prompts you to download the application to the target device. This pathname and filename are used for subsequent builds.

Here are the steps for building, downloading, and running the application:

1. **Select Build⇔Set Active Configuration.**

   This displays the Set Active Project Configuration dialog box. This dialog box contains a list of all the valid project configurations.

   For emulation mode, select the WCE x86em Release or Debug project.

   For Hitachi SH3 chips, select the WCE SH Release or Debug project.

   For an NEC, Phillips, or other MIPS processor, select the WCE MIPS Release or Debug project.

   (The project is selected from the project list in the Set Active Project Configuration dialog box. For this sample code, select Release, because you aren't going to debug the code.)

2. **Build the application by choosing Build⇔Build MFCFirst.exe, or press F7.**

   Your application is now built and the Remote Executable and Filename dialog box appears when the build operation is complete.

3. Select Yes in the Remote Executable and Filename dialog box.

This dialog box confirms the downloading of your application to the Windows CE device or the emulation environment object store. After clicking Yes, the application downloads, and the message MFCFirst.exe - 0 error(s), 0 warning(s) appears in the output window in Developer Studio. The most likely reason for errors at this stage is the communications link between your PC and Windows CE device is not working correctly.

4. Execute the application by selecting Build⇨Execute MFCFirst.exe.

You now see your application running either on the Windows CE device or in the emulation environment, depending on the project you select in the Set Active Project Configuration dialog box.

This MFC application already has much more functionality than the API application that I show you how to create in Chapter 3. The MFC application has a menu and a functional toolbar, and it displays File Open and File Save dialog boxes as appropriate. Before I show you how to add more functionality, I explain each of the classes that the AppWizard creates for you.

Exploring the MFC Classes

When you create the sample Windows CE MFC application that I discuss throughout this chapter, the AppWizard creates the following classes. (Immediately after each class name, I list the MFC class from which the class derives.)

✔ CMFCFirstApp (CWinApp): The class that represents the application itself.

✔ CMFCFirstDoc (CDocument): The class that is responsible for saving, loading, and managing any data required by your application.

✔ CMFCFirstView (CView): The class that is responsible for displaying and editing the data associated with CMFCFirstDoc. Note that the view is responsible only for the client area of the application window, as shown in Figure 4-6.

✔ CMainFrame (CFrameWnd): The class that manages all aspects of the application window except the client area (which is managed by CMFCFirstView).

✔ CAboutDlg: (CDialog): The class that displays the default About box.

Figure 4-7 shows each of these classes expanded in the class view. This view shows the members that are implemented by the AppWizard. In the following sections, I provide an overview of the important features of these classes.

The client area managed by CMFCFirstView

The application window managed by CMainFrame

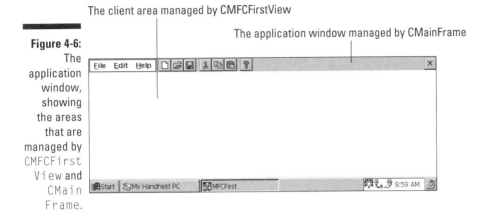

Figure 4-6:
The
application
window,
showing
the areas
that are
managed by
CMFCFirst
View and
CMain
Frame.

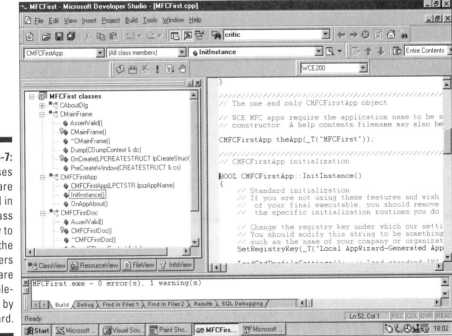

Figure 4-7:
The classes
that are
expanded in
the class
view to
show the
members
that are
imple-
mented by
AppWizard.

CMFCFirstApp (CWinApp)

The `CMFCFirstApp` class represents the application and implements the `WinMain` function and message-processing loops that I describe in Chapter 3.

The application has only one global variable, `theApp`, which is a `CMFCFirstApp` class object. This class object is created when the application is run, and it performs all the necessary initialization. The following is the declaration, which is in the file MFCFirst.cpp:

```
CMFCFirstApp theApp(_T("MFCFirst"));
```

This statement calls the `CMFCFirstApp` constructor, which takes a string that specifies the name of the application.

The `_T` macro is used to declare a Unicode string. For more details, refer to "Changing to Unicode Strings" in Chapter 3.

The `InitInstance` member function of `CMFCFirstApp` is called by the MFC to initialize various MFC objects when the application is first run. You can place your own application initialization code in this function.

CMFCFirstDoc (CDocument)

The `CMFCFirstDoc` class is responsible for storing all the data associated with a document that can be managed by the application. If you're writing a drawing application, the document is the drawing; for a word processor, the document is the formatted text document.

The `OnNewDocument` member function of `CMFCFirstDoc` is called whenever the user chooses File⇨New. You should perform any document-related initialization in this function.

You use the `Serialize` member function to load and save a document to a file. This process uses an *archive object,* which I describe in Chapter 18.

CMFCFirstView (CView)

The `CMFCFirstView` class is responsible for displaying a view of the data that's held in the `CMFCFirstDoc` class. It is important that you maintain this distinction in your applications — ensure that the view does not store document-type data and that the document does not display data to the user.

When using the MFC with Windows 95 and Windows NT programs, an application may have multiple views on a single document. For example, if you are writing a spreadsheet application, you may have a worksheet view and a chart view of the data. In Windows CE, you typically have only a single view on the document. Even though you may only have a single view, separating the storing of the document from the view of the document makes your applications easier to write and change in the future.

The OnDraw member function of CMFCFirstView is called by MFC whenever the view of the document's data needs to be redrawn.

Obviously, the view needs access to the document so that the view can get the data to draw. It does this by calling a CMFCFirstView function called GetDocument. This function returns a pointer to the CMFCFirstDoc object that stores the data for the view.

Code Listing 4-1 shows the default code that the AppWizard writes when the sample application is created.

Code Listing 4-1

```
void CMFCFirstView::OnDraw(CDC* pDC)
{
    CMFCFirstDoc* pDoc = GetDocument();
    ASSERT_VALID(pDoc);

    // TODO: add draw code for native data here
}
```

At present, CMFCFirstDoc stores no data, and the CMFCFirstView has no code in OnDraw to draw the view of the data — that's part of writing your application! Together, CMFCFirstDoc and CMFCFirstView implement the *document/view architecture* that's provided by MFC. I show you how to store and draw data in the section "Working with Documents and Views" later in this chapter.

You can use the ASSERT_VALID macro to test whether a pointer variable contains a valid pointer to a class object. Using this macro helps to make your applications more robust, because you can detect pointer problems before they cause an error. The code to test the validity of the pointer is only called in the debug version of your application.

CMainFrame (CFrameWnd)

The CMainFrame class contains code to manage the application window, which includes the command bar and the associated menu and buttons.

The `OnCreate` member function of `CMainFrame` creates the command bar and adds the buttons. Chapter 5 shows how to add your own buttons to the command bar.

CAboutDlg (CDialog)

The application's Help⇨About MFCFirst menu command displays a default About dialog box. This dialog box is implemented by the `CAboutDlg` class. The dialog box itself is displayed from the `OnAppAbout` member function of the `CMFCFirstApp` class. Chapter 6 shows you how to create dialog boxes.

Working with Documents and Views

In this section, I describe a simple example of implementing code for the document/view architecture. Specifically, I show you how to implement a simple drawing application. The application tracks the movement of the stylus over the view by drawing a series of lines.

Don't forget, Windows CE devices use a *stylus* instead of a mouse. One major difference between a stylus and a mouse is that you can track the stylus being moved by the user only if the stylus comes in contact with the screen, whereas, you can track a mouse in Windows NT or Windows 95 even when the mouse buttons are not held down.

Follow these steps to complete the application:

1. **Provide a mechanism in the** `CMFCFirstDoc` **document class to store the *x* and *y* coordinates of where the stylus has been moved.**

2. **Write these functions in** `CMFCFirstDoc` **to enable the** `CMFCFirstView` **class to handle the following tasks:**

   • Add an *x,y* coordinate to the list of coordinates.

   • Return a specific *x,y* coordinate.

   • Return the number of *x,y* coordinates currently held.

3. **Write code in** `CMFCFirstView` **to track the movement of the stylus.**

4. **Write code in** `CMFCFirstView` **to redraw the view when it needs to be updated.**

In the following sections, I outline these steps to implement drawing in the MFCFirst application.

Storing the coordinates

The CMFCFirstDoc document class must be able to store an unknown number of *x,y* coordinates. You could create an array, but how big would you make it? You would need to write code that increases the size of the array as it becomes full, and that's nasty work!

The answer lies in the MFC collection classes. These classes provide array storage for various data types. The MFC collection classes for arrays are very flexible because the arrays grow automatically as they become full.

The *x* and *y* values are both 2-byte WORD integer values, so you need a 4-byte DWORD data type to store one *x,y* coordinate. You can therefore use a DWORD array to store coordinates.

The MFC collection classes contain CDWordArray, which allows DWORD values to be stored in array format. You need to add a CDWordArray class object to the CMFCFirstDoc class. Follow these steps to do so:

1. **Be sure that you're displaying the Class View in the workspace window.**

   You should see the list of classes displayed.

   You can refer to the section called "Exploring the MFC Classes," earlier in this chapter, if you're not sure how to display this class list.

2. **Right-click CMFCFirstDoc, and select Add Member Variable from the pop-up menu that appears.**

   The Add Member Variable dialog box appears, as shown in Figure 4-8.

Figure 4-8:
Adding a member variable to the CMFCFirst Doc class.

3. **Enter the following information into the Add Member Variable dialog box:**

   - Variable Type: **CDWordArray**

   - Variable Declaration: **m_points**

   - Access: **Private**

   The Static and Virtual check boxes allow you change the type of function being created. Generally, you won't need to use these check boxes.

4. **Click OK.**

   The variable declaration is added to the class, and the class view updated to include the new variable.

The array is given *private access* — that is, the view class does not have direct access to the array. Instead, you can write access functions that provide controlled access to the array. This technique is called encapsulation. *Encapsulation* is the process by which you create functions that provide access to a variable (that is, to store a value in the variable or retrieve the current value stored in the variable) rather than allow direct access to the variable itself. This allows you to write code that verifies the values being assigned to the variable. Using encapsulation makes applications more robust, because the values being placed in variables can be verified.

Next, you need to add three functions to CDWordArray to allow a point to be added to the array and a point to be retrieved from the array, and to provide the number of points to be returned.

First, follow these steps to create a function to add a coordinate to the array:

1. **Right-click CMFCFirstDoc, and choose Add Member Function from the pop-up menu that appears.**

   As shown in Figure 4-9, the Add Member Function dialog box appears.

Figure 4-9:
Adding the
AddPoint
member
function
to the
CMFCFirst
Doc class.

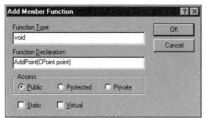

2. **Enter the following information into the dialog box, and then click OK:**

   - Function Type: **void**

   - Function Declaration: **AddPoint(CPoint point)**

   - Access: **Public**

   You pass the *x,y* coordinate to this function using the MFC class CPoint. This class has two member variables, x and y, for storing the coordinate.

   Developer Studio takes you directly to this new function when OK is clicked so that you can write the contents of the function.

3. **Add the following single line (shown in boldface in Code Listing 4-2) to this new function.**

Code Listing 4-2

```
void CMFCFirstDoc::AddPoint(CPoint point)
{
    m_points.Add(MAKELONG(point.x, point.y));
}
```

CDWordArray has an Add member function that allows you to add a DWORD value to the end of the array. The size of the array increases automatically if required.

The CPoint class object passed into this function contains two member variables, x and y, which the MAKELONG macro combines to form a DWORD value. The CPoint class doesn't provide automatic conversion from a CPoint to a DWORD.

Strictly speaking, point.x and point.y are LONG (4 byte) values, whereas the preceding code treats them as WORD (2-byte) values. I can safely make this assumption in this application because the coordinates used to track the stylus never exceed 65536.

You also need to add a function to return the number of points that are currently held in the array. Follow these steps:

1. **Right click CMFCFirstDoc, and select Add Member Function from the pop-up menu that appears.**

   The Add Member Function dialog box is displayed.

2. **Enter the following information in the dialog box, and then click OK:**

   - Function Type: **int**

   - Function Declaration: **PointCount**

   - Access: **Public**

3. **Add the following boldface line in Code Listing 4-3 to this new function.**

Code Listing 4-3

```
int CMFCFirstDoc::PointCount()
{
    return m_points.GetSize();
}
```

This function uses the `GetSize` member function of the `CDWordArray` class to return the number of elements that are currently held in the array.

The final function that you need to add to the `CMFCFirstDoc` class returns a coordinate that is stored in a particular index location in `CDWordArray`. Follow these steps:

1. **Right-click CMFCFirstDoc, and choose Add Member Function from the pop-up menu that appears.**

   The Add Member Function dialog box appears.

2. **Enter the following information in the dialog box, and then click OK:**

   • Function Type: **CPoint**

   • Function Declaration: **GetPoint(UINT index)**

   • Access: **Public**

3. **Add the following boldface line, shown in Code Listing 4-4, to this new function.**

Code Listing 4-4

```
CPoint CMFCFirstDoc::GetPoint(UINT index)
{
    return m_points.GetAt(index);
}
```

The `GetAt` member function of `CDWordArray` returns the value that's held in the specified index location. The first element is numbered 0, the second is 1, and so on.

The `GetAt` function returns a `DWORD` value, but the `GetPoint` function returns a `CPoint` class object. The `CPoint` class supports automatic conversion from a `DWORD` value to a `CPoint` class object.

That completes the additions that you need to make to the `CMFCFirstDoc` class. This type of code is very typical of code that's added to the document. You use private member variables to store data in the document, and public member functions are provided to allow `CMFCFirstView` to have controlled access to the data.

The view only has access to the document's data through the three functions that are implemented in this section (AddPoint, PointCount, and GetPoint). The mechanism that the document uses to store the points (CDWordArray) is hidden from the view.

Tracking the stylus

In this section, I explain how the view tracks the stylus and draws the lines. Remember that the view is responsible for interacting with the user and displaying the data that's held in the document.

Whenever the stylus is moved over the view, Windows CE sends the window a WM_MOUSEMOVE message. Refer to Chapter 3 for information on messages and how windows handle them.

When using the MFC, you create a relationship between a message (such as WM_MOUSEMOVE) and a member function in an MFC class (such as CMFCFirstView). MFC then ensures that this member function is called whenever the message is received. The information about this relationship is maintained in a *message map*.

Creating message maps is quite difficult, but fortunately the Developer Studio has a *Class Wizard* to automate the task. You can run the Class Wizard by choosing View⇨Class Wizard, but because you are going to constantly enter and exit the Class Wizard, you should use the keyboard shortcut, Ctrl+W.

Follow these instructions to create a message map for the WM_MOUSEMOVE message in the CMFCFirstView class:

1. **Run the Class Wizard by pressing Ctrl+W.**

2. **Ensure that CMFCFirstView is selected in the Class name list.**

3. **Ensure that CMFCFirstView is selected in the Object IDs list.**

4. **Scroll down the Messages list until you locate WM_MOUSEMOVE, and then select it, as shown in Figure 4-10.**

5. **Click Add Function.**

   The Class Wizard adds a function called OnMouseMove in the CMFCFirstView class that is mapped to the WM_MOUSEMOVE message.

6. **Click Edit Code.**

   The Class Wizard closes and takes you to the implementation of the new function.

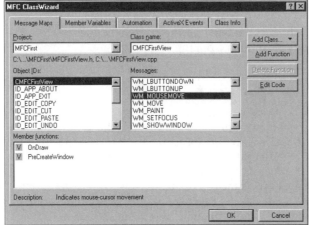

Figure 4-10:
Creating a
message
map for
WM_MOUSE
MOVE in
CMFCFirst
View.

Note that `OnMouseMove` is passed the following two arguments:

```
void CMFCFirstView::OnMouseMove(UINT nFlags, CPoint point)
```

The first argument, `nFlags`, contains information about which keys were pressed when the message was generated (such as Ctrl, Shift, or Alt). The second argument, `point`, contains the *x,y* coordinate of where the stylus was located when the message was generated.

Remember that the function `OnMouseMove` is called by the MFC whenever the message `WM_MOUSEMOVE` is received from Windows CE. You never call this function yourself.

You need to write code to perform three tasks:

- ✔ Get a pointer to the document.
- ✔ Draw the line from the last point to the new point.
- ✔ Add the point to `CDWordArray` in the `CMFCFirstDoc` class using the `AddPoint` member.

First, the following code gets the pointer to the document:

```
CMFCFirstDoc* pDoc = GetDocument();
ASSERT_VALID(pDoc);
```

As usual, you call the `GetDocument` function (which is a member of `CMFCFirstView`) to get a pointer to the document class object. You call the `ASSERT_VALID` macro to check that this is a valid pointer.

The line should only be drawn if a valid last point exists. You use the CMFCFirstDoc function PointCount to return the number of points. If the return value is 0, this is the first point to be added, and no last point exists. If a last point exists, you use the CMFCFirstDoc function GetPoint to return the last point — this is the last element in the array.

Finally, you use the CMFCFirstDoc function AddPoint to add this point to the array. The code is as shown in Code Listing 4-5.

Code Listing 4-5

```
void CMFCFirstView::OnMouseMove(UINT nFlags, CPoint point)
{

    CMFCFirstDoc* pDoc = GetDocument();
    ASSERT_VALID(pDoc);

    if(pDoc->PointCount() > 0)
    {
        UINT nLastPoint = pDoc->PointCount() - 1;
        CPoint LastPoint = pDoc->GetPoint(nLastPoint);
        CDC *pDC = GetDC();
        pDC->MoveTo(LastPoint);
        pDC->LineTo(point);
        ReleaseDC(pDC);
    }
    pDoc->AddPoint(point);
}
```

You need to add the code to the CMFCFirstView::OnMouseMove function you just created:

1. **Remove all the code between the opening and closing brackets in this function.**

   The CMFCFirstView::OnMouseMove function should now look like Code Listing 4-6.

Code Listing 4-6

```
void CMFCFirstView::OnMouseMove(UINT nFlags,
            CPoint point)
{
}
```

2. Add the code shown above between the opening and closing brackets.

You now need to add the code shown above, starting with the line:

```
CMFCFirstDoc* pDoc = GetDocument();
```

and finishing with:

```
pDoc->AddPoint(point);
```

The implementation of OnMouseMove, created by the AppWizard, contains a call to the base class implementation of OnMouseMove in the CView class. I've removed this call because it's not necessary. If you are uncertain as to whether to call the base class implementation, call it as the last line in your function.

After you add the code, you should compile and run your application. You now have a simple drawing application! To draw a line, simply move the stylus across the view. Remember that the stylus must touch the screen to generate the WM_MOUSEMOVE messages that your application responds to.

If you hide the MFCFirst application (for example, by clicking the desktop icon) and then reshow it, the diagram is lost! This happens because you don't have any redrawing code yet.

Drawing in a view

In the preceding section, you draw a line in a view using the code shown in Code Listing 4-7.

Code Listing 4-7

```
CDC *pDC = GetDC();
pDC->MoveTo(pLast);
pDC->LineTo(point);
ReleaseDC(pDC);
```

In Windows CE, Windows 95, and Windows NT, you cannot draw directly onto a window. First, you must obtain a *device context* that's associated with the window and then draw onto the device context. Don't worry about what a device context is — think of it as a link between your drawing instructions (for example, draw a line from here to there) and the window where the drawing instruction is actually displayed. Remember that a view *is* a window, so to draw onto the view, you must first get a device context for the view.

The GetDC function returns a pointer to a CDC class object. CDC is the MFC class that implements device contexts.

After you have the pointer to the CDC object, you can call drawing functions on the device context to draw on the window. I use the following two functions:

- ✔ MoveTo, which moves the current drawing position to the given point.
- ✔ LineTo, which draws a line from the current drawing position to the give point.

It's important that you release the device context when you've finished drawing. You do this by calling the ReleaseDC function and passing the pointer to the CDC class object as the only argument.

You can find more information on drawing in Windows CE in Chapter 7.

The GetDC and ReleaseDC functions are actually implemented in an MFC class called CWnd. This class represents all the window functions that are supported by Windows CE. The CView class is derived from CWnd and therefore has access to all the CWnd functions.

Keeping up to date

Your fine works of art are not maintained if you hide the MFCFirst application window and then redisplay it. This problem occurs because the only drawing code in the application responds to the stylus being moved.

To correct this problem, you must add code that can redraw the entire diagram at any time.

Windows CE notifies a window that it needs to be redrawn by sending a WM_PAINT message. In response, the window should redraw itself.

Views receive WM_PAINT messages (because they are windows), but it is more common to add your redrawing code to the view's OnDraw function. The AppWizard created this function for you with the code in Code Listing 4-8.

Code Listing 4-8

```
void CMFCFirstView::OnDraw(CDC* pDC)
{
    CMFCFirstDoc* pDoc = GetDocument();
    ASSERT_VALID(pDoc);

    // TODO: add draw code for native data here
}
```

Notice that this function passes you a pointer to a device context in the pDC argument. You should not call GetDC or ReleaseDC!

The code that redraws the diagram needs to determine the number of points that are stored in the document, and then get each point and draw a line to the next point. Use the code shown in Code Listing 4-9.

Code Listing 4-9

```
void CMFCFirstView::OnDraw(CDC* pDC)
{
    CMFCFirstDoc* pDoc = GetDocument();
    ASSERT_VALID(pDoc);

    CPoint p1, p2;
    for(int i = 0; i < pDoc->PointCount() - 1; i++)
    {
        p1 = pDoc->GetPoint(i);
        p2 = pDoc->GetPoint(i + 1);
        pDC->MoveTo(p1);
        pDC->LineTo(p2);
    }
}
```

Follow these steps to implement this code:

1. **Locate the implementation of** CMFCFirstView::OnDraw.

   Expand the CMFCFirstView class in the ClassView window, and double-click OnDraw. This takes you to the implementation of CMFCFirstView::OnDraw.

2. **Remove the comment line**.

   The TODO comment politely reminds you that you should add code to this function to handle drawing. Delete this comment line.

3. **Add the drawing code to** CMFCFirstView::OnDraw.

   You now need to add the code that redraws the diagram. This is the code that starts with the line

   ```
   CPoint p1, p2;
   ```

   and finishes with the lines

   ```
   pDC->LineTo(p2);
   }
   ```

After you add this code, you can compile and test your application. You now find that the your diagram is redrawn correctly when your application window is redisplayed.

A La Carte Menus with MFC

Follow these steps to add a menu item to an MFC application:

1. **Add the menu item to the menu that the AppWizard creates.**

2. **Add a message map for the new menu handler.**

   This message map defines a function that is called when the user chooses the menu.

3. **Add code to make the menu do something!**

In this section, I show you the steps that are required to add a menu item that clears all the points that are associated with the diagram. You can add this menu item to the existing Edit menu in MFCFirst.

You need to decide which class is to handle the menu command. You can put your menu handler in one of the following locations:

✔ CMainFrame or CMFCFirstApp: Place menu handlers here that don't refer to a document or a view. For example, menus that allow users to set preferences should be handled by CMainFrame or CMFCFirstApp. Note that the About dialog box is displayed from code in CMFCFirstApp.

✔ CMFCFirstDoc: Place menu items that affect the data contained in the document, but not the way it is displayed, in CMFCFirstDoc. For example, you should place a menu item that empties all the points from your drawing application in CMFCFirstDoc.

✔ CMFCFirstView: Place menu items that affect the way the data is displayed, but not the data itself, in CMFCFirstView. For example, a zoom option for the diagram should be handled by CFMCFirstView.

Adding the menu item

The AppWizard creates a menu called IDR_MAINFRAME, and you should modify this menu to add new items. The section "Designing a Menu" in Chapter 5, shows you how to add new items to a menu.

Follow these instructions to add a new item to the Edit menu:

1. **Open** IDR_MAINFRAME **in the Resource View.**

2. **Click the Edit menu in** IDR_MAINFRAME **to display the existing Edit menu items.**

3. **Double-click the dotted box at the end of the Edit menu.**

   The Menu Properties dialog box is displayed.

4. **Enter** ID_EDIT_CLEARALL **for the identifier and** Clear All **for the Caption.**

5. **Press Enter.**

Creating the menu handler

You add the menu handler for `ID_EDIT_CLEARALL` using the Class Wizard. As I discuss in the preceding section, you need to decide which class is to handle the menu item.

The Clear All option changes the data in the document (it empties `CDWordArray`). The Clear All option should therefore be handled by the document.

So, to add the menu handler, follow these steps:

1. **Run the Class Wizard by pressing Ctrl+W.**

2. **Select CMFCFirstDoc from the Class name list.**

3. **Select ID_EDIT_CLEARALL from the Object ID list.**

4. **Select COMMAND in the messages list, as shown in Figure 4-11.**

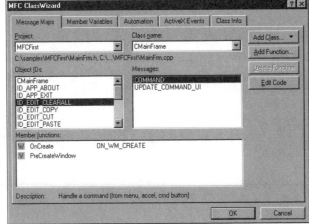

Figure 4-11:
Creating a
menu
handler for
`ID_EDIT_`
`CLEARALL.`

5. **Click the Add Function button.**

The Class Wizard prompts you to accept the default function name (`OnEditClearall`).

6. **Click OK.**

7. **Click the Edit Function button.**

The Class Wizard window closes, and the code for the new function appears.

Now you're ready to implement the code to empty all the points. The `RemoveAll` member function of `CDWordArray` removes the points from the array. The document must also notify the view that it needs to update the diagram because it's been changed by the document. The document does this by calling the `UpdateAllViews` function, passing `NULL` as the argument.

Add the following (Code Listing 4-10) to `OnEditClearAll`.

Code Listing 4-10

```
void CMFCFirstDoc::OnEditClearAll()
{
    m_Points.RemoveAll();
    UpdateAllViews(NULL);
}
```

Implementing OnNewDocument

In this section, I show you how to handle the File⇨New menu command in your application. The `CMFCFirstDoc` document class function `OnNewDocument` is called when the user creates a new document. You must place code in the `OnNewDocument` function to reinitialize any document variables.

In the case of this application, you must remove the points in the `CDWordArray` object by calling `RemoveAll`. The AppWizard creates the `OnNewDocument` function, so you only need to add the following boldface in Code Listing 4-11. The code then calls the base class implementation `CDocument::OnNewDocument`. Next, the `RemoveAll` member of the `CDWordArray` class is called for the `m_points` object. This removes all the elements stored in the array. Finally, the value `TRUE` is returned indicating that the initialization for the new document succeeded.

Code Listing 4-11

```
BOOL CMFCFirstDoc::OnNewDocument()
{
    if (!CDocument::OnNewDocument())
        return FALSE;

    m_points.RemoveAll();
    return TRUE;
}
```

Chapter 5

Using the Command Bar

In This Chapter

▶ Creating a command bar

▶ Adding a menu

▶ Using standard and customized buttons

▶ Adding tooltips to command bar buttons

*I*n Windows NT and Windows 95, an application has a caption bar, a toolbar, and a menu bar. In Windows CE, these are all combined into a single *command bar* — a unique user interface control that maximizes the available screen area.

While the single command bar means that the menus and toolbars are generally smaller and contain less options, this is generally not a problem, because Windows CE applications have less functionality and fewer commands than their Windows NT and Windows 95 counterparts.

You can place any of the following items on a command bar (see Figure 5-1):

✔ Menus

✔ Buttons

✔ Combo boxes

✔ Adornments (Close box, OK button, and Help button)

You generally add command bars to application windows (the main window displayed by your application), but because command bars are just another control, you can, in fact, add command bars to any window.

Figure 5-1:
A command
bar.

All the code shown in this chapter is from the sample code that's included in the \samples\cbar.dsw workspace on the enclosed CD-ROM. This code creates a fully featured command bar with a menu, buttons, and a combo box, and the code shows you how to respond when the user selects the buttons, selects the menu items, and changes the combo box selection.

Creating Command Bars

Before you go ahead and create a command bar you need to follow some steps to ensure that your application has set the stage for creating a command bar. After following these steps, you can then create the command bar by calling CommandBar_Create. Follow these steps:

1. **Add a global variable in your application to store the handle that is returned when you create it.**

   Add the declaration shown in boldface at the beginning of your source file as follows in Code Listing 5-1.

   ### Code Listing 5-1

   ```
   LRESULT CALLBACK WndProc(HWND, UINT, WPARAM, LPARAM);
   HINSTANCE  hInst = NULL;

   HWND       hWndCB = NULL; // Handle to command bar

   int WINAPI WinMain(HINSTANCE hInstance,
               HINSTANCE hPrevInstance,
               LPTSTR lpCmdLine, int nCmdShow )
   ```

   A command bar is one of the *common controls*. The header file commctrl.h defines the functions that are used with the common controls, and this header file must be included in your source code.

2. **Add the header file** commctrl.h **to** StartApp.cpp:

   ```
   #include <commctrl.h>
   ```

   You must initialize the library that contains the common controls before you create the common controls. You do this by calling the InitCommonControls function in WinMain so that the InitCommon Controls function is called when the application first loads.

3. **Make a call to** InitCommonControls **in** WinMain **shown in boldface in Code Listing 5-2.**

Code Listing 5-2

```
RegisterClass(&wc);
InitCommonControls(); // Initialize common controls
// Save handle to create command bar
hInst = hInstance;
```

Notice how the value in the hInstance variable is copied to a global variable called hInst. You use the instance handle that's passed to your application in WinMain in many places, so programmers commonly store the value in a global variable.

You need to create the command bar after you create the application window, but before you display it to the user. Windows CE sends a WM_CREATE message to a window after it is created (but before it is displayed) so that the command bar can be created when the message is received.

Command bars are created with the CommandBar_Create function, which requires you to specify the following items:

✔ hInst: The instance handle of the application. This instance handle is a number that uniquely identifies your application. This value is passed to the application as an argument to WinMain. Refer to Chapter 3 for more information on instance and window handles.

✔ hWnd: The window handle of the window in which the command bar is to be placed. Each window you created is assigned a unique number by Windows CE, called a *handle,* and handle is returned to you when the window is created.

✔ 1: An identifier (integer number) by which the command bar can be referenced. You can give the command bar any identifier that you like.

The function returns an integer number that is a handle to the command bar — you should save this handle in a variable. You need the command bar handle to add items to the command bar.

Code Listing 5-3 shows a call to the function CommandBar_Create in response to Windows CE sending a WM_CREATE message to the application.

Code Listing 5-3

```
case WM_CREATE:
      hWndCB = CommandBar_Create(hInst, hWnd, 1);
      break;
```

Notice how you pass an integer (1) into this function that is an identifier. You can refer to the command bar either through the handle that is returned when it is created (stored in hWndCB) or by the identifier, if you know the window that is the parent of the command bar.

Adding Adornments

You add adornments (the "?" for help, the "X" indicating close, and the OK button) by calling the CommandBar_AddAdornments function. You must supply the following items:

- ✔ hwndCB: The command bar handle to which the menu is to be added. This handle is the one that is returned when CommandBar_Create is called.

- ✔ dwFlags: Pass 0 if you only want an "X" close button. Use the constant CMDBAR_HELP if you want a Help button, or use CMDBAR_OK to get an OK button. For both a Help and an OK button, combine the two constants with the C OR operator (for example, CMDBAR_HELP | CMDBAR_OK).

- ✔ 0: This argument is reserved, and you must pass it as 0. Currently, this argument serves no purpose, but it may be used in the future.

Following user-interface guidelines

You must make sure that your application follows the Windows CE user-interface guidelines — you don't want your application to stand out from others because the user interface looks or behaves differently than other popular applications, such as Microsoft Pocket Word and Excel. The following guidelines for using command bars can help you meet most users' expectations:

- ✔ An application window in Windows CE does not have a caption bar. The text that is usually displayed in the caption bar is displayed in the application button in the Windows CE taskbar.

- ✔ You should only display a menu in the command bar, not in the window itself.

- ✔ While a menu *can* be placed anywhere in the command bar, you *should* always place it on the left side.

- ✔ You should follow the standard order for menus (File, Edit View, Insert, Tools, Window, and Help). You don't have to use all these menus, however — only those that apply to your application.

- ✔ Command bar buttons can have tooltips, and I recommend that you add them to your application.

You can use this code to call `CommandBar_AddAdornments`, which adds a Help button to the command bar, as follows:

```
CommandBar_AddAdornments(hWndCB, CMDBAR_HELP, 0);
```

TIP

You should always add the adornments last, after the menu, buttons, and controls have been added.

Adding a Menu with the API

Menus are the primary way in which an application presents its functionality to the user. Unlike Windows 95 and Windows NT applications, Windows CE menus are contained in the command bar and are not directly part of the application window.

You add menus using the `CommandBar_InsertMenubar` function, which requires the following information:

- ✔ `hwndCB`: The command bar handle to which the menu is to be added. This handle is the one that's returned when `CommandBar_Create` is called.
- ✔ `hInst`: The instance handle of the application.
- ✔ `ID_MAINMENU`: The identifier of the menu. You specify this identifier in the Menu Properties dialog box when the menu is created using the Developer Studio Resource Editor.
- ✔ `0`: The index position for the menu. The index position specifies where on the command bar you intend to add the menu. The first position is 0, the second is 1, and so on. Because you should always place menus on the left side of the command bar, you should always pass 0.

The following is an example of calling `CommandBar_InsertMenubar`:

```
CommandBar_InsertMenubar(hWndCB, hInst, IDR_MAINMENU, 0);
```

Designing the menu

You store a menu as a resource in the application. The Resource Editor in the Developer Studio allows you to create and edit menus. First, you need to create a resource file for your project and then create the menu. Follow these steps:

1. **Choose File⇨New in Developer Studio.**

   The New dialog box appears.

2. **Select Resource Script from the list of available file types.**

3. **Enter cbar.rc for the filename, and click the OK button.**

   This creates a resource file and adds it to the project. It also opens the file in the editor. You need to close the file cbar.rc before you can use the Developer Studio Resource Editor.

4. **Choose File⇨Close to close the resource file.**

   A Resource tab has been added to the workspace window. Selecting this tab gives you access to the Developer Studio Resource Editor.

5. **Select the ResourceView tab in the workspace window.**

6. **Right-click CBar resources from the list in the ResourceView window, and choose Insert from the popup menu.**

   Selecting this command displays the Insert Resources dialog box, which allows you to select the type of resource that you're adding (see Figure 5-2). You are adding a menu.

Figure 5-2:
The Insert Resource dialog box allows you to select the type of resource to add.

7. **Select Menu from the Resource Type list, and choose New.**

   Every menu has a unique identifier (an integer number) by which the menu is known — by default, the new menu uses IDR_MENU1 as the identifier. You set this identifier after creating the menu.

8. **Right-click IDR_MENU1 in the resource list under the "Menu" section in the ResourceView window, and select Properties from the popup menu.**

9. **Enter IDR_MAINMENU into the ID edit box, and press Enter.**

   Now you can design the menu. You should see a gray bar, with a dotted box on the left side, if you look in the menu editor window. The menu editor window is automatically opened when you create or open a menu in the ResourceView. The menu editor window is displayed to the right of the ResourceView window. This is an empty menu bar.

10. Double-click the dotted box in the menu bar that is displayed in the editor window.

This displays the Menu Item Properties window for the new drop-down menu. The only item that you need to change is the caption for the menu.

11. Enter &File **in the Caption edit box, and press Enter.**

An empty File menu is added to the menu bar.

12. Click the File label.

You should see two dotted boxes and the label File (see Figure 5-3). You add menu items to the File drop-down menu by double-clicking the dotted box below the File label. You can add new drop-down menus by double-clicking the dotted box to the right of the File label.

You can change the order of menu items or drop-down menus in the menu by dragging and dropping from one location to another.

13. Double-click the dotted box below the File label to display the Menu Item Properties dialog box.

Click here to add a new menu item.⌐ ⌐ Click here to add a new menu.

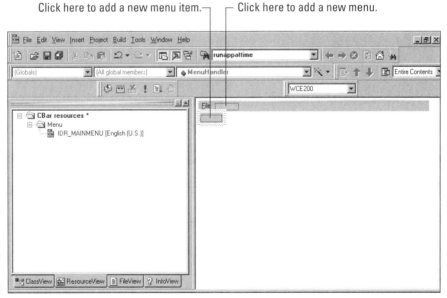

Figure 5-3:
The two
dotted
boxes allow
you to add
new menus
and new
menu items.

14. Enter ID_FILE_EXIT **into the** ID **(identifier) box, type** E&xit **into the Caption edit box (see Figure 5-4), and press Enter.**

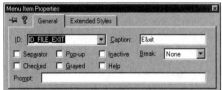

Each menu item has a unique integer identifier. The program uses this identifier to determine which menu item was selected by the user.

The menu design is now complete, so it's time to find out how to display the menu in the command bar, and to respond to a menu item being selected.

Adding the menu to the command bar

To add the menu to the command bar, add a call to the CommandBar_ InsertMenuBar function immediately after you create the command bar itself.

The call to CommandBar_InsertMenubar requires you to pass the following information:

- ✔ The command bar handle to which the menu is to be added.
- ✔ The instance handle of the application.
- ✔ The identifier of the menu. This is IDR_MAINMENU, which you specified earlier.
- ✔ Where to place the menu. If you pass 0, the menu is placed at the left side of the command bar.

Code Listing 5-4 shows the call to CommandBar_InsertMenubar (in bold-face) after the command is created but before the adornment (that is, the Close box) is added.

Code Listing 5-4

```
case WM_CREATE:
        hWndCB = CommandBar_Create(hInst, hWnd, 1);
        CommandBar_InsertMenubar(hWndCB, hInst,
            IDR_MAINMENU, 0);
        CommandBar_AddAdornments(hWndCB, 0, 0);
        break;
```

The following steps show how to add the code required to display the menu in the command bar:

1. **Add the call to** `CommandBar_InsertMenubar` **shown using boldface in the previous code.**

   The menu identifiers (such as `IDR_MAINMENU`) are defined in the header file `resource.h`. This file was created automatically when the resource file was added to the project. You must add the header file to cbar.cpp so that the compiler can reference the identifiers.

2. **Insert** `resource.h` **into cbar.cpp by adding the include line shown in boldface in Code Listing 5-5.**

Code Listing 5-5

```
#include <windows.h>
#include <commctrl.h>
#include "resource.h"
```

3. **Build and run your application — the menu bar appears.**

   You can build and run your application in one go by selecting <u>B</u>uild⇨<u>E</u>xecute in the Developer Studio.

Responding to menu item selections

Of course, the Exit menu doesn't do anything yet! You have to write code that responds to the user selecting the menu.

Windows CE sends a `WM_COMMAND` message to the window that contains the command bar and the menu whenever the user selects a menu item. You must write a message handler in `WndProc` to respond to a menu item that is being selected.

The `WM_COMMAND` message passes the identifier of the menu item that was selected in the lower 2 bytes of the `WPARAM` value. Remember that the `WPARAM` value is 4 bytes long. The macro `LOWORD` allows you to extract the value that is contained in the lower 2 bytes of a 4-byte integer; you then need to test this value for equality to `ID_FILE_EXIT`.

If the value in the lower 2 bytes is equal to ID_FILE_EXIT, the Exit menu item has been selected, and you need to terminate the application.

The easiest way to terminate the application is to close the main application window. The DestroyWindow function takes a single argument that is the handle of a window to be closed (hWnd, which is the handle to the main application window). DestroyWindow results in a WM_DESTROY menu being sent to the window that is being closed. The WndProc function already has a message handler for WM_DESTROY, which calls PostQuitMessage. This terminates the application.

You could simply call PostQuitMessage in the WM_COMMAND message handler instead of calling DestroyWindow. However, I recommend using the technique that I've described in this section, because any termination code that you place in the WM_DESTROY message handler is executed, regardless of how the application is closed.

Code Listing 5-6 shows the WM_COMMAND handler, along with the other message handlers in WndProc.

Code Listing 5-6

```
LRESULT CALLBACK WndProc(HWND hWnd, UINT message,
                         WPARAM uParam, LPARAM lParam )
{
    switch (message)
    {
    case WM_DESTROY:
        PostQuitMessage(0);
        break;
    case WM_COMMAND:
        if(LOWORD(uParam) == ID_FILE_EXIT)
            DestroyWindow(hWnd);
        break;
    case WM_CREATE:
        hWndCB = CommandBar_Create(hInst, hWnd, 1);
        CommandBar_InsertMenubar(hWndCB, hInst,
            IDR_MAINMENU, 0);
        CommandBar_AddAdornments(hWndCB, 0, 0);
        break;
    default:
        return (DefWindowProc(hWnd, message,
            uParam, lParam));
    }
    return (0);
}
```

Adding Standard and View Buttons

Windows CE provides a standard set of buttons that can be added to a command bar. Windows CE stores these buttons in two bitmaps; one contains the *standard* buttons, and the other contains the *view* buttons. Multiple buttons are stored in a single bitmap, because this is more efficient and it saves memory.

Standard buttons

Each button has an identifier by which it is referred. The standard button images are shown in Figure 5-5. Their identifiers are shown in Table 5-1.

Table 5-1	Standard Buttons and Their Identifiers
Identifier	*Purpose*
STD_FILENEW	File⇨New menu command
STD_FILEOPEN	File⇨Open menu command
STD_FILESAVE	File⇨Save menu command
STD_CUT	Edit⇨Cut menu command
STD_COPY	Edit⇨Copy menu command
STD_PASTE	Edit⇨Paste menu command
STD_UNDO	Edit⇨Undo menu command
STD_REDO	Edit⇨Redo menu command
STD_FIND	Find
STD_REPLACE	Find and replace
STD_DELETE	Delete
STD_PRINTPRE	File⇨Print Preview menu command
STD_PRINT	File⇨Print menu command
STD_PROPERTIES	Display a property dialog box for an object (such as a file)
STD_HELP	Allow access to the help system

Figure 5-5:
The standard buttons.

You don't have to display all the icons when using standard buttons — you can always select only those that are appropriate for your application.

View buttons

You generally use the view buttons when you are displaying a list (like that displayed by Explorer) and you want your users to be able to specify the type of information that is displayed. These buttons are particularly useful if you are using the list control to display data. The view buttons are shown in Table 5-2 and also appear in Figure 5-6.

Table 5-2	View Buttons and Their Identifiers
Identifier	*Purpose*
VIEW_SORTNAME	Sort by name
VIEW_SORTSIZE	Sort by size
VIEW_SORTDATE	Sort by date
VIEW_SORTTYPE	Sort by type
VIEW_DETAILS	Display full details
VIEW_LIST	Display in list format
VIEW_SMALLICONS	Display small icons
VIEW_LARGEICONS	Display large icons
VIEW_PARENTFOLDER	Display the parent folder of the current folder
VIEW_NETCONNECT	Connect to a network resource
VIEW_NETDISCONNECT	Disconnect from a network resource
VIEW_NEWFOLDER	Create a new folder

Figure 5-6:
The view
buttons.

You may find that the standard and view buttons provide only some of the buttons that you need for your application. In this case, you can use the appropriate standard and view buttons, and then add your own buttons.

Order in the buttons!

The standard buttons should always appear in the following order:

- ✔ New
- ✔ Open
- ✔ Save
- ✔ Print
- ✔ Cut, Copy, and Paste

To use standard and view buttons you must do the following:

- ✔ Load the appropriate bitmaps (standard and/or view, as appropriate).
- ✔ Specify the buttons to be displayed, the order of the display, and the locations of the spaces between the buttons.

Loading bitmaps

You use the `CommandBar_AddBitmap` function to load a bitmap in preparing to display buttons. You must supply the following information when adding the standard or view bitmap described in the previous section:

- ✔ hWndCB: The command bar handle to which the menu is to be added. This handle is the one that's returned when `CommandBar_Create` is called.
- ✔ HINST_COMMCTRL: The instance handle where the bitmap is loaded. Use HINST_COMMCTRL when loading standard bitmaps.
- ✔ The value IDB_STD_SMALL_COLOR or IDB_VIEW_SMALL_COLOR, which specifies either standard or view bitmap, respectively.
- ✔ 0: The number of button images in the bitmap that is being added. You should pass 0 when loading the standard or view bitmap.
- ✔ 16,16: The size of the buttons in the bitmap. Command bar buttons should always be 16 pixels by 16 pixels.

Calling this function does not display the bitmap — the call just makes it available for display. You need to call this function for each of the bitmaps that you want to use to create buttons.

You usually call this function directly after creating the command bar. Code Listing 5-7 is sample code that you can use in your applications to load the standard bitmap.

Code Listing 5-7

```
CommandBar_AddBitmap(hWndCB, HINST_COMMCTRL,
    IDB_STD_SMALL_COLOR, 0, 16, 16);
```

Displaying buttons

After you've loaded the bitmap or bitmaps that are required for the buttons in your command bar, you need to call the CommandBar_AddButtons function to display them.

While you call CommandBar_AddBitmap for each bitmap that you plan to use for the buttons, you only call CommandBar_AddButtons one time. You provide information on all the buttons that are to be created, regardless of which bitmap the image comes from.

You specify the buttons to be displayed by creating an array of TBBUTTON structures. Each element in the array specifies the details for one button. You use the TBBUTTON structure to specify the following information for each button:

 ✔ The identifier of the button image in the bitmap. I later describe how to specify this value if you have multiple bitmaps loaded.

 ✔ The command identifier that the button is associated with. This is the identifier that you gave to the menu command that the button is associated with.

 ✔ The initial state that the button is to have (for example, checked or unchecked, or enabled or disabled).

 ✔ The style of the button. This is usually either TBSTYLE_BUTTON (for a standard button) or TBSTYLE_CHECK (for a button that indicates an on/off or checked/unchecked state).

Creating a static array of TBBUTTON structures is the easiest way of defining the buttons to use. In Code Listing 5-8, I place a separator (space) before the buttons, and then I define three buttons for File⇨New, File⇨Open, and File⇨Save.

Code Listing 5-8

```
static TBBUTTON tbButtons[] = {
{0, 0, 0, TBSTYLE_SEP },
{STD_FILENEW , IDM_FILE_NEW, TBSTATE_ENABLED,
            TBSTYLE_BUTTON },
{STD_FILEOPEN , IDM_FILE_OPEN, TBSTATE_ENABLED,
            TBSTYLE_BUTTON },
{STD_FILESAVE, IDM_FILE_SAVE, TBSTATE_ENABLED,
            TBSTYLE_BUTTON },
};
```

Declaring a separator

You should include separators in your toolbar to group the buttons. If you have a menu, you need to add a separator at the beginning of the TBBUTTON array to separate the menu and buttons. That's what I've done in the following TBUTTON array:

```
{0, 0, 0, TBSTYLE_SEP },
```

You should set the style value for the button to TBSTYLE_SEP and leave all the other values set to 0.

Specifying buttons

You initialize each TBBUTTON structure for the three buttons in a similar way. Refer to Code Listing 5-9.

Code Listing 5-9

```
{STD_FILENEW , IDM_FILE_NEW, TBSTATE_ENABLED,
            TBSTYLE_BUTTON },
```

First, you specify the bitmap to be used. For standard bitmaps, you use the STD_ constants to specify which of the button images in the bitmaps are to be used. In the previous code, STD_FILENEW selects the File⇨New button.

Buttons are generally associated with menu items through the menu's identifier. In this example, IDM_FILE_NEW is the identifier that is given to the File⇨New menu command when it is created in the menu editor. When this File New button is clicked, Windows CE sends a WM_COMMAND message to the window specifying IDM_FILE_NEW as the menu identifier. Therefore, clicking this button executes the same code as choosing File⇨New.

Creating and initializing static arrays

You can create and initialize arrays with values. You determine the number of elements in the array by the number of initialized elements that are provided. For example, you could write the following declaration for a simple array of integers:

```
static int myArray[] = {
   0,1,2,3,4 };
```

In this case, I declare an integer array with unknown size ([ ]). I then specify five initializers in braces, and this creates the array with five elements.

You can also create static arrays of structures. In this case, you specify the initializers for the structure members in braces within the initialization of the array (which is in braces, too). So, in the TBBUTTON array declaration for the button bar, I declare four array elements, each storing a TBBUTTON structure.

In many cases, you need to determine the number of elements in the array. The easiest way to do this is to use the sizeof operator in the following way:

```
sizeof(tbButtons)/
   sizeof(TBBUTTON)
```

This determines the overall size of the array in bytes and divides the array by the size of the structure in bytes. This expression, therefore, returns the number of elements in the array.

You have specified all three buttons with the TBSTYLE_BUTTON style. This specifies buttons that can be clicked. You can create buttons that toggle up and down when the user presses them. To create these types of buttons, you specify the TBSTYLE_CHECK style in place of TBSTYLE_BUTTON.

You can enable or disable buttons when they are first displayed. Passing TBSTATE_ENABLED ensures that they are initially enabled. You should pass 0 for the button state member to disable the button when it's displayed.

Adding the buttons

After you declare the TBBUTTON array, you must call CommandBar_AddButtons to add the buttons to the command bar. You need to pass the following information:

- ✔ The command bar handle to which the buttons should be added
- ✔ The number of buttons (TBBUTTON structures) that are declared in the TBBUTTON array
- ✔ A pointer to the TBBUTTON array

You can use this code with the TBBUTTON array called tbButtons to add buttons to a command bar, as follows in Code Listing 5-10.

Code Listing 5-10

```
CommandBar_AddButtons(hWndCB,
    sizeof(tbButtons)/sizeof(TBBUTTON),
    tbButtons);
```

Using multiple bitmaps

You can call `CommandBar_AddBitmap` multiple times when initializing your command bar so that you can use button images from several bitmaps. For example, you can make the following calls (shown in Code Listing 5-11) to load both the standard and view bitmaps.

Code Listing 5-11

```
CommandBar_AddBitmap(hWndCB, HINST_COMMCTRL,
    IDB_STD_SMALL_COLOR, 0, 16, 16);
CommandBar_AddBitmap(hWndCB, HINST_COMMCTRL,
    IDB_VIEW_SMALL_COLOR, 0, 16, 16);
```

Managing multiple bitmaps is a bit more tricky, because the bitmap identifier now takes into account all the bitmaps that are loaded into the command bar. You can think of it as if each bitmap is appended to the previously loaded bitmap. Therefore, when you specify the button identifier in the second bitmap, you must add to the identifier the number of bitmaps in the first bitmap.

An example can make this concept clearer. The last button in the standard bitmap is `STD_PRINT`, and its button number is 14. The first button is `STD_CUT`, and its button number is 0. The first button in the view bitmap is `VIEW_LARGEICONS`, and its button number is 0.

If both the standard and view bitmaps are loaded, the bitmap identifier for `VIEW_LARGEICONS` is 15, which can be expressed using the following constants:

```
STD_PRINT + 1 + VIEW_LARGEICONS
```

You can expand the TBBUTTON array called tbButtons to include another separator and the `VIEW_PARENTFOLDER` button from the view bitmap as follows in Code Listing 5-12.

Code Listing 5-12

```
static TBBUTTON tbButtons[] = {
{0, 0, 0, TBSTYLE_SEP },
{STD_FILENEW ,    IDM_FILE_NEW,   TBSTATE_ENABLED,
         TBSTYLE_BUTTON },
{STD_FILEOPEN , IDM_FILE_OPEN, TBSTATE_ENABLED,
         TBSTYLE_BUTTON },
{STD_FILESAVE, IDM_FILE_SAVE, TBSTATE_ENABLED,
         TBSTYLE_BUTTON },
{0, 0, 0, TBSTYLE_SEP },
{STD_PRINT + 1 + VIEW_PARENTFOLDER,IDM_VIEW_PARENT_FOLDER,
          TBSTATE_ENABLED, TBSTYLE_BUTTON }, };
```

Adding Your Own Button Images

The standard and view bitmaps provide button images for most of the common commands that your application is likely to require. On some occasions, however, you must design your own buttons.

You may be tempted to try and make the standard or view bitmap buttons "fit" the command that your application requires. Avoid doing this, because the standard and view bitmap buttons have specific purposes that are part of the standard user interface that is provided by Windows CE.

Follow these steps to add your own button images:

1. **Add a bitmap of the correct size to the project.**

2. **Load this bitmap when the command bar is initialized.**

3. **Specify the button images in the** TBBUTTON **array.**

The sample application in the \samples\cbar\cbar.dsw workspace adds a new bitmap with a toolbar image for Next and Previous. You should use the resource view to see how the bitmap is created.

Creating the bitmap

First, you must create a bitmap of the correct size. Each button's image is 16 x 16 pixels. The height of the bitmap should, therefore, be 16 pixels, and the width should be the number of button images multiplied by 16. The following steps are required to create the bitmap:

1. **Select the Resource View in the workspace window.**

2. **Insert a new bitmap by choosing Insert⇨Resource, selecting Bitmap, and clicking the New button.**

3. **Change the identifier of the bitmap through the bitmap's Properties dialog box. The sample application uses** `IDB_CMDBAR` **for the bitmap identifier.**

4. **Choose Image⇨ToolbarEditor.**

5. **Set the Button Height edit box to 16 and the Button Width edit box to 16, and click OK.**

6. **Use the drawing tools to create the two button images (see Figure 5-7).**

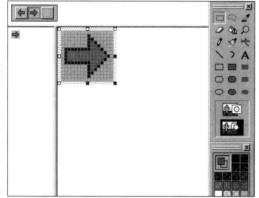

Figure 5-7: Images designed for the Next and Previous buttons.

The bitmap that you create in the Resource Editor has three button images. The fourth (with the dotted box) is not created until you start editing it. I'm only using two of the three images — you can leave blank buttons at the end of a bitmap that you can use later.

Loading your bitmap

You must load your bitmap along with any of the standard bitmaps that your application requires. You should be aware of two main differences when loading your own bitmaps:

✔ When you loaded the standard or view bitmaps, you specified `HINST_COMMCTRL` for the instance handle. You must now use the instance handle of your own application (`hInst`).

✔ You *must* specify the number of button images in the bitmap. This number is 3 in the example shown in Figure 5-7.

In Code Listing 5-13, the call to `CommandBar_AddBitmap` loads the bitmap that is shown in Figure 5-7.

Code Listing 5-13

```
CommandBar_AddBitmap(hWndCB, hInst,
    IDB_CMDBAR, 3, 16, 16);
```

Make this call after the other calls to `CommandBar_AddBitmap`, which load the standard and view bitmaps.

Using your toolbar buttons

You should extend the `TBBUTTON` structure to include definitions for your own buttons. However, be careful when setting the bitmap identifiers, because you must allow for all the bitmaps that have been loaded for the command bar.

In the sample application `CBar`, the standard bitmap (with 15 buttons) and the view bitmap (with 12 buttons) are loaded. Therefore, you specify the first button in `IDB_CMDBAR` by writing `STD_PRINT + VIEW_NEWFOLDER + 2`.

Code Listing 5-14 shows the `TBBUTTON` array called `tbButtons` expanded to include initializations for the buttons in the new button bitmap.

Code Listing 5-14

```
static TBBUTTON tbButtons[] = {
{0, 0, 0, TBSTYLE_SEP },
{STD_FILENEW , IDM_FILE_NEW, TBSTATE_ENABLED,
    TBSTYLE_BUTTON },
{STD_FILEOPEN , IDM_FILE_OPEN, TBSTATE_ENABLED,
    TBSTYLE_BUTTON },
{STD_FILESAVE, IDM_FILE_SAVE, TBSTATE_ENABLED,
    TBSTYLE_BUTTON },
{0, 0, 0, TBSTYLE_SEP },
{STD_PRINT + 1 + VIEW_PARENTFOLDER,IDM_VIEW_PARENT_FOLDER,
    TBSTATE_ENABLED, TBSTYLE_BUTTON },
{0, 0, 0, TBSTYLE_SEP },
{STD_PRINT + VIEW_NEWFOLDER + 2,
    IDM_VIEW_PREV, TBSTATE_ENABLED, TBSTYLE_BUTTON },
{STD_PRINT + VIEW_NEWFOLDER + 3,
    IDM_VIEW_NEXT, TBSTATE_ENABLED, TBSTYLE_BUTTON },
};
```

Adding Combo Boxes

You can add combo boxes (or, drop-down lists) to a command bar. These combo boxes allow users to select, for example, font sizes, font names, or other list options. The combo box is managed using standard Windows CE combo box functions and messages after you have created the combo box.

You use the `CommandBar_InsertComboBox` function to add a combo box to a command bar, and you must pass the following information:

- ✔ `hWndCB`: The handle of the command bar where the combo box is to be added.
- ✔ `hInst`: The instance handle of your application.
- ✔ `120`: The width of the combo box in pixels.
- ✔ `ID_CMDCOMBO`: An identifier (integer value) that is used to identify the combo box. You would normally use a `#define` statement to declare this value, as follows:

```
#define    ID_CMDCOMBO   100
```

- ✔ `10`: The button position for the combo box. Each menu, separator, button, and combo box is located at a button position. You number these items from the left, beginning with 0.

The `CommandBar_InsertComboBox` function returns a window handle to the new combo box. You then use this window handle when calling Windows CE to identify the combo box. You should declare a variable (which is typically global) to store the return value. The following is an example:

```
HWND   hCmdCombo = NULL;
```

You can use the code in Code Listing 5-15 to add combo boxes to your own command bars.

Code Listing 5-15

```
hCmdCombo = CommandBar_InsertComboBox(hWndCB,
      hInst,
      120,
      CBS_DROPDOWNLIST,
      ID_CMDCOMBO,
      10);
```

After you create the combo box, you can add strings by sending a `CB_ADD` `STRING` message to the combo box. Code Listing 5-16 is an example of adding a single string to the combo box.

Code Listing 5-16

```
SendMessage(hCmdCombo, CB_ADDSTRING, 0,
     (LONG)TEXT("Option 1"));
```

In this case, you send the combo box a `CB_ADDSTRING` message, with the string pointer being passed as the last argument. Each message has a `WPARAM` and `LPARAM` value, which specifies the data that is associated with the message; you often have to cast values to a `WPARAM` or `LPARAM` value. I explain sending messages more fully in Chapter 6.

You send notification messages from the combo box when, for example, the user changes the current selection. You handle these messages similarly to the way that you select menu items. Code Listing 5-17, from the CCmd sample on the enclosed CD-ROM, shows you how code can be executed when the user changes the combo box selection.

Code Listing 5-17

```
case WM_COMMAND:
    if(lParam == (LPARAM)hCmdCombo)
    {
        if(HIWORD(uParam) == CBN_SELCHANGE)
            MessageBox(hWnd, TEXT("Selection changed"),
                szTitle, MB_OK);
    }
    else
        MenuHandler(hWnd, LOWORD(uParam));
    break;
```

Windows CE sends the `WM_COMMAND` message to the `WndProc` window message handler function when a menu item or control in that window generates a notification. The `lParam` value contains the handle of the control that generates the message (I'm checking for `hCmdCombo` in this case), and the top 2 bytes of `uParam` contain the notification message. You use the `HIWORD` macro to extract the top 2 bytes from `uParam`. In this case, the notification message is `CBN_SELCHANGE`.

Adding Tooltips

Windows CE displays tooltips for command bar buttons when the user keeps the button pressed for a short period of time.

You may find that tooltips don't work under emulation. You should test the tooltips for your command bar on a Windows CE device.

You can only display tooltips for buttons, not menus or combo boxes.

The first step in creating tooltips is to create an array of strings that contain the text of the tooltips. Use Code Listing 5-18.

Code Listing 5-18

```
WCHAR *szTooltips[] = {
    NULL,
    &TEXT("New Button"),
    &TEXT("Open Button"),
    &TEXT("Save Button"),
    &TEXT("Folder button"),
    &TEXT("Prev button"),
    &TEXT("Next button"),
};
```

The NULL value in the first element of this array is for the menu. Although the menu cannot display a tooltip, you must specify an element in the szTooltips array for the menu.

Next, call the CommandBar_AddToolTips function to add the tooltips to the command bar. You must pass the following information:

- hWndCB: The handle of the command bar.
- 7: The number of elements in the szTooltips array.
- szTooltips: A pointer to the array of tooltip strings.

Make your call to CommandBar_AddToolTips before calling CommandBar_AddAdornments, as follows:

```
CommandBar_AddToolTips(hWndCB, 7, szTooltips);
```

Using Command Bars with MFC

All the information about command bars that I describe in previous chapters applies to using command bars in MFC applications, but creating new buttons is easier.

All the buttons that are used in the command bar are contained in the IDR_MAINFRAME toolbar. The toolbar is created automatically when the application is created using the AppWizard.

Note that MFC applications do not use the standard and view bitmaps that I describe earlier in this chapter.

You can set the identifiers for each button using the Toolbar Button Properties dialog box, shown in Figure 5-8. This allows you to associate a button with a menu command.

The standard IDR_MAINFRAME menu is already added by the AppWizard to the command bar, so you don't need to do this.

The CMainFrame::OnCreate method calls the necessary code to create the command bar and to add the buttons. The CFrameWnd class (from which CMainFrame is derived) contains member functions that call the command bar functions that I describe earlier in the chapter. Some examples of these functions are shown in Table 5-3.

Figure 5-8:
Designing
command
bar buttons
in MFC
applications.

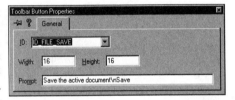

Table 5-3	Member Function Examples
CFrameWnd Method	*Corresponding Command Bar Function*
AddBitmap	CommandBar_AddBitmap
InsertButtons	CommandBar_AddButtons
InsertComboBox	CommandBar_InsertComboBox
AddAdornments	CommandBar_AddAdornments
InsertMenu	CommandBar_InsertMenubar

To provide additional features on your command bar in an MFC application, you should add the calls to the CFrameWnd class members, which are shown in this table, to the CMainFrame::OnCreate method.

Chapter 6

Creating Dialog Boxes

• •

In This Chapter

▶ Designing dialog boxes for Windows CE

▶ Using the correct styles for a Windows CE dialog box

▶ Creating dialog box message functions

▶ Responding to notification messages

• •

*I*n this chapter, I show you the important differences between Windows CE dialog boxes and those developed for Windows 95 and NT. The most important difference is that Windows CE dialog boxes do not have the typical OK and Cancel buttons. Instead, the dialog box caption bar displays the OK and X icons, which represent these buttons (see Figure 6-1).

Figure 6-1:
A Sample
Dialog Box.

Style Guide for Dialog Boxes

Many of the same design rules for Windows NT and 95 dialog boxes apply to Windows CE. Dialog boxes in Windows CE, however, are much smaller, and they have fewer controls and less-complex user interactions. Remember that a Windows CE dialog box is probably more difficult to use because of the smaller keyboard. Furthermore, interactions involving the stylus are more difficult than interactions with a mouse.

Remember that Windows CE devices do not have a mouse. Instead, a stylus is used to tap items on the screen to select or otherwise interact with them.

Try to follow these general guidelines when designing dialog boxes for Windows CE:

✔ Create simple dialog boxes with only a few, large controls.

Controls should be at least 23 pixels high and 23 pixels wide, or 38 x 38 pixels if you expect the user to interact with the stylus.

✔ Use a non-boldface font for all labels and text in controls.

Your best bet is to use the default MS Sans Serif 8-point font.

✔ If the dialog box contains OK and Cancel (X) buttons, place them both in the caption and not in the dialog box itself.

If the dialog box has OK and Cancel button functions that perform the same task, add an OK button to the caption and disable the caption's Cancel button.

Creating Dialog Boxes Using the API

Creating a dialog box involves designing the layout of the controls (such as edit boxes and radio buttons), and then writing code that responds to the user carrying out actions (for example, tapping a radio button).

The \samples\DlgDisplay.dsw workspace on the enclosed CD-ROM contains source code and dialog box designs that show you how to add dialog boxes to your applications. You can copy the source code directly into your own application and use it as a starting point to develop your own dialog boxes.

Use the following general steps to create a dialog box:

1. **Design the dialog box (which defines the layout of the controls) in the Developer Studio Resource Editor.**

   This is the fun bit! The Resource Editor is a graphical tool that allows you to place the controls in a dialog box, and to arrange them exactly the way you want. The dialog box is called IDD_DLGSAMP in the DlgDisplay.dsw workspace on the CD-ROM.

2. **Create a message-processing function to handle messages and interactions from the dialog box.**

The message processing function is very similar to the window message processing function (WndProc) described in the section "Declaring message-handling functions" in Chapter 3. This function is called OptionsDlgProc in the file DlgDisplay.cpp on the CD-ROM.

3. **Make a call to display the dialog box from a menu item, button, or other user-interface component**.

   Dialog boxes are most frequently displayed in response to the user selecting a menu command. The dialog box IDD_DLGSAMP appears when the user selects the menu item IDM_FILE_OPTIONS in DlgDisplay on the sample CD-ROM.

Designing the dialog box

You create dialog boxes by using the Resource Editor in the Developer Studio. Use the following steps to create a new dialog box in an application:

1. **Select the Resource View tab in the Workspace window.**

   The resource view tab displays a list of all the resources, including dialog boxes, in your project. You can also add new dialog boxes from the resource view.

2. **Choose Insert⇨Resource menu, select Dialog from the Resource Type list, and then select New.**

   This menu displays the Insert Resource dialog box, which contains a Resource Type list containing a list of all the different types of resources that can be added to a project. You should choose Dialog from the Resource Type list.

   This creates a standard Windows NT/95 dialog box. You now need to make the following changes for Windows CE.

3. **Delete the OK and Cancel buttons that are created by default in the dialog box.**

   Select the OK button in the dialog box that you just created, then press Delete. Repeat for the Cancel button.

4. **Right-click anywhere in the dialog box you've created, and choose Properties from the popup menu that appears.**

   The Dialog Properties dialog box appears.

5. **Change the X Pos and Y Pos edit boxes to 20 and 20, respectively.**

   The X Pos and Y Pos values specify the position of the upper-left corner of the dialog box when the dialog box is displayed.

6. **While still in the Properties window for the dialog box, click the Extended Styles tab.**

7. Check the Caption Bar OK (WCE Only) style.

After you change this style, the dialog box appears with the OK button in the caption bar.

You can choose Layout⇨Test in Developer Studio to review the dialog box's design. Note that this does *not* show the OK button in the caption bar because Windows NT does not support this feature.

If you're adding a dialog box to your API application, be sure that you add a resource (RC) file to your project. This is described in the section "Designing the menu" in Chapter 5.

You can now design the dialog box using the standard Developer Studio techniques. I show the layout of the controls for the sample dialog box in DlgDisplay.dsw in Figure 6-1. Use the following steps to create the dialog box design:

1. Display the dialog box's property window by right-clicking the dialog box and choosing Properties.

This displays the Dialog Properties dialog box.

2. Set the dialog box's identifier to IDD_DLGSAMP and the caption to Sample Dialog box.

The General tab in the Dialog Properties dialog box contains the Identifier combo box for setting the dialog box's identifier and the Caption edit box for setting the text for your dialog box's caption.

3. Add a static text control, and set the caption to Options: in the static text control's property window.

You display this window by right-clicking the static text control and choosing Properties from the pop-up menu that appears. This displays the Text properties dialog box.

4. Add a drop-down list box to the dialog box, right-click the combo box and select Properties from the pop-up menu that appears.

This displays the Combo Box Properties dialog box. Set the identifier for the combo box to IDC_OPTIONS in the combo box's property window.

Keep in mind that a combo box is a dialog box that includes a drop-down list.

The drop-down list box works differently in Windows CE than it does in Windows NT or Windows 95. Unless the drop-down list box is deeper than about five lines, the vertical scrollbar does not appear. It is important to use the following steps whenever you add a combo box in Windows CE:

1. Select the combo box with a single click.

Note that sizing boxes are displayed around it (as shown in Figure 6-2).

Click the gray down-arrow button.

Figure 6-2:
Enabling
the sizing
box.

All the sizing boxes for the combo box (except the left and right box, which are used for changing the width of the combo box), are disabled.

2. Click the gray down-arrow button in the combo box itself.

The sizing box at the bottom center is now enabled and is shown as a blue box. You can now use this sizing box to change the depth of the drop-down list box (see Figure 6-3).

Figure 6-3:
Changing
the depth
of the drop-
down list.

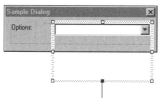

Use the blue box to increase the depth of the listbox.

3. Use the blue sizing box to increase the depth of the drop-down list box so that it is more than five lines deep.

Creating the dialog box message function

Each dialog box must have a function that manages the messages sent to the dialog box by Windows CE. This function is called a *dialog box message function*. You can add code to this function to respond to actions taken by the user. The following code sample is the function declaration for the dialog box function from DlgDisplay.dsw:

```
int CALLBACK OptionsDlgProc(HWND hDlg, UINT uMsg,
    WPARAM wParam, LPARAM lParam)
```

You call this function whenever a message is generated for the dialog box, including notification messages.

Windows CE must provide information about what the user has done in the dialog box, so that the code you add to the function can respond appropriately. This information is passed to the function using the following paramaters:

- ✔ hDlg: The handle (unique reference value) to the dialog box.

- ✔ uMsg: The message ID. This is WM_COMMAND for messages being sent from a control in the dialog box.

- ✔ wParam and lParam: Data that is specific to each type of message.

The function returns TRUE if it handles the message or FALSE if it does not.

Code Listing 6-1 shows the code used as a starting point for a dialog box message function. This dialog box message function has code that handles the following two messages:

- ✔ The WM_INITDIALOG message. You send this just before the dialog box is displayed to the user. You should add code to initialize the controls (for example, by adding strings to a combo box) in response to this message.

- ✔ The WM_COMMAND message. You send this when a control needs to notify the dialog box of some event. The LOWORD of wParam contains the identifier of the control that is sending the message. In this case, the code calls EndDialog if either the OK button or Cancel button sends a notification message. This message is sent to the dialog box when the user clicks one of the buttons.

Code Listing 6-1

```
int CALLBACK OptionsDlgProc(HWND hDlg, UINT uMsg,
    WPARAM wParam,
    LPARAM lParam)
{
    switch(uMsg)
    {
    case WM_INITDIALOG:
        return (TRUE);
```

```
case WM_COMMAND:
    switch (LOWORD(wParam))
    {
    case IDOK:
        EndDialog(hDlg, IDOK);
        break;
    case IDCANCEL:
        EndDialog(hDlg, IDCANCEL);
        break;
    }
    return (TRUE);
}
return (FALSE);
}
```

You call the `EndDialog` function when either the OK button or Cancel button is tapped. This function closes the dialog box whose handle is specified in the first argument (`hDlg`). You use the second argument (`IDOK` or `IDCANCEL`) to specify which button was tapped to close the dialog box.

Initializing dialog box controls

You often need to initialize controls with specific values or give them a particular appearance before the dialog box is displayed to the user. You can add this initialization code in response to the `WM_INITDIALOG` message being received. For example, in DlgDisplay.cpp, you load the combo box with some strings.

You make controls do things by sending them messages. To send these messages, you need the window handle of the control. You must obtain this handle at runtime using the `GetDlgItem` function, passing the dialog box's window handle and the identifier of the control (which you set in the dialog box editor), as follows:

```
HWND hCombo;
hCombo = GetDlgItem(hDlg, IDC_OPTIONS);
```

After you obtain a handle of the control (`hCombo`), you can send messages to the control (such as `CB_ADDSTRING`) using the `SendMessage` function. You need to provide additional information for the message, such as, which string to add to the dialog box. The `SendMessage` function requires you to pass the following data to provide this additional information:

✔ hCombo: The window handle of the control to which the message is to be sent.

✔ CB_ADDSTRING: The message to be sent.

✔ wParam and lParam: Two 4-byte values that contain additional information about the message being sent.

The data that you pass to SendMessage depends on the message being sent. In the case of CB_ADDSTRING, you pass a pointer to the string in the last argument and cast it to an LPARAM. You can use Code Listing 6-2 in DlgDisplay.cpp to add strings to the dailog box, as follows.

Code Listing 6-2

```
HWND hCombo;
    switch(uMsg)
    {
    case WM_INITDIALOG:
        hCombo = GetDlgItem(hDlg, IDC_OPTIONS);
        SendMessage(hCombo, CB_ADDSTRING, 0,
            (LPARAM)TEXT("Option 1"));
        SendMessage(hCombo, CB_ADDSTRING, 0,
            (LPARAM)TEXT("Option 2"));
```

Getting control notifications

Controls can send the dialog box message function notification messages in a WM_COMMAND message when some event occurs. You've already seen an example of this when the OK button notifies the dialog box that it's been tapped. This is a simple case, because the OK button can only notify the dialog box of one event (it has been tapped), so you don't need to further investigate the type of event.

Controls can send the dialog box message function notification messages in a WM_COMMAND message when some event occurs. For example, the OK button sends the message WM_COMMAND to the dialog box message function whenever it is tapped. The dialog box message function responds by closing the dialog box.

The OK button is a simple case, because the button only sends one notification message (called the *button has been clicked notification*). Other controls can sends many different notification messages. For example, a dialog box may send a notification such as "user selected a string from the list box," or "user has typed text into the combo box." In this case, you need to further investigate which type of notification event is being sent by the control.

Combo boxes (drop-down list boxes) have a number of different notification messages that all begin with *CBN* (which stands for *combo box notification*). For example, the combo box sends `CBN_CLOSEUP` when the user closes the list box part of the control.

The control passes the notification message in the top two bytes of the message's `wParam` value. You can use the `HIWORD` macro to extract the notification code. Use Code Listing 6-3 to display a message box when the user double-taps the combo box.

Code Listing 6-3

```
case WM_COMMAND:
    switch (LOWORD(wParam))
    {
        case IDC_OPTIONS:
            if(HIWORD(wParam) == CBN_CLOSEUP)
                MessageBox(hDlg, TEXT("Listbox Closed!"),
                    szTitle, MB_OK);
            break;
        case IDOK:
```

Responding to the dialog box closing

You need to write code that does something with the data that the user enters when the user taps the OK button. For example, in Code Listing 6-4, the string that's currently selected in the combo box is displayed to the user in a message box using the `GetWindowText` function to retrieve the text that's associated with a control. In your application, you probably take the data from the controls and store the data in variables to allow the data from the controls to be used after the dialog box has been closed.

Code Listing 6-4

```
case IDOK:
    TCHAR szBuffer[20];
    hCombo = GetDlgItem(hDlg, IDC_OPTIONS);
    GetWindowText(hCombo, szBuffer, 10);
    MessageBox(hDlg, szBuffer, szTitle, MB_OK);
    EndDialog(hDlg, IDOK);
    break;
```

Notice how you call the `GetDlgItem` function whenever the handle to the dialog box is required. This is necessary because each new message results in a new call to the `OptionsDlgProc` function being made by Windows CE, and you must reinitialize `hCombo`.

Displaying the dialog box

In the DlgDisplay.cpp sample source code, the dialog box is displayed in response to the user choosing File⇨Options. You use the `DialogBox` function to display the dialog box, and this requires the following information:

- ✔ `hInst`: The application's instance handle.

- ✔ `IDD_DLGSAMP`: The dialog box's identifier. Note that you must use the `MAKEINTRESOURCE` macro to convert this integer identifier to a string value, because `DialogBox` expects a string.

- ✔ `hWnd`: The window handle that is to be the parent window of the dialog box. This is the application window in this case.

- ✔ `OptionsDlgProc`: The function that is to handle the messages from the dialog box. I describe this function in the previous section.

This information tells Windows CE which dialog box to display and which dialog message function handles messages from the dialog box.

The code in Code Listing 6-5 displays the dialog box. The return value from `DialogBox` is the second argument that's passed to `EndDialog` when the user closes the dialog box. This allows the caller of `DialogBox` to determine if the OK button or Cancel button was tapped.

Code Listing 6-5

```
case IDM_FILE_OPTIONS:
    if(DialogBox(hInst, MAKEINTRESOURCE(IDD_DLGSAMP),
            hWnd, OptionsDlgProc) == IDOK)
        MessageBox(hWnd, TEXT("OK pressed"), szTitle, MB_OK);
    break;
```

A few more odds and ends

To program dialog boxes you need to further understand the following items:

- ✔ **The messages to send to controls to make them do something:** These messages are documented under the names of the controls to which they apply. For example, you can search the online help for *Combo Box Messages* to find a list of the other messages that you can send to a combo box.

✔ **The notification messages that a control can send you:** Search the online documentation under the name of the control, for example, `Combo Box Notifications`.

✔ **Window functions that can be used on controls:** For example, `GetWindowText` can retrieve the text in text boxes, static text boxes, and combo boxes, and you can call `GetWindowTextLength` to find the number of characters in the window's text.

Creating Dialog Box Forms with the MFC

Programming dialog boxes using MFC in Windows CE is almost identical to performing this task in Windows 95 and NT. You should, however, follow the user interface style guidelines that are detailed in "Style Guide for Dialog Boxes," near the beginning of this chapter. You can then follow the steps in "Designing the dialog box" to build Windows CE style dialog boxes in MFC applications.

The \samples\DlgMFC.dsw workspace contains the source code for an MFC application that displays a dialog box from the File➪Options menu command. The code in this section is taken from this application. The dialog box created in this application is the same as that in Figure 6-1.

When designing a Windows CE dialog box, you generally delete the OK and Cancel buttons that are created by the Resource Editor because they are displayed as icons in the dialog box's caption bar. You should create the dialog box's class and add the message handlers for the OK and Cancel buttons *before* deleting the buttons in the dialog box editor. If you don't do this, you may not see `IDOK` and `IDCANCEL` in the dialog box's list of controls, and you won't be able to add message handlers for them.

Chapter 7

Drawing Using the MGDI

• •

In This Chapter

▶ Drawing in API applications

▶ Drawing in MFC applications

▶ Using `Polyline` in place of `MoveTo` and `LineTo`

▶ Using `DrawText` in place of `TextOut`

▶ Finding out about missing drawing functions in Windows CE

• •

*1*n Windows 95 and Windows NT, programmers use the *graphics device interface* (GDI) to support drawing onto windows, which includes the output of text, drawing lines, filling shapes, and printing. In Windows CE, *multiplatform graphics device interface* (or MGDI) replaces GDI. The MGDI is a set of functions that implements all the drawing capabilities supported by Windows CE. The MGDI supports many of the same functions as the GDI, but you will find that a significant number of GDI facilities are not present in MGDI.

You must use MGDI functions to display *everything* that appears in a window, including text, lines, and the drawing of bitmaps. In this chapter, I show you how to draw onto your application window using MGDI functions, and explain some of the differences between the MGDI and GDI.

Drawing Using the API

You can write two different types of drawing code in a Windows CE API application:

> ✔ **Code that draws in the window in response to some event.** For example, if you write a drawing program, you may need to draw a line to where the user taps the stylus. In this case, you draw the line immediately as the stylus tap event is received by your application. I call this *drawing on the fly*.

✔ **Code that redraws the window when the display is out of date.**
Windows CE sends the application a WM_PAINT message indicating that
the window must be redrawn. This happens, for example, when the
application window is brought to the foreground. Windows CE does not
store the image that you have drawn in a window. You are responsible
for redrawing the image whenever the window is redisplayed (after being
hidden). So, you must be prepared to redraw your window at any time.

In both cases, your code must use a *device context* onto which you draw —
that is, you cannot draw directly onto a window. You use different methods
to get a device context; it depends on whether your application is drawing
on the fly or the window function has received a WM_PAINT message.

You find the code demonstrating these two drawing techniques in the
workspace \samples\drawAPI\drawAPI.dsw. Through these samples, you
can experiment with different drawing techniques by modifying and testing
this code. I describe some ways to draw text and graphics in the two
following sections.

Understanding device contexts

In Windows CE, you can't draw onto a window — it's just not allowed.
Instead, you need to obtain a *device context* for the window. You don't need
to worry too much about what a device context is. Think of it as a link
between the function calls that you make to draw text or graphics, and the
window in which you want the drawing to be displayed. The device context
contains information about how drawing will take place. This includes, for
example, the font to use when drawing text or the color to use when drawing lines.

When you request a device context, you're returned a handle to the device
context. This handle is an integer value that represents the device context.
After you receive a device context, you can then call MGDI functions to draw
onto the device context. Any drawing that you perform onto the device
context appears in the window that the device context is associated with.

Drawing on the fly

The first step is to figure out how to draw in response to an event. Code
Listing 7-1 shows code that draws circles in response to the user tapping the
application window.

Codo Licting 7-1

```
case WM_LBUTTONDOWN:
    HDC hDC;
    int x, y;
    x = LOWORD(lParam);
    y = HIWORD(lParam);
    hDC = GetDC(hWnd);
    Ellipse(hDC, x, y, x + 20, y + 20);
    ReleaseDC(hWnd, hDC);
    break;
```

The circle is drawn at the point where the user taps. This drawing involves three steps:

1. **Get a device context.**

   You must declare an `HDC` variable, and then call the Windows CE function `GetDC` to get a handle for a device context for a window. The function `GetDC` is passed the handle of a window with which the device context is associated.

   ```
   HDC hDC;
   hDC = GetDC(hWnd);
   ```

2. **Call drawing functions.**

   The MGDI contains a set of functions that you can call to draw text and graphics. These functions are called just like any other Windows CE functions. You use MGDI functions to draw onto the device context (which results in the drawing being displayed on the window).

   In this circle-drawing example, the x,y coordinate at the point where the user taps is obtained from the `HIWORD` and `LOWORD` values in the `lParam` that's passed with this message. The `Ellipse` MGDI function is then called, and is passed the coordinates of the top-left and bottom-right corners of the rectangle that bounds the ellipse to be drawn.

   ```
   x = LOWORD(lParam);
   y = HIWORD(lParam);
   Ellipse(hDC, x, y, x + 20, y + 20);
   ```

3. **Release the device context.**

   Call the Windows CE function `ReleaseDC` to release memory associated with the device context and to mark the end of drawing. The function `ReleaseDC` is passed the handle of the window, `hWnd` and the device context, `hDC`.

   ```
   ReleaseDC(hWnd, hDC);
   ```

This drawing does not *stick* — by this I mean that any drawing you do on the window is lost if the user hides the window and then redisplays it. The window will be blank.

WM_PAINT messages

A WM_PAINT message is sent by Windows CE to a window whenever part or all of the window needs to be redrawn. Your application stores appropriate data in variables so that the window can be redrawn at any time. Generally, it's easiest just to redraw the entire window, regardless of how much actually needs to be redrawn. Therefore, I recommend that you redraw the entire window when all or part of the window needs redrawing.

In the case of the circle-drawing sample application (Code Listing 7-1), you have to store each *x,y* coordinate where the user taps the window. In response to a WM_PAINT message, you must write code to redraw every circle at the appropriate location.

The file called DrawAPI.cpp on the CD-ROM contains all the code for storing the coordinates and redrawing in response to the WM_PAINT message.

When an application receives a WM_PAINT message, you obtain a device context by calling the BeginPaint function (Code Listing 7-2). This function is passed a window handle and pointer to a PAINTSTRUCT structure. Windows CE places a valid display context handle in the hdc member of the PAINTSTRUCT structure. After executing the drawing code, call EndPaint, passing the same window handle and pointer to the PAINTSTRUCT structure.

Code Listing 7-2

```
case WM_PAINT:
        PAINTSTRUCT  ps;
        hdc = BeginPaint(hWnd, &ps);
        // insert drawing code here
        EndPaint(hWnd, &ps);
        break;
```

Never call GetDC and ReleaseDC in response to receiving a WM_PAINT message. Also, never call BeginPaint or EndPaint except in response to a WM_PAINT message. If you don't follow these rules, the device context that you obtain will be invalid, and your application will fail.

Understanding the Client Area

Your application can only draw in the *client area* — the area within the window frame. You can determine the size of the client area by calling the function `GetClientRect` and passing it the window handle and a pointer to a `RECT` structure, as shown in Code Listing 7-3.

Code Listing 7-3

```
RECT rClient;
GetClientRect(hWnd, &rClient);
```

The `RECT` structure has four members: `top`, `left`, `bottom`, and `right`. Together the members define the top-left and bottom-right coordinates of a rectangle. The top and left values are always 0 after calling `GetClientRect`. The bottom and right members of `RECT` contain the height and width of the client area of the window, as shown in Figure 7-1.

Top-left
(0,0)

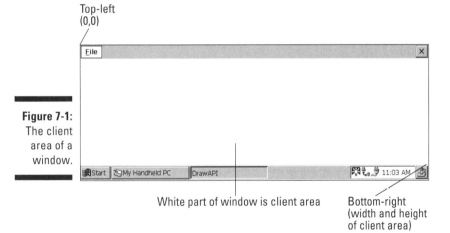

Figure 7-1:
The client
area of a
window.

White part of window is client area   Bottom-right
(width and height
of client area)

In Windows 95 and Windows NT applications, you can draw anywhere in the client rectangle. This is also true of Windows CE, with the exception of where the window has a command bar (the command bar occupies part of the client area). Determine the height of the command bar and then start drawing underneath it. The function `CommandBar_Height` returns the height of the command bar and takes a single argument, which is the command bar's handle.

So, to adjust the `RECT` structure returned from `GetClientRect`, add Code Listing 7-4 to your application.

Code Listing 7-4

```
RECT rClient;
GetClientRect(hWnd, &rClient);
rClient.top += CommandBar_Height (hWndCB);
```

As an example of how to use the RECT returned from GetClientRect, the sample application drawAPI (located on the CD-ROM in the workspace \samples\drawAPI\drawAPI.dsw,) draws a rectangle around the client rectangle just inside the frame of the window (see Figure 7-2).

The code shown in Code Listing 7-5, draws the rectangle by calling the Rectangle function. The Rectangle function is passed the display context (from the PAINTSTRUCT structure) and the top-left and bottom-right coordinates for the rectangle to be drawn. The call adds and subtracts 10, in order to draw the rectangle 10 pixels in from the window's frame.

Figure 7-2:
A rectangle and circles drawn within the window's client area.

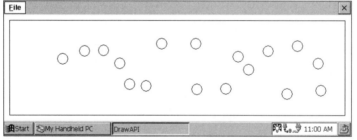

Code Listing 7-5

```
case WM_PAINT:
        PAINTSTRUCT  ps;
        hdc = BeginPaint(hWnd, &ps);

        RECT rClient;
        GetClientRect(hWnd, &rClient);
        rClient.top += CommandBar_Height (hWndCB);
        Rectangle(ps.hdc,
            rClient.left + 10,  rClient.top + 10,
            rClient.right - 10, rClient.bottom - 10);

        EndPaint(hWnd, &ps);
        break;
```

Drawing Using the MFC

When drawing in an MFC application, you must obtain a device context just as with API applications. The major difference between using the MFC and using the API is that you don't get a device context by calling the function GetDC. Instead, MFC provides a CDC class. The CDC class is used for all drawing in an MFC application. All of the drawing functions (such as the Rectangle function used in the previous section) are represented by member functions in the CDC class. Use the following steps for drawing on the fly using the CDC class:

1. **Get a pointer to a** CDC **class object.**

   The MFC GetDC member function returns a pointer to a CDC class object for a window. GetDC returns a CDC class object for your view if you execute the following code in your CView class:

   ```
   CDC *pDC = GetDC();
   ```

2. **Use the** CDC **class object for drawing.**

   In this example, the CDC class Rectangle member function is used to draw a rectangle using the coordinates 10,10 and 20,20.

   ```
   pDC->Rectangle(10, 10, 20, 20);
   ```

3. **Release the** CDC **class object.**

   This call deletes the device context that was obtained by calling GetDC.

   ```
   ReleaseDC(pDC);
   ```

Chapter 4 shows a complete example of drawing using the CDC class, that includes drawing on the fly and drawing in response to a WM_PAINT message.

When drawing in an API application, you have to allow for the height of the command bar, as it's part of the client area. MFC applications, however, automatically allow for this height — the 0,0 coordinate is just below the command bar.

Drawing Text

Many programmers grew up with the TextOut function for drawing a single line of text at a specified coordinate. Over the past years, the TextOut function has been going out of vogue, and finally, with the release of Windows CE, TextOut is relegated to the has-been function list.

Making do without a current drawing location

Windows NT and Windows 95 both support the concept of a *current drawing position,* which defines the coordinate where drawing takes place. Many, but not all, GDI functions use the current drawing location as the starting point for drawing. Two functions, MoveTo and LineTo, are used for drawing lines in Windows NT and Windows 95. The function MoveTo moves the current drawing location to a new point. The function LineTo draws from the current drawing location to a given point. So, to draw a line from 10,10 to 40,50, you can write:

```
MoveTo(hDC, 10, 10);
LineTo(hDC, 40, 50);
```

The current drawing location was a casualty of moving the Windows 95 and Windows NT APIs to the smaller Windows CE. The consequence of having no current drawing location is that any Windows NT or Windows 95 function using the current drawing location is not supported in Windows CE.

Actually, many of the functions that use the current drawing location are obscure, and you probably won't miss them. However, MoveTo and LineTo are used frequently, so replacements must be found — the function PolyLine replaces MoveTo and LineTo.

While you won't find MoveTo and LineTo in the Windows CE API, they *are* present in the MFC class CDC. The programmers who write the MFC missed MoveTo and LineTo so much they wrote their own.

Because MoveTo and LineTo are not supported in the Windows CE API, you should use PolyLine for drawing lines. This function takes three arguments:

✔ The display context handle to draw to. This is the HDC handle obtained from calling GetDC.

✔ A pointer to an array of POINT structures containing the coordinates to draw lines between. Each POINT variable has an x and y member that are used to store the coordinate. You should specify two points if you want to draw a single line. The first point is the start coordinate and the second point is the end coordinate for drawing the line.

✔ An integer specifying the number of points in the POINT structure array. When drawing a single line, this integer should be 2.

In this source code fragment, the PolyLine function is used to draw a line from the point 100,100 to the point 150,150. These coordinates are specified in the POINT array pPnt:

```
HDC hDC;
hDC = GetDC(hWnd);
POINT pPnt[2];
pPnt[0].x = 100; pPnt[0].y = 100;
pPnt[1].x = 150; pPnt[1].y = 150;
Polyline(hDC, pPnt, 2);
ReleaseDC(hWnd, hDC);
```

Instead, savvy programmers (that's you!), use the more powerful DrawText. This function has the advantage over TextOut in that multiline text can be formatted within a rectangle. The downside is that DrawText is slightly more complex to call:

```
DrawText(hDC, lpStr, -1, &rRect, DT_CENTER | DT_WORDBREAK);
```

DrawText is passed the following arguments:

- ✔ **Device context handle:** The device context handle (hDC) to draw the text onto.

- ✔ **The text to draw:** A pointer to the string to print (lpStr). This can include new line (\n) characters.

- ✔ **Length of text to draw:** The number of characters in the string to be printed. If the string is NULL terminated, you can pass -1 and DrawText works out the length.

- ✔ **Formatting rectangle:** A pointer to a RECT structure specifying the rectangle coordinates within which the text is printed.

- ✔ **Formatting options:** Constant values that define how the text is formatted. You can combine multiple formatting options using the C OR operator. For example, DT_CENTER | DT_WORDBREAK specifies that the text should be horizontally centered and that lines should automatically wrap with line breaks placed between words.

In Code Listing 7-6, look for the following:

- ✔ The string lpStr points to a string constant containing three lines.

- ✔ The RECT structure rRect is initialized by a call to the Windows CE function SetRect. The function SetRect takes four arguments which are top, left, right and bottom integer values that are set in the RECT structure.

  This function call initializes the structure to contain the coordinates 40,100 and 200,200.

- ✔ The GetDC function is called to obtain a device context on which to draw the text.

- ✔ DrawText is called using the arguments described earlier in this section.

Code Listing 7-6

```
LPTSTR lpStr = TEXT("First line\nSecond line\nThird Line");
RECT rRect;
SetRect(&rRect, 40, 100, 200, 200);
hDC = GetDC(hWnd);
DrawText(hDC, lpStr, -1, &rRect, DT_CENTER | DT_WORDBREAK);
ReleaseDC(hWnd, hDC);
```

The call to DrawText results in text being drawn that

- ✔ Is formatted within the rectangle
- ✔ Is centered horizontally
- ✔ Has line breaks inserted between words

All functions that take a RECT parameter always require that you pass a pointer to the RECT structure.

What Else Is Missing in the MGDI?

The MGDI is missing a number of graphics functions and facilities that you may be used to calling for Windows 95 and Windows NT. Here are some of the more common functions that Windows CE does *not* support:

- ✔ **Non-client drawing:** In Windows NT and Windows 95, you can draw outside of the client area, which allows you to override the drawing of a window's caption bar and frame. You can't draw in the non-client area in Windows CE.

- ✔ **Mapping modes:** Windows CE supports only the default MM_TEXT mapping mode. This means that you're limited to using the pixel coordinate system in which the origin (0,0) is located at the top left of the client area.

- ✔ **Mouse Cursors:** Windows CE does not allow you to use custom mouse cursors. Most Windows CE devices allow you only to display the hourglass-shaped wait cursor, which is displayed when your application is performing lengthy operations. You can use the calls in Code Listing 7-7 to display the hourglass wait cursor, and then hide it.

Code Listing 7-7

```
SetCursor(LoadCursor(NULL, IDC_WAIT));
// Lengthy processing here
SetCursor(NULL);
```

Chapter 8

Exploring Other Development Environments

. . . .

In This Chapter

▶ Windows CE Toolkit for Visual Basic 5.0

▶ Windows CE Toolkit for Visual J++

▶ Other development environments that you probably can do without

. . . .

*W*indows CE is an operating system and, as such, is not limited to or built for any particular development language. Throughout this book, I describe how to build Windows CE applications by using C or C++ with the API, or by using C++ with the MFC. These tools allow you to write the most efficient and best-performing applications.

To be perfectly honest, though, the API and MFC are not everyone's cup of tea! You can use other development environments, including Microsoft Visual Basic and Microsoft Visual J++ (using the Java language) to create great Windows CE applications. This chapter gets you started.

Windows CE Toolkit for Visual Basic 5.0

Microsoft Visual Basic is the most popular development environment for Windows 95 and Windows NT, so it makes sense that you can use Visual Basic to create Windows CE applications. The Windows CE Toolkit for Visual Basic 5.0 (which I refer to as *Pocket VB,* just to save space and time) is an add-in for Microsoft Visual Basic 5.0 that allows programmers to develop Windows CE applications. This add-in brings Windows CE programming to nearly all PC developers. (After all, very few programmers out there haven't done *something* with a Visual Basic application.)

What's in the box?

Pocket VB provides all the additional tools necessary to build Windows CE applications, including the following:

- ✔ **Add-ins for Visual Basic:** These add-ins allow you to build and compile projects under Windows CE.

- ✔ **The emulation environment:** This environment allows you to run and debug Pocket VB applications on a desktop PC.

- ✔ **A setup wizard:** This wizard automates the production of a setup program that installs Pocket VB on a Windows CE device.

Because this product is an *add-in* for Visual Basic 5.0, you must first have Visual Basic 5.0 installed before you can use Pocket VB. You can then use the standard Visual Basic development environment to build the application (as shown in Figure 8-1).

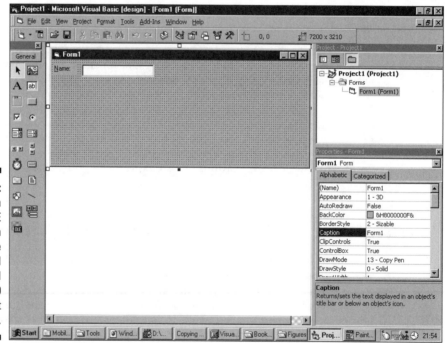

Figure 8-1:
Building a
Windows CE
application
using the
standard
Visual
Basic 5.0
development
environment.

Building Pocket VB applications

Building a Pocket VB application with Visual Basic 5.0 is similar to building standard Windows 95 or Windows NT applications, but you may find important differences — not so much in how Pocket VB applications are constructed, but in what items are missing. For a list, see the upcoming section entitled "What's missing in Pocket VB?"

In the following sections, I give you just a flavor of what developing with Pocket VB is like, but don't expect you to be able to use the information in the following sections to create Pocket VB-based applications, as it's outside the scope of this book.

Creating a project

To start building an application, you must create a *project.* You then use the project to store information about the files used to build the application. The project also stores information about the application options, which you can select or change.

First, you must create a new project and then you must select wce from the list of project types in the New Project dialog box (as shown in Figure 8-2).

Figure 8-2:
You create
Pocket VB
applications
by selecting
wce as the
project
type.

Developing an application

You develop Pocket VB applications by using the standard Visual Basic techniques. However, you need to consider all the inherent differences that Windows CE imposes on your application. These differences (which are the same as those imposed on Visual C++ applications) include the changes to the user interface, the small amount of available memory, and slower processors.

Running the application

You can run your Pocket VB applications either under emulation on your desktop PC or on the target Windows CE device. You need to consider the following important points when writing applications with Pocket VB:

✔ Pocket VB applications require a set of *run-time files,* which contain code that is required to run any Pocket VB applications. The run-time files are shared by all Pocket VB applications running under Windows CE. The total size of these files is about 650K. You can download these files onto your Windows CE device by choosing Tools⇨Download Remote Files in Visual Basic.

✔ Most manufacturers of Windows CE 2.0 devices probably include the Pocket VB run-time files in the device's ROM (which means that your users don't need to install the run-time files). This feature saves valuable RAM in the Windows CE device. However, you should still include the run-time files with your setup application, just in case the ROM on the Windows CE device on which your application is being installed does not contain run-time files.

✔ With ordinary Visual Basic applications, you can run an application from within the development environment without having first built the application. However, this is not the case with Pocket VB applications. You must first choose File⇨Make Project in Visual Basic. The Project dialog box appears, and then you can select the name of the file to be used for the .exe file, and close the dialog box. Then you choose Run⇨Project to run the application on the target Windows CE device.

✔ A Pocket VB application file has the filename extension .pvb. You can run these application files on any target Windows CE device, regardless of the type of processor (SH3, MIPS, and so on) that the device uses. This feature means that you need to build only one .pvb file to support all Windows CE devices.

✔ Pocket VB supports *remote debugging,* which means that you can run your application on a Windows CE device and debug it from your desktop PC.

What's missing in Pocket VB?

As you can imagine, program developers had to leave quite a lot out of Visual Basic to squeeze it onto Windows CE devices. The Pocket VB programming language and facilities end up resembling a cross between Visual Basic for Applications (VBA) and VBScript, rather than the full Visual Basic language.

Here's a brief list of what's missing in Pocket VB. (Note that this list is not exhaustive — you may find other differences as you work through applications.)

✔ **Data types:** The only data type supported in Pocket VB is the *variant* data type. Therefore, *all* variables must be declared variant. The variant data type can store data in all the standard data types (such as integer, float, string, and so on), and functions exist for determining the underlying data type of the data stored in a variant. User-defined types (`Type...End Type`) are not supported.

✔ **Classes:** You cannot create your own classes in Pocket VB. You must rely on modules, functions, and procedures for organizing your code.

✔ **Collections:** You cannot create your own collections of objects in Pocket VB. You should use variable arrays instead. Arrays of all sorts are covered in *C For Dummies,* Volumes I and II, by Dan Gookin and *C++ For Dummies,* 2nd Edition, by Steven R. Davis (both published by IDG Books Worldwide, Inc.).

✔ **Multiple Document Interface (MDI) forms:** Pocket VB does not allow applications to use the MDI interface. You are limited to Single Document Interface (SDI), which typically has a main application window from which dialog boxes can be displayed.

✔ `On Error Goto`: Pocket VB does not support `On Error Goto` error handling. Instead, you must manually check for errors after executing statements.

Windows CE 2.0 Toolkit for Visual J++

The Windows CE 2.0 Toolkit for Visual J++ add-in does for Java what Windows CE Toolkit for Visual Basic 5.0 does for Visual Basic. With this add-in, you can write applications by using Java and run them on the Windows CE 2.0 Java Virtual Machine.

The Java Virtual Machine (VM) is effectively an application that runs Java applications. Java applications are compiled to byte codes that are independent of any processor or operating system. The job of the VM is to interpret these byte codes and translate them into appropriate instructions on the target device.

Java applications on Windows CE devices may run slower than you expect, especially if your application performs complex calculations. However, a Just In Time (JIT) compiler takes the Java byte code and compiles it on the fly directly into machine code for the local processor, which then executes the machine code. This step makes Java code execution much faster. The first release of the Windows CE Java VM does not have a JIT compiler.

The add-in allows you to create Java language projects that are compiled on the desktop machine and then downloaded to the target Windows CE device or emulation environment, where the applications execute. The add-in supports remote debugging.

The Windows CE 2.0 Java VM is designed to be included in ROM. So, many Windows CE devices should already include the VM (and therefore the capability of running Java applications). You do have the option of installing the Virtual Machine and standard classes in RAM if they are not present in ROM.

Part II
Discovering the Unique Features of Windows CE

THE GREAT THING ABOUT WINDOWS CE 2 PROGRAMMING IS, IT'S MADE SOFTWARE DEVELOPMENT AS EASY AS PUTTING ONE FOOT IN FRONT OF THE OTHER.

In this part . . .

*W*indows CE has a few tricks up its sleeve that allow you to create really cool applications. In this part, I explain two essential ingredients in any Windows CE application: How to create a setup program that runs from a desktop PC and how to add Hypertext Markup Language (HTML) help files. Then, I introduce you to Windows CE databases, which allow you to store and retrieve data quickly and efficiently (but probably aren't the type of databases that you're used to). Finally, I show you how to access the Windows CE address book in your new applications.

Chapter 9

Creating a Setup Program

. . . .

In This Chapter

▶ Creating an install script

▶ Calling the load functions to perform a setup

▶ Locating the uninstall script

. . . .

*Y*our applications will need to be copied from a Windows NT or Windows 95 PC onto a Windows CE device. You can't rely on users copying the files into the correct location, however, so you should provide a setup program that automates the copying of the files to the correct location. You perform four tasks to create a setup program, and I explain each of these tasks in this chapter. By the end of the chapter, you'll be able to create professional-looking setup applications with very little coding.

Remember that the setup program runs on the *desktop* PC under Windows 95 and Windows NT. Your users need to create a connection between the desktop PC and Windows CE device before running your setup program.

The Remote API (RAPI) is a set of functions that can be called from an application running on a desktop machine to automate the setup of an application. Setting up an application includes:

✔ Adding registry entries required by an application

✔ Copying the files into the correct locations

✔ Adding shortcuts to your application (for example, on the Windows CE desktop)

In Chapter 17, I describe the Windows CE Registry. Chapter 16 tells you about shortcuts.

Writing a setup program can be a little tricky (I never get it right the first time!), so I provide a generic setup program that you can modify for your own applications. It is located in the folder \samples\GenSetup on the CD-ROM. You can copy this project to your local hard drive and then modify the code to match your application's requirements.

Four Easy Steps to Creating a Setup Program

Creating a setup program for a Windows CE application requires these four steps:

1. **Create a Developer Studio workspace.**

   Create a workspace for a desktop application (that is, an application that runs on a desktop PC under Windows 95 or Windows NT). This application can be any of the standard project types, including MFC AppWizard or Win32 Application. Be sure that the Win32 platform is selected when creating this project.

2. **Write a load script.**

   A *load script* is a text file that contains a list of commands instructing the setup process to copy files, install registry entries, and create shortcuts. I'll show you how to write a load script further on in this chapter, in the section entitled — oddly enough — "The load script."

3. **Call the load functions.**

   Add code to your desktop application to call the *load functions*. These functions provide a user interface that indicates progress to the user, including the following:

   • Initialize the connection between the desktop PC and Windows CE device.

   • Determine whether the application has already been loaded.

   • Determine if sufficient free space exists on the Windows CE device.

   • Find out what type of CPU the target Windows CE device has.

   • Execute the load script to perform the installation.

4. **Name the files to install.**

   Be sure that all the files required by the setup program are correctly named and in the correct directory.

Each of these steps is described in detail in the following sections.

Creating the setup application

The setup process is run on a desktop PC application running under Windows NT or Windows 95. You can create an application whose only job is to install a Windows CE application, or you can add the setup code to an existing Windows 95 or Windows NT application.

The sample workspace GenSetup.dsw on the CD-ROM was created using the Win32 application project type and is designed to run on Windows NT or Windows 95. This means that it will have a WinMain function, but the application will not display an application window. Instead, WinMain executes the load functions one by one, and then exits.

When you open the file GenSetup.dsw, you see the following global variable declarations. Modify these values for your own setup program:

- **Program title:** The name used by the setup program to display in the title of message boxes.

  ```
  LPTSTR lpszTitle = "SetupEG Application";
  ```

- **Application name:** The name of the application you are installing. This is typically the name of the exe file without the .exe extension. This name must be unique, otherwise you get a message indicating that the application is already installed on the Windows CE device.

  ```
  LPTSTR lpszSetupTarget = "Cardfile";
  ```

- **Storage space in bytes:** The amount of storage space required on the Windows CE device. This is used to ensure that setup has sufficient space to proceed, by the progress indicator. The progress indicator shows how much of the file copying has been completed.

  ```
  DWORD dwFreeSpaceRequired = 26000;
  ```

- **Install directory:** The directory on the Windows CE device where the application will be installed.

  ```
  LPTSTR lpszInstallDir = "\\Cardfile";
  ```

Don't forget to include two backslashes in a path name, because the backslash character is used as an escape character in C/C++.

If you build your own setup program you need to do the following to allow your application to access the load functions:

- Include the file ppcload.h in your source code.

  ```
  #include <ppcload.h>
  ```

✔ Add the ppcload.lib file to the linker settings in your project. The linker settings specify options the linker uses when building the application's exe. Follow these steps:

1. **Choose Project⇨Settings in Developer Studio.**

   This brings up the Project Settings dialog box, which displays a list of the configurations on the left side and a series of tabs on the right.

2. **Click the Link tab.**

   This displays the list of link options that can be changed.

3. **Choose All Configurations from the Settings For combo box.**

   The library must be added to the debug and release build, so it's important to add the library for all configurations.

4. **Add ppcload.lib.**

   Add the text `ppcload.lib` to the end of the Object/Library edit box, taking care to add a space before it.

5. **Click OK.**

   The changes you make are accepted and the dialog box closes.

The load script

The load script contains commands that specify:

✔ Registry entries you can add to the Windows CE device's Registry (see Chapter 17 for more on the Registry).

✔ Files you can copy.

✔ A list of shortcuts you can create.

This file is a straightforward text file, so you can create it using Developer Studio or Notepad.

The filename used to save the load script must have a .load extension, and the base filename must be the same as the string that `lpszSetupTarget` points to. In the GenSetup sample of the CD-ROM, the load script file has the filename Cardfile.load.

The load script contains a series of comments (using the C++ `//` comment character) and commands (such as using `copy` to copy a file from the desktop PC to a Windows CE device).

The load script for GenSetup uses three commands:

✔ **copy:** This command copies a file from a path on the desktop PC to a path on the Windows CE device:

- The first argument specifies the file's location on the desktop PC. If you use a period (.), the directory from which your setup program was run is used.

- The second argument specifies the folder on the Windows CE device that you copy the file to. If you use a period (.), then you use the directory that lpszInstallDir points to.

✔ **createShortCut:** This command creates a shortcut icon in a specified folder on the Windows CE device. The command takes three parameters:

- The first argument specifies the folder on the Windows CE device where you create the shortcut. \Windows\Desktop specifies that the shortcut appear in the desktop window.

- The second argument specifies the name of the file you use for the shortcut. This should be the name of your application (Cardfile, in the sample) and the .lnk extension.

- The third argument is the application file to which you make the shortcut.

✔ **exit:** Terminates the script.

It is important that you always use the .lnk extension for the shortcut file, otherwise your shortcut doesn't work. Windows CE only recognizes short-cut files that have the .lnk extension.

Code Listing 9-1 contains the load script for the GenSetup sample on the CD-ROM.

Code Listing 9-1

```
// Sample installation script for Cardfile application.
// Copy the two files associated with the application
copy . . cardfile.exe
copy . . cardfile.htc

// Create a shortcut on the desktop to the application
createShortcut \Windows\Desktop
        "Cardfile.lnk" . cardfile.exe
// Exit the script
exit
```

Calling the load functions

You need to call the following load functions in your desktop setup application. You can see all the code associated with these functions in the file GenSetup.cpp.

Load_Init

This function should be called first to initialize communications with the Windows CE device. It does not take any arguments. Only continue with the setup if this function returns LOAD_SUCCESS. Code Listing 9-2 shows how to call Load_Init and to handle errors.

Code Listing 9-2

```
if(Load_Init() != LOAD_SUCCESS)
{
    // report error to user
    return FALSE;
}
```

Load_AlreadyInstalled

This function is used to determine whether the application is already installed on the Windows CE device. If it is, you can't continue with the setup. The user must use the Control Panel on the Windows CE device to uninstall the application first. This function takes a single argument that is the name of the application (without the .exe extension). The sample uses lpszSetupTarget, which points to the string Cardfile. This is the name of the application being installed — you should use the name of your own application. Code Listing 9-3 shows how to call the function Load_AlreadyInstalled.

Code Listing 9-3

```
if(Load_AlreadyInstalled(lpszSetupTarget))
{
    // report error to user
    Load_Exit();
    return FALSE;
}
```

You must call Load_Exit before exiting the application. This closes down communications with the Windows CE device.

Load_PegFreeSpace

This function returns the amount of free space in the object store, which is where files are stored in a Windows CE device. You should use the return value to check that sufficient space is available for the setup. Code Listing 9-4 shows how to call `Load_PegFreeSpace` and to test that sufficient space is available on the Windows CE device.

Code Listing 9-4

```
DWORD dwFreeSpace = Load_PegFreeSpace();
if(dwFreeSpace < dwFreeSpaceRequired)
{
    // report error to user
    Load_Exit();
    return FALSE;
}
```

Load_PegCpuType

You also need to call `Load_PegCpuType` to determine the type of CPU the Windows CE device is using. This returns a string, such as SH3 or MIPS. This information is used later to determine which Windows CE executable file should be installed. Code Listing 9-5 shows a declaration of a string buffer called `szCPU` and a call to `Load_PegCpuType` to fill the string buffer with the CPU type.

Code Listing 9-5

```
TCHAR szCPU[20];
Load_PegCpuType(szCPU);
```

Load

The Load function initiates the setup, and copies the files, registers items in the registry, and creates shortcuts. This function takes two arguments.

- ✔ **Window Handle:** The first argument is a handle of a window that is to be the parent for any windows that the setup process displays. If you don't have a window (as is the case in GenSetup) you can pass `NULL`.

- ✔ **Command String:** The second argument is more complex. It is to a pointer to a string that contains seven items that specify how the setup should proceed. There are six strings and one integer value. Double quotes should enclose all six strings, and there should be a space between each of the seven items. The items are:

  - **CPU type:** The CPU type used by the Windows CE device. You can use the string returned from calling `Load_PegCpuType`.

- **Application name:** The name of the target application. This is the string that `lpszSetupTarget` points to (which is `Cardfile` in the sample).

- **The installation directory:** This is the string that `lpszInstallDir` points to (which is `\\Cardfile` in the sample).

- **The number of bytes to be copied:** You can use the value stored in the variable `dwFreeSpaceRequired`.

- **The user name:** This is not currently used by Windows CE, so this should be an empty string (that is, two double quotation marks with nothing in between).

- **The company name:** Again, this is not currently used by Windows CE and should be an empty string.

- **Script file:** The name of the load script file. This is Cardfile.Load in the sample.

You can use `sprintf` to build up this string using the following code. Notice how `\"` is used to insert a double quote mark into the string in Code Listing 9-6.

Code Listing 9-6

```
TCHAR szCmdLine[400];
sprintf(szCmdLine,
        "\"%s\" \"%s\" \"%s\" %d \"\" \"\" \"%s.load\" ",
        szCPU,    // cpu type, from calling Load_PegCpuType
        lpszSetupTarget,    // name of application
        lpszInstallDir,    // installation directory
        dwFreeSpaceRequired,// number of bytes to install
        lpszSetupTarget);  // name of command file.
```

The function Load is called with two parameters: The first is the window handle that will be the parent for any dialog boxes displayed by the setup process, and the second is the string `szCmdLine`.

```
Load(NULL, szCmdLine)
```

The function Load returns the value `LOAD_SUCCESS` if the setup was successful, otherwise an error code is returned. The sample file GetSetup.cpp contains a function called `ReportLoadError` that reports an error returned by Load.

Load_Exit

You should always call `Load_Exit` in your setup program if you called `Load_Init` — even if the setup process failed. This function takes no arguments.

```
Load_Exit();
```

Naming the files

The files you reference in the install script must be located in the correct directories — this is typically the same directory as the install script itself.

You should try to provide an .exe for each of the CPUs supported by Windows CE. The common CPUs are SH3 and MIPS. Each .exe should be named with the extension .exe.sh3 and .exe.mips. In the sample on CD-ROM two Cardfile .exe extensions are present in the same directory as the install script.

```
Cardfile.exe.SH3
Cardfile.exe.MIPS
```

The sample workspace GenSetup.dsw has been setup so that the program GenSetup.exe is built in the \samples\GenSetup directory and not \samples\GenSetup\debug. This is to ensure that the setup program GetSetup.exe is located in the same directory as the install script, and all the files that are to be installed.

Uninstall Scripts

The load process automatically creates an uninstall screen on the Windows CE device if the setup process succeeded. This file is located in the \Windows folder on the Windows CE device, and is named using the application name (Cardfile, in the sample program) with the extension .Unload. The unload file is used by the Control Panel's Remove Programs icon.

Installing Shared Libraries

You must be careful when installing Dynamic Link Libraries (DLLs) or other shared libraries. These libraries should always be installed in the \Windows folder. The folder search order used by Windows CE for locating DLLs is different from Windows NT and Windows 95. Chapter 15 describes Dynamic Link Libraries and where they are located in Windows CE.

Since several applications may be sharing a DLL, Windows CE maintains a usage count of how many installed applications need to use the DLL. The DLL is only removed from the Windows CE device if this usage count is zero (that is, no other installed applications are using the DLL).

You should use the `copyShared` command in an install script for DLLs and other shared libraries. The `copyShared` command takes the same arguments as copy.

```
copyShared . \Windows htmlview.dll
```

Creating Registry Items

Registry items are stored under keys. (A *key* is the name by which the Registry item is known and referenced.) Registry keys can be added into the Windows CE registry by using the `RegKeyCreate` command. Registry values can be added using the `RegString` or `RegInt` commands, depending on whether the data is a string or an integer. Chapter 17 describes the Registry and how keys and values are organized.

The `RegKeyCreate` command creates a new key in the Registry. It takes three arguments:

- ✔ The key under which the new sub-key is created
- ✔ The sub-key's name
- ✔ The value 0 if the sub-key is not to be removed by the uninstall script, or 1 if the sub-key is to be removed

For example, the following command creates a sub-key called `Software\MyCompany\ObjStr` under the key `HKEY_CURRENT_USER`, and is removed by the uninstall script.

```
regKeyCreate HKEY_CURRENT_USER Software\MyCompany\ObjStr 1
```

The command `regString` can be used to set values into a key. It takes a key, a sub-key, a removal flag (0 or 1), the value's name (Default, in this case), and the string value (`"TestValue"`) to be set.

```
regString HKEY_CURRENT_USER Software\MyCompany\ObjStr 1
        Default "TestValue"
```

You should enter the `regKeyCreate` and `regString` commands all on one line.

Chapter 10

Building Help Files

*U*sers of your applications use Windows CE so that they can carry less stuff around, right? So, you've got to figure that they're not going to heave any manuals around with them either. The answer? Help files.

Help files for Windows CE applications should be concise (consisting of short, specific instructions) and small — after all, they occupy valuable memory. The contents of a Windows CE help file typically contains a list of how-to topics — not an exhaustive list of each of the program's functions that you would find with Windows NT or Windows 95 applications. You can add bitmaps to your help files, but be sure to assess how much they will really help the user; bitmaps can use up lots of memory.

You write your Windows CE help files by using Hypertext Markup Language (HTML), and the help files are displayed to the user with the peghelp.exe application. The contents of Windows CE help files are actually displayed using a Pocket Internet Explorer window in the peghelp.exe application. You can use a wide range of HTML tags to format your help file, but Windows CE help files typically use just a few simple tags.

You don't need a compiler to create Windows CE help files, unlike Windows 95 and Windows NT help systems.

The sample workspace \samples\SamHelp\SamHelp.dsw is an MFC application that has a Windows CE help system created for it. The sample help files provide a template that you can copy into your own workspaces.

Structure of a Windows CE Help System

Creating a help system for a Windows CE application requires that you create the following files:

- ✔ **Content file:** A singe Content file (with an .htc extension) that contains a list of hyper jumps to the sections.

  Place the content file in the \windows directory.

- ✔ **Section files:** Section files (with .htp extensions) that contain the text for each section. The section files can have jumps to other section files.

  You can also place the section files in the \windows directory. You can put them in other directories if you like, but you must ensure that the content file's jumps have fully qualified pathnames to the directory where the section files reside.

Your setup program will probably install the help files automatically into the correct location. Add `copy` commands to your setup "load" script to install the help files automatically, along with the application itself. See Chapter 9 for information about creating a setup application.

Creating HTML Files

You can create HTML files by using a wide variety of editors, including Microsoft Word for Windows and Microsoft Front Page. However, the formatting in Windows CE help files is usually so simple that you can create the files by using the Developer Studio.

HTML formatting consists of a series of *tags,* which are instructions to the HTML viewer (such as the Pocket Internet Explorer) about how to display the text. These tags are enclosed in angled brackets, which look like this: ⟨ and ⟩.

Each HTML file has two tags: The ⟨HTML⟩ tag marks the start of the file, and the ⟨/HTML⟩ tag marks the end of the file. There are usually two sections within an HTML file, the *head* and the *body.* The <HEAD> and </HEAD> tags identify the start and end of the head section, respectively, and the <BODY> and </BODY> tags mark the start and end of the body section, respectively.

You can find out more about HTML tags and formatting in the book *HTML For Dummies,* 3rd Edition, by Ed Tittel and Stephen N. James (IDG Books Worldwide, Inc.).

You can create the HTML files in Developer Studio and add them to the workspace. The HTML files then become part of your application, and managing the files becomes easier.

To create an HTML file in Developer Studio, follow these steps:

1. **Choose File⇨New menu.**

   This step displays the list of different file, project, and workspace types that you can create with Developer Studio.

2. **Select the Files tab.**

   Selecting this tab shows you a list of all the file types that you can add to the project.

3. **Select HTML Page for the file type.**

   Developer Studio recognizes HTML files and color-codes the tags.

4. **Enter the name of the HTML file.**

   HTML files typically have an .htm or .html file extension. For Windows CE help files, they should have an .htc extension for content files or .htp extension for section files.

5. **Click OK.**

   Clicking OK creates the file and opens it in the Developer Studio ready for editing.

Developer Studio creates a skeleton HTML file for you (Code Listing 10-1). The skeleton HTML file includes some extra tags that you either delete or modify to create your Windows CE help files.

Code Listing 10-1

```
<HTML>
<HEAD>
<META NAME="GENERATOR"
      Content="Microsoft Developer Studio">
<META HTTP-EQUIV="Content-Type"
      content="text/html; charset=iso-8859-1">
<TITLE>Document Title</TITLE>
</HEAD>
<BODY>
<!- Insert HTML here ->
</BODY>
</HTML>
```

When creating a content file, be sure to use the extension .htc, and for section files, use .htp. Developer Studio uses an .htm extension if you don't specify an extension.

Formatting the Content File

You have just one content file in your Windows CE help system, and it should have an .htc extension. This file contains a series of hypertext jumps to the content .htp files. Your content file should contain the following:

- ✔ **The** `meta http-equiv` **tag shown in Code Listing 10-2:** You can remove other tags in the `HEAD` section.

- ✔ **A heading 5 title for your content file:** This is enclosed in `<H5>` and `</H5>` tags.

- ✔ `<MENU>` **and** `</MENU>` **tags:** The menu tags enclose a list of sections (topics) in the help file. Separate each line by a `<li>` tag.

- ✔ `<A>` **and** `</A>` **anchor tags:** These tags denote a hypertext jump to another file. The files are named something like `"file:Subject1.htp"`, and the text between the `<A>` and `</A>` tags (for example, "Section 1 Help topic") is the clickable text for the hypertext jump.

Code Listing 10-2

```
<HTML>
<HEAD>
<META http-equiv=refer content="">
</HEAD>
<BODY>
<H5>SamHelp Contents</H5>
<MENU>
<li><a href="file:Subject1.htp">Section 1 Help topic</a>
<li><a href="file:Subject2.htp">Section 2 Help topic</a>
<li><a href="file:Subject3.htp">Section 3 Help topic</a>
<li><a href="file:Subject4.htp">Section 4 Help topic</a>
</MENU>
</BODY>
</HTML>
```

Formatting the Section Files

Chances are, you'll have multiple section files with .htp extensions. The names should be the same as the filenames used in the anchor tag `<A>` in the Content file. A section file consists of the following:

✔ A `meta http-equiv` **tag, as shown in Code Listing 10-3:** The `content` chould be the name of the content file. The content tag allows the Contents button in Windows CE help to return to the contents file `SamHelp.htc`.

✔ **Standard HTML formatting commands within the** `<BODY>` **section:** In Code Listing 10-3, a level 2 heading is enclosed in `<H2>` and `</H2>` tags. Normal text (that is, text not enclosed in `<H2>` and `</H2>` HTML tags) follows, and this normal text includes some bold text within `<B>` and `</B>` tags. Use the `<P>` tag to mark the end of a paragraph.

Code Listing 10-3

```
<HTML>
<HEAD>
<meta http-equiv=refer content="file:SamHelp.htc"">
</HEAD>
<BODY>
<H2>Subject 1</H2>
This is the text that is contained in <B>Subject 1</B>.<P>
Each subject file will contain text in a similar format.
</BODY>
</HTML>
```

Using Windows CE with the API

You must launch the Windows CE help system in response to the user's selecting the help option in your application. To do this, you need to create a new process. You can use Code Listing 10-4 to display help — just change the name of the .htc file.

Code Listing 10-4

```
PROCESS_INFORMATION pi;
CreateProcess(TEXT("peghelp.exe"),
    TEXT("file:\\Cardfile.htc"),
    NULL,NULL,FALSE,0,NULL,NULL,NULL, &pi);
CloseHandle(pi.hProcess);
CloseHandle(pi.hThread);
```

Chapter 13 contains information about creating processes, including how to use `CreateProcess` and the arguments that are passed to it.

Using Windows CE Help with MFC

When creating an application, you can specify that your application will have Windows CE help files by using the AppWizard.

In Step 2 of the AppWizard, select the Windows CE Help check box (see Figure 10-1). Notice that selecting this option enables the Help Contents File edit box, which specifies the name of the contents file. SamHelp.htc is the name of the contents file in Figure 10-1.

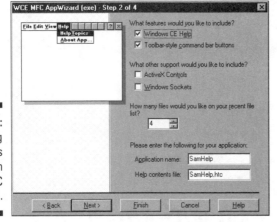

Figure 10-1:
Specifying
Windows
CE help in
an MFC
application.

The code necessary for displaying the Windows CE help system is automatically included in the MFC application.

Chapter 11

Using Databases

*Y*ou may know about desktop databases and server-based databases, but Windows CE databases are quite different. In this chapter, I show you examples of how you can create and open databases, how you can create to retrieve data quickly, and how you can read and write to databases. I also show you an example of how to access Windows CE databases from your desktop PC applications.

The workspace \samples\cardfile\cardfile.dsw contains the complete code for a cardfile application written using the API. The data for the cards (a title and associated text) is stored in a Windows CE database. This code shows you how to write a fully functional Windows CE application that uses databases, which is also a useful application in which to store your data.

Not Your Average Desktop Database

Windows CE databases have a simple structure — they contain rows of data known as *records*. Each record consists of *properties* of a standard data type (for example, an integer or a string), in which individual data items (also known as fields) are stored. In this respect, a Window CE database is like a table in a standard database system.

If you use standard desktop database systems, you may be surprised to find that the properties in a record don't need to be the same as the properties in another record. Take a look at Figure 11-1.

Figure 11-1
A sample WIndows CE database.

Author Number #1	Name	Address	Record Type: Author
Author Number #1	Book Title #1		Record Type: Title
Author Number #1	Book Title #2		Record Type: Title
Author Number #2	Name	Address	Record Type: Author
Author Number #2	Book Title #3		Record Type: Title
Author Number #2	Book Title #4		Record Type: Title

In the example shown in Figure 11-1, the first record stores information about an author, and the second and third records store information about the two books written by that author. The Author Number property relates the data in these records together. You generally also include a property called Record Type that indicates the type of record it is (that is, an Author record or Title record). Figure 11-2 shows how the data looks in my database.

Figure 11-2.
Sample data for the database.

1	John O'Toole	157, Main Street	A
1	Woodcraft Made Simple		T
1	Making Joinery Fun		T
2	Johnny Scott	1321 Old Creek	A
2	Sailing around the world		T
2	Shipwreck!		T

You generally place all the data associated with your application in a single database. It is easier and more efficient to open a single database in your application rather than opening lots of databases.

If you use ordinary databases, such as Microsoft Access, you know about splitting the data up into different tables — each table containing similar information. For example, you may have a table with information about authors and another table with information about books. You then use Structured Query Language (SQL) statements to join these tables together. You don't do this with Windows CE databases — all the data goes into a single database and you don't use SQL to query these databases from your application; you must write calls to functions to manipulate the data.

Databases are stored in memory and in Windows CE devices, memory is in short supply! Structure your databases to minimize memory usage — for example, you may be tempted to use an author's name rather than a number to relate records, but a name takes more memory than a number, because a name is duplicated on all title records.

Getting Databases to Work

In this section, I show you how to create, open, and close databases. In general, your applications will probably create a database when the application is first run, and the database will be given a name. After you create a database, the database can be opened and records read from it or written to it. Finally, you must close the database.

Creating a database

You create databases with the CeCreateDatabase function. You must pass the following arguments to this function:

- **Database name:** The name of the database, which can be up to 32 characters in length and follows the usual naming rules for objects in the object store (see Chapter 17 for more information on the object store). Databases are placed in the \Databases folder.

- **Database type:** An integer that identifies the type of the database. Database type specifies the type of database being created and can be used to search for databases of particular types. In this case, I assume that all databases that hold author information will be given the type 45000. At some later time, I could create another database called Authors 2, with the same type of identifier, and then use the database search facility to search for all author databases by using the type identifier.

- **Index information:** The last two parameters (passed as 0 and NULL), are used to pass index information. I describe how to use indexes in the section "Indexing for Speed," later in this chapter. In this case no indexes have been created.

Code Listing 11-1 is a simple example of how to create a database.

Code Listing 11-1

```
CEOID oiDB;
const DWORD DW_DBTYPE = 45000;
oiDB = CeCreateDatabase(TEXT("Authors 1"),
    DW_DBTYPE, 0, NULL);
```

If the function call is successful, an object identifier is returned (see Chapter 17 for more information). The *object identifier* represents the database that has been created in the object store.

If you write applications that must run on Windows CE 1.0 as well as Windows CE 2.0, call the `PegCreateDatabase` function instead — it works in exactly the same way. All of the database functions described in this chapter that start with "Ce" have equivalent functions that start with "Peg" that work on Windows CE 1.0.

You may have spotted a problem — what's to stop two programmers using the same type identifier? The simple answer is — nothing. Therefore, you want to pick numbers that are unlikely to be used by other database types.

You cannot access a database that has been created using `CeCreateDatabase` — you must first open it using `CeOpenDatabase`. I show you how to call `CeOpenDatabase` in the section "Opening a database."

Opening a database

After a database has been created, it can be opened using `CeOpenDatabase`. You can use the same function to open existing databases. This function takes the following arguments:

- **Object identifier:** The object identifier for the database (as returned from `CeCreateDatabase`).
- **Database name:** A string pointer to the name of the database to be opened.

But it didn't work!

When the function call fails, the function `Ce-CreateDatabase` returns a `NULL`. You should always check for a `NULL` value being returned from `CeCreateDatabase` and call `GetLastError` to find the number representing the error that caused the failure, as shown in the following code:

```
if (oiDB == NULL)
{

    DWORD dwLastError =
GetLastError();
    // report error

}
```

Three error values, shown in the following table, can be returned from `GetLastError`:

Error	Meaning
ERROR_DISK_FULL	The object store has run out of memory.
ERROR_INVALID_PARAMETER	An index specification was coded incorrectly — this is unlikely in this case, because no indexes were specified!
ERROR_DUP_NAME	A database with this name already exists in the object store.

✔ **Index:** The index that specifies the order of the records when they're retrieved (which I explain in the section "Indexing for Speed").

✔ **Flags:** 0 or the flag `CEDB_AUTOINCREMENT`. When you specify the `CEDB_AUTOINCREMENT` flag, the current record pointer is moved to the following record after reading a record. I discuss flags when describing how to read records in the section "Reading Records."

✔ **Window handle:** A window handle (HWND) that receives notification messages when another application changes the database (while you have it open).

Opening a new database

You can specify the database that you want to open by either using the first argument (object identifier) or the second argument (database name). When a database is created, the function `CeCreateDatabase` returns an object identifier, and this can be passed as the first argument. The second argument can specify the name of the database, or is `NULL` if the object identifier is specified. You can use Code Listing 11-2 to open a database that was created by calling `CeCreateDatabase`.

Code Listing 11-2

```
HANDLE hAuthor;
hAuthor = CeOpenDatabase(&oiDB, NULL, 0, 0, NULL);
if(hAuthor == INVALID_HANDLE_VALUE)
{
    DWORD dwLastError = GetLastError();
    // report error
}
```

Notice how a pointer to the object identifier, obtained using the C/C++ address & operator, is passed as the first parameter and all the other parameters have default values.

`CeOpenDatabase` returns a handle that refers to the open database. A return value of `INVALID_HANDLE_VALUE` indicates failure, and the values returned by `GetLastError` are shown in Table 11-1.

Table 11-1	CeOpenDatabase Error Numbers
Error	*Meaning*
`ERROR_NOT_ENOUGH_MEMORY`	Windows CE is out of memory and the memory associated with the handle could not be allocated.

(continued)

Table 11-1 (continued)

Error	Meaning
ERROR_INVALID_PARAMETER	An index specification was coded incorrectly — unlikely in this case, because no indexes were specified.
ERROR_FILE_NOT_FOUND	The object identifier is invalid, and the database could not be found.

Opening an existing database

Opening existing databases is just as easy as opening a new database. You should initialize the oiDB variable to zero and pass a pointer to it as the first parameter. This tells the function that we're not specifying the database by object identifier. The second parameter contains the database name. Code Listing 11-3 shows how to open an existing database called Authors 1.

Code Listing 11-3

```
oiDB = 0;
hAuthor = CeOpenDatabase(&oiDB, TEXT("Authors 1"),
    0, 0, NULL);
```

As an added bonus, CeOpenDatabase returns the object identifier in oiDB. This can be used to get database information (such as the number of bytes of storage being used) using the CeOidGetInfo function.

Closing a database

When you finish using a database, close it using the CloseHandle function — every open database has memory associated with it. You must always minimize the memory used by your application — when you finish accessing a database, close it. Code Listing 11-4 shows you how to close the database that you open in the section "Opening an existing database."

Code Listing 11-4

```
if(CloseHandle(hAuthor) == FALSE)
{
    // could not close database
}
```

Notice that you pass the *handle* hAuthor, not the *object identifier* oiDB. Remember that the handle (which is an integer number) refers to the open database, and the object identifier (which is also an integer number) refers to the actual database in the object store.

You would usually write and read records before closing the database! I show you how to write records in the section called "Writing Records" and read records in the section called "Reading Records," both later in this chapter.

The function InitDB in the sample Cardfile.dsw workspace shows how to create a database and open it, or to open an existing database. You can use this source code if your application needs to create a database (if the database does not exist) and then open the database.

Deleting a database

You can delete a database and all the data in that database, by calling the function CeDeleteDatabase. This function takes a single argument that is the object identifier of the database. The database object identifier is returned when you open the database (this is the variable oiDB in Code Listing 11-3). So, to delete a database you can use Code Listing 11-5.

Code Listing 11-5

```
if(!CeDeleteDatabase(g_oidDatabase))
{
    // could not delete the database
}
```

If the database you try to delete is currently open, the call to CeDeleteDatabase fails. You should close the database first before attempting to delete it.

Database Properties

Windows CE stores data in a database in *properties.* Each property has a unique identifier (which is an integer number you use to refer to a specific property) and a data type (which specifies the type of data you're storing in the property). You need to use properties when reading data from and writing data to a Windows CE database.

Specifying a property

Each property in a record has two important pieces of information:

  ✔ **Property identifier:** A property identifier (number) that is used for the same property for all records. You decide the value to use.

✔ **Data type:** A data type for indicating the type of data that is stored with the property.

What, no names? Yes, that's right — a number, not a name, always identifies properties. You probably want to define constants for the properties you use, as shown in Code Listing 11-6.

Code Listing 11-6

```
const WORD HHPR_AUTHOR_NUMBER = 10;
const WORD HHPR_AUTHOR_NAME = 11;
```

You can use any integer number that you like for your field numbers — you just need to ensure that all the fields in your database have different values.

The data types you can use are shown in Table 11-2.

Table 11-2	Property Data Types
Data Type	*Corresponding Windows Data Type and Description*
CEVT_I2	INT — 16-bit signed integer
CEVT_I4	LONG — 32-bit signed integer
CEVT_UI2	UINT or WORD — 16-bit unsigned integer
CEVT_UI4	ULONG or DWORD — 32-bit unsigned integer
CEVT_LPWSTR	LPCSTR — Pointer to a null terminated string
CEVT_FILETIME	A FILETIME structure — stores access times for a file
CEVT_BLOB	A CEBLOB structure — stores large binary data (for example, bitmaps)

A property is specified using the CEPROPID data type. CEPROPID is a four-byte value that contains two pieces of information:

✔ **Data type:** The lower (first) two bytes contain a value indicating the data type.

✔ **Property identifier:** The upper (last) two bytes contain the identifier.

The macro MAKELONG is used to combine these two numbers to form the CPROPID.

So, to specify a property, declare a variable of type CEPROPID. The MAKELONG macro is used to combine the property's data type (CEVT_LPWSTR) and the property's identifier (HHPR_AUTHOR_NAME).

```
CEPROPID propAuthorName;
propAuthorName = MAKELONG(CEVT_LPWSTR, HHPR_AUTHOR_NAME);
```

Specifying the data for a property

Use a CEPROPVAL structure to specify the data associated with a property. This structure is used when reading and writing records.

Each property being read from or written to the record must have its own CEPROPVAL structure. The structure contains:

- ✓ CEPROPID: A CEPROPID structure defining the property's data type and identifier.

- ✓ wLenData: A wLenData member, which is not used and can be ignored.

- ✓ wFlags: This is usually set to 0, unless you want to delete the property from a record, in which case it is set to CEDB_PROPDELETE.

- ✓ CEVALUNION: A CEVALUNION union that contains the data associated with the property.

Code Listing 11-7 shows the declaration of the CEPROPVAL structure.

Code Listing 11-7

```
typedef struct _PEGPROPVAL {
    CEPROPID    propid;
    WORD        wLenData;
    WORD        wFlags;
    CEVALUNION  val;
} CEPROPVAL;
```

The CEVALUNION union has a member for each of the data types shown in Table 11-3.

Table 11-3   The CEVALUNION Union Members and Data Types

Data Type	Corresponding Data Type
CEVT_I2	iVal
CEVT_I4	lVal
CEVT_UI2	uiVal
CEVT_UI4	ulVal
CEVT_LPWSTR	lpwstr
CEVT_FILETIME	filetime
CEVT_BLOB	blob

So, if your property is a `CEVT_I4` (which is a `LONG` value) you can write the code in Code Listing 11-8.

Code Listing 11-8

```
CEPROPVAL propAuthorNumber;
propAuthorNumber.propid = MAKELONG(CEVT_I4,
    HHPR_AUTHOR_NUMBER);
propAuthorNumber.wFlags = 0;
propAuthorNumber.val.lVal = 100;
```

In the case of a long pointer to a string, you can either use a character array or a pointer (such as is returned from `LocalAlloc` — see Chapter 13 for information on allocating memory with `LocalAlloc`). In Code Listing 11-9, I declare a string buffer called `szAuthorName`, and then use `wcscpy` (the Unicode version of `strcpy`) to copy an author's name into the buffer. A `CEPROPVAL` structure is then initialized to set the value and property information.

Code Listing 11-9

```
TCHAR szAuthorName[100];
wcscpy(szAuthorName, TEXT("H.G. Wells"));

CEPROPVAL propAuthorName;
propAuthorName.propid = MAKELONG(CEVT_LPWSTR,
    HHPR_AUTHOR_NAME);
propAuthorName.wFlags = 0;
propAuthorName.val.lpwstr = szAuthorName;
```

Writing Records

Records can be written to an open database. You need to specify the data type of fields (that are called *properties* in Windows CE database) and the data itself. Keep in mind that the structure of each record must be specified, as this is not set when the database is created.

The structure of records

Individual data items are stored in properties, and a record can have many properties. Properties can be written to a new record or an existing record, either individually or in groups. So, you can:

✔ **Create** a new record and with a new property.

✔ **Add** another new property to this record at a later stage.

✔ **Update** an existing property in the record.

✔ **Delete** a property without deleting the record.

How about that for flexibility? All of this can be done through the function `CeWriteRecordProps`.

Time to write

When writing records, the `CPROPVAL` structures, described in the section "Database Properties," can be passed to `CeWriteRecordProps` to write a record.

First, Code Listing 11-10 is an example of writing a new record that contains just the author number. You must declare and initialize the `propAuthorNumber` as described in the previous section before calling this code. The following parameters are passed to `CeWriteRecordProps` when writing a new record:

✔ **Open database handle:** The handle (`hAuthor`) representing the open database to write to.

✔ **Write record flag:** 0 indicates that a new record is to be written.

✔ **Number of properties to write:** 1 specifies the number of properties to write.

✔ **Properties to write:** A pointer to a `CPROPVAL` structure containing the property specification (`&propAuthorNumber`).

Code Listing 11-10

```
CEOID oiRec;

oiRec = CeWriteRecordProps(hAuthor, 0, 1,
        &propAuthorNumber);
if (oiRec == NULL)
{
    DWORD dwLastError = GetLastError();
    // report error
}
```

`CeWriteRecordProps` returns an object identifier for the new record. If the returned object identifier is `NULL`, you should call `GetLastError` to determine what caused the error. The values, shown in Table 11-4, can be returned from `GetLastError`.

Table 11-4	CeWriteRecordProps Error Numbers
Error	**Meaning**
ERROR_NOT_ENOUGH_MEMORY	Windows CE is out of memory and the memory associated with the handle could not be allocated.
ERROR_INVALID_PARAMETER	An index specification was coded incorrectly — unlikely in this case because indexes are not being used.

Notice that each record has an unique record object identifier — this is not the same as the object identifier returned when the database was created. The *record object identifier* is used to refer to a specific record in a database.

You can now write additional properties to this database record using the records object identifier (oiRec) returned from calling CeWriteRecordProps. Note that the oiRec variable is passed as the second argument — this specifies the record to be updated.

```
oiRec = CeWriteRecordProps(hAuthor, oiRec, 1,
    &propAuthorName);
```

The return value from calling CeWriteRecordProps is the same value passed to it in oiRec unless the function fails — in which case it will be NULL.

You may think that this looks like hard work if CeWriteRecordProcs has to be called one time for every property. Luckily, we can pass multiple CPROPVAL structures at a time. Code Listing 11-11 shows an example.

Code Listing 11-11

```
CEOID oiRec;

TCHAR szAuthorName[100];
wcscpy(szAuthorName, TEXT("H.G. Wells"));

CEPROPVAL propAuthorProps[2];
propAuthorProps[0].propid = MAKELONG(CEVT_I4,
    HHPR_AUTHOR_NUMBER);
propAuthorProps[0].val.lVal = 100;
propAuthorProps[1].propid = MAKELONG(CEVT_LPWSTR,
    HHPR_AUTHOR_NAME);
propAuthorProps[1].val.lpwstr = szAuthorName;

oiRec = CeWriteRecordProps(hAuthor, oiRec, 2,
    propAuthorProps);
```

Notice that I create an array of CPROPVAL with two elements. I then refer to each element through an index of 0 or 1. If you're more adventurous, you can use LocalAlloc to allocate memory for these structures.

But wait! Where has the & gone from in front of propAuthorProps? Because this is now an array, it is effectively a pointer, so you don't need to get a pointer to it. Putting an & in front of propAuthorProps is incorrect — this creates a pointer to a pointer.

It is much more efficient and faster to make a single call to CeWriteRecordProps with multiple CEPROPVAL structures instead of making lots of calls with a single CEPROPVAL structure.

The file db.cpp in the workspace \samples\cardfile\cardfile.dsw contains a function called SaveCurrentCard. This function saves the information associated with a card (the title and the text) to an open database. This code shows you how to write multiple properties to a record in one call to CeWriteRecordProps.

Indexing for Speed

You can use indexes to make record retrieval faster. Indexes serve two purposes:

- ✔ Indexes allow records to be located quickly.
- ✔ Indexes determine the order in which records are retrieved.

You can create an index for a particular property in a database. Then, as new records are added, Windows CE adds index information for that property. After an index has been created, you can search the database using that index — this allows you to locate a particular record containing a value in the indexed property that matches the value you're searching for.

While indexes speed up searching for records, they make adding, updating, and deleting records slower. Only index those properties that you will frequently search on.

Specify the index when you create the database, using CeCreateDatabase. When the database is opened using CeOpenDatabase, you specify which index will be used. The selected index determines the order in which records are returned.

While you can create up to four indexes in a Windows CE database, you can only use a single index at a time — specify the index you want to use when you call CeOpenDatabase. When you want to use a different index, you must first close the database by calling CloseHandle, and then reopen the database using CeOpenDatabase, specifying a different index.

Creating indexes

Indexes are created at the same time the database is created using the function CeCreateDatabase. The specification for each index is contained in a SORTORDERSPEC structure. You must supply two pieces of information for each index:

- **The property to be indexed:** A CEPROPID structure specifying the property to be indexed.

- **How to index the property:** A value specifying how the property should be indexed. It can be one or more of the values in Table 11-5 combined using the C | operator :

Table 11-5	Property Indexing Values
Value	*Purpose*
PEGDB_SORT_DESCENDING	The sort is done in descending order. By default, the sort is done in ascending order.
PEGDB_SORT_CASEINSENSITIVE	The sort order for records is not case sensitive.
PEGDB_SORT_UNKNOWNFIRST	Records that do not contain this property are placed before all the other records. By default, such records are placed after all other records.

Records don't all have the same properties, so a record might not have a property that's used as an index.

In the authors database described in the section called "Not Your Average Desktop Database" (in this chapter), you may want to add an index for the Author Number and the Author Name.

Code Listing 11-12 shows you how to create two indexes when creating an authors database — the steps go like this:

1. Create a two-element array of SORTORDERSPEC **structures.**

2. **Initialize this array with the property identifiers for the two properties.**

   Set dwFlags to 0 in both cases (this specifies the default sort order).

3. **Pass the array** sort **to** CeCreateDatabase **as the last parameter.**

   Use the number 2 to specify the number of indexes being specified.

Code Listing 11-12

```
SORTORDERSPEC sort[2]; // Sort order descriptions

sort[0].propid = MAKELONG(CEVT_LPWSTR, HHPR_AUTHOR_NAME);
sort[0].dwFlags = 0;
sort[1].propid = MAKELONG(CEVT_I4, HHPR_AUTHOR_NUMBER);
sort[1].dwFlags = 0;

oiDB = CeCreateDatabase(TEXT("Authors 1"),
    DW_DBTYPE, 2, sort);
```

Specifying an index when opening the database

You can create up to four indexes, but only one index can be used at any one time — you specify the index you want to use when calling CeOpenDatabase. The third argument to CeOpenDatabase specifies the identifier of the property whose index is to be used. In the Code Listing 11-13, the database is opened using the Author Name property as the indexed field.

Code Listing 11-13

```
hAuthor = CeOpenDatabase(&oiDB, NULL,
    MAKELONG(CEVT_LPWSTR, HHPR_AUTHOR_NAME)
    , 0, NULL);
```

The function InitDB in the file db.cpp in the workspace \samples\ cardfile\cardfile.dsw shows how to create and open a cardfile database with a single index.

Seeking records

When a database is opened, the database's record pointer is set to the first record based on the selected index. This is the record that is read by calling the function CeReadRecordProps (unless the record pointer is first moved by calling `CeSeekDatabase`). Reading properties, using the `CeReadRecordProps` function, is described in the section "Reading Records."

With `CeSeekDatabase`, you can move the current record pointer by specifying:

✔ An identifier that specifies how to seek. The identifiers are shown in Table 11-6.

✔ The property value to search for (or where in the database to seek to).

Table 11-6	CeSeekDatabase Seek Identifiers
Identifier	*Seek Technique*
CEDB_SEEK_PEGOID	Seek directly to a record using its record object identifier. The record identifier is returned when the record is added.
CEDB_SEEK_VALUESMALLER	Find a record using the current index to locate the record with the index value that is just smaller than that specified in the call to CeSeekDatabase.
CEDB_SEEK_VALUEFIRSTEQUAL	Find the first record that has an index value equal to the value specified in the call to CeSeekDatabase.
CEDB_SEEK_VALUENEXTEQUAL	Find the next record that has an index value equal to the specified value.
CEDB_SEEK_VALUEGREATER	Find the next record that has a value greater than or equal to the specified value.
CEDB_SEEK_BEGINNING	Seek the specified number of records forwards from the first record specified by the current index.
CEDB_SEEK_CURRENT	Seek the specified number of records backwards or forwards from the current record using the current index.
CEDB_SEEK_END	Seek the specified number of records back from the last record using the current index.

To call `CeSeekDatabase,` you must specify the following arguments:

- ✔ **Open database handle:** The handle returned when the database is opened.

- ✔ **Seek identifier:** One of the seek identifiers listed in Table 11-6.

- ✔ **The value to search for:** The nature of the value depends on the seek identifier specified.

- ✔ **Record offset:** A pointer to a `DWORD` value in which the offset (in records) will be returned from the start of the database for the located record.

Code Listing 11-14 shows a simple call to `CeSeekDatabase` to locate the first (0) record in the database, using the index specified when the database opens.

Code Listing 11-14

```
DWORD dwIndex;
CEOID pOIDRec;
pOIDRec = CeSeekDatabase(hAuthor,
    CEDB_SEEK_VALUEFIRSTEQUAL, 0, &dwIndex);
```

The call to `CeSeekDatabase` returns an object identifier of the located record (or null, if the function fails).

Seeking a value

You must initialize a `CEPROPVAL` structure when searching for a particular value. This structure defines the property, the property's type, and the value to search for.

You can only seek on a property if that property is indexed (which you specify when you create the database) and if that index is selected when the database is opened.

For example, in Code Listing 11-15, the structure variable `propAuthorProps` has been initialized with the `propid` for the Author Number property, and the `lVal` value has been set to 100.

Code Listing 11-15

```
CEPROPVAL propAuthorProps;

propAuthorProps.propid = MAKELONG(CEVT_I4,
      HHPR_AUTHOR_NUMBER);
propAuthorProps.val.lVal = 100;

pOIDRec = CeSeekDatabase(hAuthor,
      CEDB_SEEK_VALUEFIRSTEQUAL, (DWORD)&propAuthorProps,
      &dwIndex);
```

Notice that I pass a pointer to `propAuthorProps` to `CeSeekDatabase`, and this must be cast to a `DWORD`. You want to follow this procedure, because the third argument to `CeSeekDatabase` is normally passed a number (for example, the number of records to seek forward or back). However, when using `CEDB_SEEK_VALUEFIRSTEQUAL`, a `CEPROPVAL` pointer must be passed to this same argument, and so, `propAuthorProps` must be cast to avoid a compiler error.

When you open a database with the `CEDB_AUTOINCREMENT` flag, the record pointer automatically moves to the next record after a call to `CeReadRecordProps`. If you don't specify the `CEDB_AUTOINCREMENT` flag, the record pointer does not move, and another call to `CeReadRecordProps` rereads the same record.

Reading Records

After you move the current record pointer to a particular record, you can read the property values using the function `CeReadRecordProps`. Use this function to retrieve all property values or only those property values that you specify.

Remember that the record to be read is the one pointed to by the current record pointer. You can use `CeSeekDatabase` to move to a particular record.

You must allocate memory so that `CeReadRecordProps` can return the data for the properties. You can take on this responsibility yourself, but you'll probably find it much easier to get `CeReadRecordProps` to do this for you. Just remember to free the memory allocated by `CeReadRecordProps` after you finish using the property values.

Reading all properties

While reading all property values in a record is the easiest technique to use (because you don't need to specify *which* records to read), you should only read all properties if you really want all the property values — this makes your application more efficient.

To read all the properties for the current record, pass the following arguments to CeReadRecordProps:

- ✔ **Open database handle:** hAuthor, the handle to an open database.

- ✔ **Memory allocation flag:** CEDB_ALLOWREALLOC, a flag indicating that CeReadRecordProps should allocate the memory for the properties.

- ✔ **Number of properties actually read:** &cProps, a pointer to an unsigned short variable into which CeReadRecordProps places the number of properties returned.

- ✔ **List of properties to be returned:** The value NULL, indicating that all property values should be returned.

- ✔ **Return property values:** & props, a pointer to a CEPROPVAL pointer variable. CeReadRecordProps places a pointer into this variable, which points at the returned property values (stored in CEPROPVAL structures).

- ✔ **Size of property values buffer:** &cbBuf, a pointer to a DWORD variable into which CeReadRecordProps places the size of the memory allocated for the property values, in bytes.

Code Listing 11-16 shows how to call CeReadRecordProps to read all property values.

Code Listing 11-16

```
CEOID pOIDRec;
DWORD cbBuf;
CEPROPVAL *props = NULL;
unsigned short cProps;

pOIDRec = CeReadRecordProps(hAuthor,
    CEDB_ALLOWREALLOC,
    &cProps,
    NULL,
    (LPBYTE*)&props,
    &cbBuf);
```

If you request `CeReadRecordProps` to allocate memory for you, it is imperative that you set the `props` pointer to be `NULL` before calling `CeReadRecordProps`. If you don't do this, `CeReadRecordProps` may mistake this value for being a pointer to memory, and attempt to access it. This will probably result in your application failing.

Notice that the pointer to the `props` variable must be cast to a `(LPBYTE*)`.

It is crucial that you free the memory used to hold the property values that are returned to you when calling `CeReadRecordProps`. I describe how to do this in the section called "Freeing memory — don't forget!"

Reading specific property values

Your applications will be more efficient if you read only those property values you want, rather than all the property values — Windows CE takes time to read each property, and memory must be allocated for each property value that is returned to your application. It takes a little more effort, but you'll find it worthwhile in the long run.

I show you how to call `CeReadRecordProps` so that only the Author Name property value is returned. First, you need to create a `WORD` array and initialize this array with the property identifiers that are to be retrieved.

```
DWORD dwPropIDs[1];
dwPropIDs[0] = MAKELONG(CEVT_LPWSTR, HHPR_AUTHOR_NAME);
```

This array needs to be passed to `CeReadRecordProps`, and the `cProps` variable must be initialized with the number of property values to be returned (which is 1 in this case), as shown in Code Listing 11-17.

Code Listing 11-17

```
cProps = 1;
pOIDRec = CeReadRecordProps(hAuthor,
      CEDB_ALLOWREALLOC,
      &cProps,
      dwPropIDs,
      (LPBYTE*)&props,
      &cbBuf);
```

Accessing property values

When you call `CeReadRecordProps`, the property values are placed in `CEPROPVAL` structures, with one structure for each property that was read.

The memory for these structures is allocated by CeReadRecordProps. From the CEPROPVAL structure, you can determine the property id, the property data type, and the value read from the database.

Finding the property identifier

Generally, the properties are returned to you in the order they are written. Don't assume a particular order (especially if the database is written by another application) — your best bet is to check the property identifiers before attempting to use the property value.

You may recall from the section "Database Properties" that the property identifier is a combination of the data type and the number you assigned to the property.

```
propAuthorName = MAKELONG(CEVT_LPWSTR,HHPR_AUTHOR_NAME);
```

This same information is contained in the CEPROPVAL array that is returned when you call CeReadRecordProps, so that you can reverse the process of making the property identifier to determine either the property's data type or its number. The HIWORD macro, when applied to the propid, will return the property number (for example, HHPR_AUTHOR_NAME). The LOWORD macro will return the data type (for example, CEVT_LPWSTR). Code Listing 11-18 checks if the first property returned in the props array is for the Author Name property.

Code Listing 11-18

```
if (HIWORD(props[0].propid) == HHPR_AUTHOR_NAME)
{
        // author name property
}
```

After you identify the property, you can use the val union contained in the CEPROPVAL structure to obtain the value for the property. The following call assigns the value returned for the Author Name property into a window using the function SetWindowText.

```
SetWindowText(hWnd, props[0].val.lpwstr);
```

Because the val member in the CEPROPVAL structure is a union, be certain of the property's data type before accessing the union members. You get garbage back if you use the wrong union member (for example, lpwstr instead of iVal).

Freeing memory — don't forget!

The memory used to store the property values is allocated by CeReadRecordProps, but you are responsible for freeing it.

If you fail to free the memory returned to you from `CeReadRecordProps`, your application will have a *memory leak*. That is, all the memory allocated by `CeReadRecordProps` will remain allocated until your application terminates. The free application memory will disappear rapidly and sooner or later, you won't have any free memory left at all.

You should free the memory after you finish accessing the property values. You need to call the `LocalFree` function, passing it the pointer to the `CEPROPVAL` pointer.

```
LocalFree(props);
```

Don't forget to free the memory returned to you from `CeReadRecordProps`. You can find more information on memory management in Chapter 13.

Deleting Properties and Records

You can delete data from a database in two ways: by deleting individual properties from a record (calling `CeWriteRecordProps`) or by deleting the entire record (calling `CeDeleteRecord`).

Deleting properties

This may sound strange, but you delete properties from a database record by calling `CeWriteRecordProps`. You create and initialize `CEPROPVAL` structures for each of the properties just as you do for adding properties, except that you set the `wFlags` member to `CEDB_PROPDELETE`. The value in the `val` union is ignored, because the property is being deleted.

After the `CPROPVAL` structure or structures are initialized, you call `CeWriteRecordProps` as normal. Code Listing 11-19 deletes the Author Number property from the current record.

Code Listing 11-19

```
CEPROPVAL propAuthorNumber;
CEOID oiRec;

propAuthorNumber.propid =
    MAKELONG(CEVT_I4,HHPR_AUTHOR_NUMBER);
propAuthorNumber.wFlags = CEDB_PROPDELETE;
propAuthorNumber.val.lVal = 0;
oiRec = CeWriteRecordProps(hAuthor, 0, 1,
    &propAuthorNumber);
```

Deleting records

You can use the `CeDeleteRecord` function to delete a record from an open database. This function takes two arguments: a handle to an open database and the object identifier for the record to be deleted.

The most difficult part of calling this function is determining the object identifier of the record to be deleted. The object identifier is returned from `CeWriteRecordProps` when properties are added, updated, or deleted, but it is unlikely that you store the object identifiers for all records. The most likely case is that you want to delete the current record. You can use the `CeSeekDatabase` to determine the object identifier of the current record (by seeking 0 records from the current record), and then pass the returned object identifier to `CeDeleteRecord`, as shown in Code Listing 11-20.

Code Listing 11-20

```
DWORD dwIndex;
CEOID pOIDRec;
pOIDRec = CeSeekDatabase(hAuthor, CEDB_SEEK_CURRENT,
    0, &dwIndex);
CeDeleteRecord(hAuthor, pOIDRec);
```

Often, Windows CE database records create a global variable that is used to store the object identifier of the current record, because it is required in many different circumstances.

Take care when deleting the current record, as any subsequent attempt to read or write from the current record will fail. The Cardfile application (located on the CD ROM in the workspace \samples\cardfile\ cardfile.dsw), moves the current record pointer on the next record (or the first record if the last record is deleted) after a record is deleted. The source for this is in the function `DeleteCard in cardedit.cpp`.

Using the MFC CE Database Classes

The MFC provides a number of classes to access Windows CE databases. The classes are:

- `CCeDBDatabase`: This class provides the main access to Windows CE databases, and has methods to create, open, close, and delete databases. Further, the `CCeDBDatabase` class has a set of methods that allows you to seek, read, write, and delete records in a database.

Accessing databases from the desktop

A neat feature of Windows CE databases is the ability to access databases on a Windows CE device directly from applications running on Windows 95 or Window NT. This means that you can load data into your Windows CE application's database in the following situations:

✔ When the application is installed (with code placed in the setup application, see Chapter 9 for more information on writing setup programs).

✔ Whenever the Windows CE device is connected to the desktop PC. This allows the data in the database to be synchronized with, say, a corporate database.

The database functions that are callable from your desktop applications are part of the Remote Application Programming Interface (RAPI). To use these functions in your desktop application you will need to:

✔ **Rapi.h:** Include the header file `rapi.h` in all source files that use the functions.

✔ **Rapi.lib:** Add the library file `rapi.lib` into the Developer Studio project. Chapter 9 tells you how to add new library files to a project.

All the database functions described in this chapter have RAPI equivalent functions, and they all have the same name. There are two important differences you must consider when using the RAPI database functions:

✔ Always call `CeGetLastError` to determine the reason why a function call failed. Don't call `GetLastError`.

✔ Always call `CeCloseHandle` to close a database, not `CloseHandle`.

✔ `CCeDBRecord`: This class is used to represent a single record in a Windows CE database. The class contains methods that allow property values to be added, updated and removed from a record. The `CCeDBRecord` class is used when a `CCeDBDatabase` class object is used to read or write records.

✔ `CCeDBProp`: This class is used to store a property and the associated data. The class, therefore, stores the same data as a single `CEPROPVAL` structure.

You should include the header file `Wcedb.h` in any .CPP file in your application that use the MFC database classes listed above.

The workspace \samples\cardfile\dbmfc.dsw is for you MFC users — the code in this application shows you how to call the MFC CE database classes. The application implements the authors database described at the start of this chapter in the section "Not Your Average Desktop Database." The application displays a list of authors in a combo box (drop-down list box) on the command bar, and uses a list control to display the titles and ISBN numbers of the books written by a selected author.

Using the CCeDBProp class

I start by describing the CCeDBProp class, which is used to specify all of the information associated with a property. You use the CCeDBProp class when calling methods in the CCeDBDatabase and CCeDBRecord classes.

The CCeDBProp requires that you specify three pieces of information to fully define a property. They are:

- **Property identifier:** The property's identifier using the SetIdent method.
- **Data type:** The property's data type using the SetType method. The class has an enumeration which includes values for all the database data types (for example, dbPropSeek.Type_Long).
- **Value:** The property's value. Two functions exist for each data type to get the property's value (for example, GetLong) and set a property's value (for example, SetLong).

Code Listing 11-21 declares a CCeDBProp class variable. The variable is initialized with an identifier (HHPR_AUTHOR_NUMBER), a data type (dbPropSeek.Type_Long), and a value (contained in the variable lAuthorNum). CCeDBProp can now search for a particular record, or to add a property value to a database record.

Code Listing 11-21

```
CCeDBProp dbPropSeek;
dbPropSeek.SetIdent(HHPR_AUTHOR_NUMBER);
dbPropSeek.SetType(dbPropSeek.Type_Long);
dbPropSeek.SetLong(lAuthorNum);
```

The CCeDBProp class serves the same purpose in MFC as the CEPROPVAL structure does in API applications.

Using the CCeDBDatabase class

The class CCeDBDatabase provides the ability to create, open, close, and delete databases. The class CCeDBDatabase also provides methods to navigate through the records in a database.

Creating and opening databases

Typically, an application needs to open the database when the application first runs. The application must also see whether the database exists, and if it doesn't, the application must go ahead and create the database.

Creating an MFC database application

Building an MFC database application is different from building a standard MFC application (which I describe in Chapter 4). Database applications don't use the standard commands on the File menu (such as File⇨Open), and they typically display records from a database in the application window. You should follow these steps to create an MFC database application:

1. **Create a project with AppWizard.**

   Use the default options, except you should specify 0 for the number of files on the Recent file list. Your application will not use the File menu commands. You can select `CListView` as the base class for the application's view if you want to display a list of records with columns in the application window. The section "Step 4 — setting class names" in Chapter 4 shows how to change the base class for the view. The sample DBMFC contains code showing how to fill the list with records in the member function `CDBMFCDoc::FillTitleList`.

2. **Include the header file Wcedb.h in stdafx.h:**

   ```
   #include <Wcedb.h>
   ```

Include the standard header file in `stdafx.h` so that the database function declarations are available to all suurce files in the workspace.

3. **Remove File and Edit menus and command bar buttons.**

   Database applications don't typically use the standard File⇨Open, File⇨Save, and File⇨Save As menu commands, so be sure to remove them. In this application, the standard Edit menu is removed, too, and the corresponding command buttons are also removed.

4. **Add Property identifier declarations.**

   Each property requires a unique identifier. Variables to hold these identifiers should be added to your application's document class (which is `CDBMFCDoc` in the DBMFC sample application). The following is one example of a declaration:

   ```
   WORD HHPR_AUTHOR_NUMBER;
   ```

   This variable is initialized in the document's constructor:

   ```
   HHPR_AUTHOR_NUMBER = 10;
   ```

After completing these steps, you can begin the database programming.

Use the following `Exists` member function of the class `CCeDBDatabase` to test whether a database exists (where `DB_NAME` the name of the database):

```
if(!CCeDBDatabase::Exists(DB_NAME))
```

Use the `Create` member function to create a new Windows CE database. The following call creates a new database with a default database identifier and no indexes:

```
m_AuthorDB.Create(DB_NAME);
```

The `Open` member function opens an existing Windows CE database. The following code opens the database whose name is specified by `DB_NAME`:

```
m_AuthorDB.Open(DB_NAME);
```

These functions call to `Create` and `Open` use default arguments for the index specifications, and, therefore, no indexes are used or created.

The `dbmfc.dsw` sample application creates (if necessary) and opens the database in the `CDBMFCDoc::OnNewDocument` member. The code in `CDBMFCDoc::OnNewDocument` ensures that the database is open before the application window appears. Indexes are used, so you can use this code as an example of how to add indexes to your own MFC applications.

Navigating through records

`CCeDBDatabase` provides the following member functions for navigating through records in a database:

- `SeekFirst`: To move to the first record.
- `SeekNext`: To move to the next record.
- `SeekPrev`: To move to the previous record.
- `SeekLast`: To move to the last record.

The `CCeDBDatabase` class member `m_bAutoSeekNext` determines whether or not the record pointer should move automatically to the next record, following a record read. The class member `m_bEOF` will have a value of `TRUE` if the last record in the database has been reached.

The member function `CDBMFCDoc::FillAuthorList` in the `dbmfc.dsw` sample application shows how to read through a database, read the record, and add data to a combo box.

Seeking records

The `CCeDBDatabase` class has a number of methods that locate records based on index values. They are as follows:

- `SeekFirstEqual`: To locate the first record with the given value.
- `SeekNextEqual`: To locate the next record with the given value.
- `SeekValueGreater`: To seek the record with an index value that is greater than or equal to the specified value.
- `SeekValueSmaller`: To see the record with an index value that is just smaller than the specified value.

The member function `CDBMFCDoc::FillTitleList` in the `dbmfc.dsw` sample application shows how to seek records in a database, read the record, and add data to a list control.

Using the CCeDBRecord class

Use the `CCeDBRecord` class when reading or writing to records. For example, the following call to `CCeDBDatabase::ReadCurrRecord` reads the current database record:

```
CCeDBRecord dbRecRecord;
if(!m_AuthorDB.ReadCurrRecord(&dbRecRecord))
    return;
```

The `CCeDBRecord` class object contains information on all the properties in the record that has been read. You can also use the `CCeDBDatabase::AddRecord` method to add new records in a similar way.

The best method to access the data that is contained in a `CCeDBRecord` class object is to retrieve a `CCeDBProp` class object pointer for the particular property that you're interested in. In Code Listing 11-22, a `CCeDBProp` pointer is obtained for the property `HHPR_AUTHOR_NAME`, and the `GetString` method is used to get the author's name for this record.

Code Listing 11-22

```
CCeDBProp*  prop;
prop = DBRecord.GetPropFromIdent(HHPR_AUTHOR_NAME);
sAuthorName = prop->GetString();
```

The member function `CDBMFCDoc::AddAuthor` in the `dbmfc.dsw` sample application shows how to set up `CCeDBProp` class objects ready for new records to be added to the database. This method also shows how to determine the author identifier to use — this should be one greater than the maximum author identifier in use.

Chapter 12

Accessing the Contacts Database

- -

In This Chapter

▶ Opening and closing the address book

▶ Opening and searching records

- -

*T*he address book database is the central storage area for all contact information on a Windows CE device. You're encouraged by Microsoft to use this database to store contact-related information, rather than create your own contact databases. The address book database is a Windows CE database called Contacts Database in the \database folder.

Windows CE provides a set of API functions that provide you with structured access to your address book database, so you don't have to know all the details of Windows CE database programming. However, I advise you to flip to Chapter 11 to discover more about how Windows CE databases work.

The workspace \samples\condb\condb.dsw contains the source code of an API application that accesses the address book. You can use this application to display the surname, e-mail address, and Web address of contacts in your address book in a list control. You can also add, delete, and update these three pieces of information. This application also contains code that you can use in your own applications to access your address book.

Address Book Essentials

The address book is essentially a Windows CE database with predefined *properties,* or fields, that store contact information. Rather than letting developers have free access to the database (and we know what would happen then), Windows CE gives you a set of API functions that provide an interface that is structured and easier-to-use than the standard Windows CE database functions.

Address book fields

Each property in the address book has an identifier (integer number) that's used to reference the property. For example, HHPR_COMPANY_NAME is used for the company name, and HHPR_SURNAME for the surname.

Getting ready to call address book functions

Before you attempt to call the address book functions described in this chapter, you must:

- ✔ **Include** addrstor.h **in your source files:** The header file addrstor.h contains all the function and structure declarations that you need for calling the address book functions.

- ✔ **Include** addrstor.lib **in the project:** You must add the library addrstor.lib to the project; otherwise, the building of the application fails with unresolved errors for each of the address book functions that you use.

Opening the address book

If your application needs to use the address book, call OpenAddressBook when your application starts. This function requires two arguments:

- ✔ **Notification Window Handle:** This hWnd is the window handle that receives notification messages whenever another application modifies the database. These message names all start with DB_PEGOID. If you're not interested in notifications, you can pass NULL for this argument.

- ✔ **Index to be used:** The property identifier of the index to be used, or NULL for no indexes.

You can use Code Listing 12-1 to open the address book.

Code Listing 12-1

```
if(!OpenAddressBook(hWnd, NULL))
    {
    return FALSE;
    }
```

Closing the address book

You'll probably want to close the address book by calling `CloseAddressBook` when your application terminates (Code Listing 12-2). This function is simple — it takes no arguments. A good place to put this call is in the message handler for the `WM_DESTROY` message in the main application window.

Code Listing 12-2

```
case WM_DESTROY:
        // close the address book
        CloseAddressBook();
        PostQuitMessage(0);
        break;
```

The AddressCard Structure

A contact record has lots of different fields, which are represented in an `AddressCard` structure that you can use to manipulate data in a single contact record. The `AddressCard` structure has `TCHAR*` pointers for all the text properties in a contact record and two `SYSTEMTIME` structures for the birthday and anniversary fields. The first part of the `AddressCard` structure is shown in Code Listing 12-3.

Code Listing 12-3

```
typedef struct _AddressCard {
    SYSTEMTIME stBirthday;
    SYSTEMTIME stAnniversary;
    TCHAR *pszBusinessFax;
    TCHAR *pszCompany;
    TCHAR *pszDepartment;
    TCHAR *pszEmail;
```

First you must declare an `AddressCard` structure and then initialize all the fields to have `NULL` values. You can do so by calling `memset` (Code Listing 12-4). You need to pass three arguments to `memset`:

- A pointer to the `AddressCard` variable
- The value to initialize with (0)
- The number of bytes to initialize (the `sizeof` operator returns the number of bytes in the `acCard` variable)

Code Listing 12-4

```
AddressCard acCard;
memset(&acCard,0,sizeof(acCard));
```

Searching and Opening Records

You can use the `GetMatchingEntry` function to search your address book. If you locate multiple records by the search, the `GetMatchingEntry` function displays a dialog box that asks you to select one particular record. The `GetMatchingEntry` function returns back the object identifier of the record found in the search. After you have the object identifier of the selected record, you can open the record by using the `OpenAddressCard` function.

Getting a property's long name

Before you can perform a search, you must first get the long text name of the property that you want to search on. You can use the function `GetPropertyDataStruct` to get a property's long name by using the following arguments:

✔ **How to specify the property:** When calling `GetPropertyDataStruct`, you need to specify how you're referring to a particular property. Generally, using the property identifier is easiest. Therefore, you pass the constant `GPDS_PROPERTY` as the first argument.

✔ **The property identifier:** The second argument specifies the property identifier whose long name you're retrieving. For example, `HHPR_SURNAME`.

✔ **Pointer to a** `PropertyDataStruct` **variable:** This variable is filled with information about the specified property. The member `pds.pszPropertyName` contains the long property name.

You can use Code Listing 12-5 to get the long property name.

Code Listing 12-5

```
PropertyDataStruct pds;
GetPropertyDataStruct(GPDS_PROPERTY, HHPR_SURNAME, &pds);
```

Performing a search

After you have the property's long name, you can perform a search by using the function `GetMatchingEntry`. You need to pass the following arguments to this function:

- ✔ **The text to search for:** This argument is a `TCHAR` buffer that contains the full or partial property value to search for. If your search locates multiple records, the function displays a dialog box from which you can select a single record.

- ✔ **The size of the search buffer:** If your search locates multiple records, the function `GetMatchingEntry` places the actual property value that you've selected into the search buffer. Therefore, you must specify the size of the buffer.

- ✔ **Long Property Name:** This argument is the long property name that you obtain from calling `GetPropertyDataStruct`.

- ✔ **Pointer to a `CEOID` variable:** The variable pointed to by this argument is filled with the `CEOID` value located by the search. You can use this value later to open the record.

- ✔ **Pointer to a `HHPRTAG` variable:** The data returned in the variable pointed to by this argument specifies the identifier of the property upon which the search was carried out. You probably won't use this information.

Code Listing 12-6 shows how to search for a surname in the address book.

Code Listing 12-6

```
TCHAR szBuffer[100];
CEOID oiFound;
HHPRTAG hprt;

wcscpy(szBuffer, _TEXT("Smyth"));
if(GetMatchingEntry(szBuffer,
    100,   pds.pszPropertyName,
    &oiFound, &hprt))
    {
    // record found
    }
```

Opening a record

Now that you know how to get the `CEOID` of a specific record in the address book, you can use this value to open the record and use the contact information. You can use the `OpenAddressCard` function for this purpose.

You need to pass the following arguments to OpenAddressCard:

- ✔ **The record's identifier:** This argument is the object identifier returned from a search by using GetMatchingEntry.

- ✔ **Pointer to** AddressCard **variable:** This structure is filled with the data for the selected record.

- ✔ **Memory allocation flag:** This flag indicates how memory should be allocated for the data in the contact record. Normally, you pass 0 unless you want to modify the data in the record.

Code Listing 12-7 shows code that you can use to retrieve data for a record.

Code Listing 12-7

```
AddressCard acFound;
if(!OpenAddressCard(oiFound, &acFound, 0))
{
    // record not found
}
```

After you've finished using the data in the AddressCard variable, you must *always* call the FreeAddressCard function. Doing so frees the memory allocated when you opened the record. You must call the FreeAddressCard function regardless of the allocation flag you specified.

```
FreeAddressCard(&acFound);
```

After you retrieve data for a card, you can reference the data for that card through the AddressCard structure that you passed to the function OpenAddressCard.

Part III
Peeking Behind the Scenes

The 5th Wave   By Rich Tennant

IN A STROKE OF SELF-RELIANCE, RAY EXTENDS THE POWER OF HIS H/PC BY TAPPING INTO THE BATTERY OF HIS SLEEPING NEIGHBOR'S HEARING AID.

In this part . . .

Okay — your application looks good and gives users some really neat features. But how does it look behind the scenes? Does your application consume too much memory? Can you improve its performance by adding threads? Is it a power hog? Can it be split up into smaller libraries of code?

In this part, I discuss how to efficiently manage memory and how to calmly react to low-memory situations. Then, I explain how you can create processes, so that you can run other applications. I take a look at how you can use threads to more efficient applications. Finally, this part looks at power management and creating dynamic link libraries (DLLs).

Chapter 13

Memory Management, Process Control, and Thread Control

• •

In This Chapter

▶ Making the most of memory

▶ Dealing with memory loss

▶ Running other applications as processes

▶ Using threads for efficient program execution

• •

Does managing memory, creating processes and starting threads leave you cold and uncomfortable? You're not alone, but understanding these topics is important if you want to write applications that run reliably and efficiently. Limiting the amount of memory used by your applications is of paramount importance: You can be sure that users will run out of memory at the most inconvenient times, such as when they're about to clinch that big deal or when they're counting beetles in the Amazon rain forest.

When an application is run, a process is created by Windows CE, and each such process has at least one thread. It is the thread that actually executes the code in your application. Managing processes and threads makes your applications run more quickly and efficiently. But be careful — dangers lurk in dark places.

On the CD-ROM that accompanies this book, you can find the sample code for this chapter, in the \samples\memman.dsw sample workspace. As you read this chapter you should view the sample code in Visual Studio. You should compile and execute the applications to see the techniques used for memory management, process control and thread control in action. You can then use copy and paste to add the code directly into your applications. See the About the CD Appendix for instructions on installing the files from the CD-ROM and how to load them into Visual Studio.

Using Memory Efficiently

All resources are, to some extent, limited; otherwise, they wouldn't be called resources! Windows CE-based devices typically have very limited memory resources. For example, on a handheld PC (H/PC) you can expect to find 4MB or 16MB of RAM (or possibly as little as 2MB of RAM). Remember that the Windows CE code, (including applications such as Pocket Word and Excel) is contained in ROM, so the operating system requires little RAM to execute. Efficient memory management is very important as there is so little memory to play with.

All Windows CE programmers take on the responsibility of using the smallest possible amount of memory. Take the oath of allegiance now!

 Don't forget that the memory in a Windows CE machine stores persistent data (consisting of file system, registry, and databases), as well as the data and code used by programs as they run (program memory). Figure 13-1 shows how memory is divided between storing persistent data and program memory.

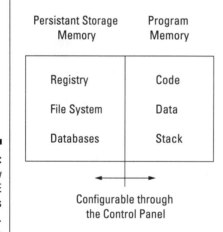

Figure 13-1: How Windows CE organizes memory.

 Often, you can add various types of memory cards to Windows CE devices to increase memory. Generally, these memory cards increase the amount of memory only for storage, and Windows CE can't use them as program memory.

Understanding how your applications use memory

When you install an application on a Windows CE machine, Windows CE saves the .exe file in compressed format in the file system storage area, which does the following:

- ✔ Uncompresses the application's code and copies the code into the program memory area.
- ✔ Allocates program memory for the stack.
- ✔ Allocates program memory for the data used by the application.

Application code

An application's code is generally read-only and is not modified during execution (so the code is called *pure*). Therefore, if memory runs short, Windows CE can remove code from the program memory area. Windows CE can reload the code from the application's file when required.

You should reduce the amount of code generated for your application. For example, make sure that code used in many different parts of your application is placed in functions.

Windows CE shares address space

In Windows 95 or Windows NT, each application has its own 4GB address space. So each application can use an address, such as 0x0000ffde. Storage must be allocated from the disk-based paging file before an address can be used to stored data. Storage is allocated in *pages,* which are typically 4K or 8K in size. Pages must be loaded into memory before data can be stored in them, and the pages are written back to the paging file when finished with. You should understand that data is held in storage (which is part of the paging file), and memory is only used by Windows NT or Windows 95 to allow this storage to be accessed by your code.

In Windows CE, however, all applications share the same 4GB address space. This address space is divided into 33 *slots* (or areas) of 32MB each, and each application is assigned its own slot. The first slot uses the address range 0 to 31MB, the second 32-63MB etc. An application can't access memory in another application's slot. Note that Windows CE has no paging file, so addresses are mapped directly onto memory.

But wait a minute! Why am I'm talking about 4GB address spaces on a Windows CE device with 2, 4, or 16MB of memory? An application must allocate physical memory before data can be stored at a particular address. Most of the address in the 4GB address space don't have memory allocated for them, and so cannot store data.

Application stack

Each application has a stack which is an area of memory used to manage function calls. Windows CE uses the stack for the following purposes:

✔ Recording each function call made by another function, so that a function can return to the function that called it.

✔ Storing data associated with the parameters passed by a function when calling another function.

✔ Storing local (or *auto*) variables declared in a function. Variable nVar is a local variable in Code Listing 13-1.

Code Listing 13-1

```
function myFunc1()
{
        int nVar;
}
```

The stack has an initial size of 1K, and it grows automatically to a maximum size of 58K. An application error occurs if Windows CE attempts to grow the stack larger than 58K.

As an application calls and returns functions, the actual amount of stack in use fluctuates. The stack space allocated to an application shrinks to the amount in use if Windows CE becomes short of memory.

Application data

An application stores data in one of three places:

✔ **The stack:** Local variables are stored in the stack (as described in the previous section).

✔ **Global (or static) data variables:** These variables are created by adding declarations outside functions, or within functions and classes where the static keyword is used.

✔ **The Heap:** Containing dynamic data created using new, malloc, LocalAlloc.

Global variables should only be used to store data that is required for the entire time the application is running. Use as few global variables as possible.

Allocating dynamic memory

Of the memory allocation techniques described in the section "Application data," dynamic memory allocation is the technique most likely to give you problems. Sooner or later, you will probably allocate memory and then forget to free it. If this happens repeatedly, you have a memory leakage. An application has a *memory leakage* when it allocates more and more memory as its running, but isn't actually using all the allocated memory, because the memory should have been freed when the application finished using it. Luckily, all memory used by your application is freed when the application terminates — so at least you can recover from such bugs.

You can dynamically allocate memory in a number of ways:

- ✔ Using the C malloc and free functions — Check out *C For Dummies*, Volumes I and II, by Dan Gookin (IDG Books Worldwide, Inc.) for more on these functions.

- ✔ Using the C++ new and delete operators. *C++ For Dummies*, 2nd Edition, by Steven R. Davis (IDG Books Worldwide, Inc.) has plenty of information for you on these operators.

- ✔ Using the Windows CE memory management functions, such as LocalAlloc.

All these techniques allocate memory for the application's heap. The *heap* is an area of memory provided by Windows CE from which an application can dynamically allocate memory. Code Listing 13-2 is an example of using LocalAlloc.

Code Listing 13-2

```
LPTSTR szDBName = NULL;    // pointer to memory
szDBName = LocalAlloc(LMEM_FIXED, 4000);
if (szDBName == NULL)
   {
   // failed to allocate memory
   }
else
   {
// use the data in szDBName. . .
// free the allocation
   LocalFree(szDBName);
   }
```

Allocating memory in different ways

Memory from the heap is allocated in pages. A page is the minimum unit in which memory can be allocated. The page size is machine-specific — for H/PC machines, the page size is typically 1K or 4K. When you allocate memory from the heap, Windows CE looks in the existing pages for available space to satisfy the allocation. If no space is available, more pages are allocated to the heap. Pages can be freed only if they are completely empty. Note that the maximum size of the heap for an application is 1MB.

If you're creating a large number of small allocations, you should consider creating your own heap, which is particularly efficient when all the allocations are the same size, or when they are only required for a short period of time. You can create your own heap by using the HeapCreate function. Then you use the HeapAlloc and HeapFree functions to allocate and deallocate memory from this heap. Note that making a single function call to HeapDestroy destroys all allocations in such a heap.

On the CD-ROM that accompanies this book, you can find the sample code in the workspace \samples\memman\memman.dsw. (The code is in SampleCreateHeap and related functions in memman.cpp.) This code shows you how to create and use your own heap in your applications.

If you need to allocate one large memory block, take a look at VirtualAlloc. It's efficient and fast, but not too easy to use! The functions SampleVirtualAlloc and SampleVirtualFree in memman.cpp show a safe and simple way of allocating large memory blocks using VirtualAlloc and VirtualFree.

Determining free program memory

Monitoring the amount of free program memory is important, especially if your application requires large amounts of memory.

The function GlobalMemoryStatus fills a MEMORYSTATUS structure with information about the current program memory state.

MEMORYSTATUS is one of those structures that requires that the first member is initialized with the size of the structure before calling the function GlobalMemoryStatus. The sizeof operator returns the size of a structure to you. Use Code Listing 13-3 to call GlobalMemoryStatus.

Code Listing 13-3

```
MEMORYSTATUS msStatus;
msStatus.dwLength = sizeof(msStatus);
GlobalMemoryStatus(&msStatus);
```

Here are the relevant MEMORYSTATUS members and their purposes:

- ✔ dwTotalPhys: Total number of bytes currently configured for program memory
- ✔ dwAvailPhys: Total number of bytes currently available for allocation

In memman.cpp in the workspace \samples\memman\memman.dsw on the CD-ROM that accompanies this book, you can find the DisplayFreeMemory function. This function makes a call to GlobalMemoryStatus and then displays the returned values in a message box. You can test this function call by choosing the OptionsÍFree Memory command in this application.

Monitoring memory usage

As you develop your application, you need to regularly check the following, using the Windows CE Remote Heap Walker:

- ✔ The amount of memory your application uses
- ✔ Potential memory leakages

In Visual Studio, choose Tools⇨Remote Heap Walker to run the Remote Heap Walker application. (Note that the Remote Heap Walker runs on your desktop PC, which is connected to the Windows CE device.) Remote Heap Walker displays the Process List window when it first runs, which contains a list of all the processes running on the Windows CE device (see Figure 13-2).

You can view the memory allocations made by any of the processes listed in the Process List window by double-clicking the appropriate row in the process list. This displays the HeapList for the selected process, which displays a single line for each of the memory allocations (for example, allocations made in your application using the LocalAlloc function). Figure 13-2 shows the HeapList for the Cardfile application.

The contents of any of the memory allocations in the heap can be viewed by double clicking the entry in the HeapList, which displays the Memory Dump window for the selected memory allocation. The Memory Dump window shows a list of each byte of data in the allocated memory using hexadecimal and the ASCII character itself. This is the data that you place in the memory block (such as strings or data in structure variables). Figure 13-2 shows the Memory Dump window for one of the memory allocations made by Cardfile.

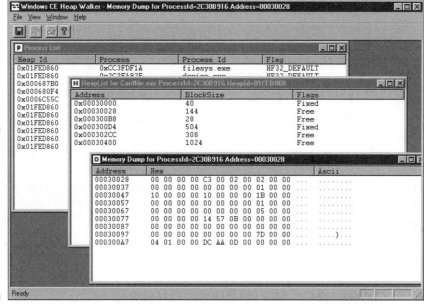

Figure 13-2:
An example
of Remote
Heap
Walker,
showing
memory
usage by
the Cardfile
application.

You can use Remote Heap Walker to monitor the memory usage of your application as your application executes. You may have a memory leak if the number of memory allocations in the HeapList window continues to grow as your application executes. You can display the memory dump of the memory allocations for each entry in the HeapList and from the contents of the memory block, determine if the memory block should have been deleted.

Hibernating when it gets cold

Even with the best-written programs, Windows CE sometimes run out of memory. Running out of memory is a serious situation with Windows CE machines, because they lack secondary storage devices (such as disk drives).

When Windows CE detects that available memory is running low, it takes several steps to free up memory. Windows CE takes this action when an application's attempt to allocate dynamic memory fails. Before returning a failure code to the application, Windows CE sends a `WM_HIBERNATE` message to visible windows, starting with the application that has been inactive the longest. Windows CE repeats this action until enough memory is freed to allow the original allocation request to succeed.

In response to a WM_HIBERNATE message, well-behaved applications do the following:

- ✔ Free any large memory blocks whose contents can be reconstructed at a later time.
- ✔ Free any Graphics, Windowing, and Events Subsystem (GWES) objects (such as windows, dialog boxes, brushes, fonts, and so on).

The functions DoHibernate and DoActivate in memman.cpp show typical code for handling WM_HIBERNATE and WM_ACTIVATE messages.

When you activate an application, it receives a WM_ACTIVATE message. If the application previously hibernated, it should recreate the necessary GWES objects and reallocate memory blocks. The application can then continue executing as normal.

You can use the application wm_hiber.exe to send WM_HIBERNATE messages to all applications or to a particular window in an application. The wm_hiber.exe application (located in the Windows CE folder \Windows in the emulation environment) allows you to test your hibernation routines.

Dealing with the lowest of the low memory situations

Windows CE begins to send WM_HIBERNATE messages when an allocation would result in the free memory dropping below 128K.

If an allocation would result in free memory dropping below 64K (the *low memory threshold*), two new rules apply, depending on the size of the request:

- ✔ If the requested allocation of memory is less than or equal to 16K, Windows CE displays a System Out of Memory dialog box and prompts the user to close applications or increase the amount of configured program memory.
- ✔ If the requested allocation of memory is less than or equal to 16K, the allocation fails (and Windows CE returns a NULL pointer). No dialog box appears.

When the user closes applications in response to the System Out Of Memory dialog box, they receive a WM_CLOSE message. Applications should not create large memory blocks in response to WM_CLOSE (for example, to save a file); otherwise, the applications fail on closing and data may be lost.

If an allocation would result in free memory dropping below 16K (the *Critical Memory Threshold*), similar rules apply, but the threshold determining if the System Out Of Memory dialog box is displayed is 8K, not 16K.

The numbers quoted here are for machines with 1K page sizes. On 4K page size machines, the hibernation threshold is 160K, the Low Memory Threshold is 96K, and the Critical Memory Threshold is 48K. The other numbers remain the same.

What's In a Process?

Whenever you run an application, Windows CE creates a process. (A *process* is really just a block of information maintained by Windows CE that describes a running application.) You can think of an application as the .exe saved in the object store; when the .exe is run, a process is created. In fact, a process is created for every instance of that application.

When a process is created, Windows CE does the following:

✔ Creates access to the code needed to run the application

✔ Sets aside memory to store the data required by the application

✔ Creates the primary thread for the application and starts it executing

Processes and threads! Is this designed to be confusing? Make sure that you understand the distinction. A *process* is really all the parts that create the environment in which the application runs. Most importantly, a process can't execute code and, therefore, can't do anything. *Threads* execute code, so a process must have at least one thread to be able to run. Think of threads as *threads of execution* (which has nothing to do with cloth and tailors).

Creating a process

All processes are started when another process calls the API function CreateProcess, which takes a multitude of parameters that can make it confusing to use. Most of these parameters are not supported under Windows CE, so I only described those that are required.

Code Listing 13-4 shows an example of how CreateProcess is used to execute Pocket Word and pass the command line parameter process — the file to be opened from the default \My Documents folder.

Processes in Windows NT, Windows 95, and Windows CE

Windows NT and Windows 95 create and destroy processes all the time, and they have a large number of processes running at any time. In fact, processes are often created to perform quite trivial, quick tasks, such as copying files or removing unwanted data from databases.

In Windows CE, a limit of 32 processes can run at one time. You should therefore avoid creating lots of small processes.

In fact, you are much less likely to need to create a process in Windows CE than in Windows NT or Windows 95.

Code Listing 13-4

```
PROCESS_INFORMATION pi;
if(CreateProcess(TEXT("pword.exe"), TEXT("process"),
      NULL,NULL,FALSE,0,NULL,NULL,NULL, &pi) == NULL)
      {
      MessageBox(hWnd,
          TEXT("Failed to start application"),
          NULL, MB_OK);
      }
else
      {
      CloseHandle(pi.hProcess);
      CloseHandle(pi.hThread);
      }
```

You can find this code in the function SampleCreateProcess in memman.cpp in the workspace \samples\memman\memman.dsw. You can copy this code into your own application, and change the text shown in italics to specify the application name and command line parameters.

Of the ten parameters, only the following three are required when calling CreateProcess in Windows CE:

- ✔ The name of the application's EXE file.

- ✔ Command line arguments (for example, the file to be opened). Use NULL if none are to be passed.

- ✔ A pointer to a PROCESS_INFORMATION structure in which information about the new process is returned. This returns kernel object handles, which are covered in the next section.

The other parameters should be passed as `NULL,NULL,FALSE,0,NULL,` `NULL,NULL`, as shown in the call to `CreateProcess` in Code Listing 13-4.

Take care when using pathnames in the application's EXE filename. The backslash is used as an escape character in C and C++, so you should use two backslashes. For example, to run `calc.exe` with a fully qualified pathname and no command line arguments, write the following:

```
CreateProcess(TEXT("\\windows\\calc.exe"), NULL,
        NULL,NULL,FALSE,0,NULL,NULL,NULL, &pi);
```

If a pathname is not specified, `CreateProcess` searches the following folders:

- ✔ The root of the PCMCIA card if it exists
- ✔ The windows (`\windows`) folder
- ✔ The root (`\`) folder of the Windows CE device

`CreateProcess` returns `FALSE` if the application can't be run. You can use `GetLastError` to find out more detailed information about the failure.

Handling kernel object handles with care

Processes, threads, and other objects created by the kernel are associated with important information. Therefore, when the kernel creates an object (such as a process), it also creates a block of data describing that object. Windows CE returns a handle to the object when it is created.

Of course, this block of information must be deleted at some stage. You may think that you can delete the information associated with a process when the process terminates, but this is not the case. You may want to access process information after the process terminates.

So how does the kernel know when to delete this data? It maintains a reference count. When the kernel gives a kernel object handle to a program, the reference count is increased by one, and when you call the function `CloseHandle`, the reference count is decreased by one. When the reference count reaches zero, Windows CE deletes the data.

The function `CreateProcess` is passed a `PROCESS_INFORMATION` structure, and the function returns a kernel object handle for the new process and the primary thread for that new process. Therefore, two kernel object handles are returned.

Personally, I don't want to find out information about the new process and thread using the kernel object handle, so I close them immediately (but only if the process is created successfully; see Code Listing 13-4). Note that the data associated with the process and thread is not deleted at this time, because the kernel keeps a reference to them while the application is running.

You must call `CloseHandle` for any kernel object handle given to you by Windows CE. If you don't, the data associated with the object is never freed.

Understanding why CreateProcess failed

Your call to `CreateProcess` may fail for many reasons, but here are the most common ones:

✔ The EXE filename you specified does not exist at the specified location or in the default search locations. Did you use double backslashes in the pathname?

✔ Windows CE already had the maximum number of processes running.

✔ Some other resource ran out, such as memory.

✔ You didn't pass a legal pointer to a `PROCESS_INFORMATION` structure.

You usually get a memory exception when you don't specify a proper pointer to a `PROCESS_INFORMATION` structure. Note that you must pass a pointer — you can't pass `NULL`.

Finishing early

You can terminate a process at any time by calling the `TerminateProcess` function and specifying the process's handle (obtained when you created the process) and a process exit code. Here is an example:

```
TerminateProcess(pi.hProcess, 0);
```

Note that you still need to close the process handle in the usual way.

Windows CE does not support process exit codes, and they should be set to zero.

To terminate your own process, you must first obtain a process handle to your process. You can do this by calling the function `GetCurrentProcess`, which takes no arguments and returns a handle (see Code Listing 13-5).

Code Listing 13-5

```
HANDLE hMyProcess;
hMyProcess = GetCurrentProcess();
TerminateProcess(hMyProcess, 0);
```

In this case, you don't have to close the handle hMyProcess because GetCurrentProcess returns a pseudo-handle. This is a special handle that says "refer to the current process, whichever that may be."

By the way, call TerminateProcess only as the last resort. Always try to finish a process through the normal channels first.

Weaving Threads

A primary thread is created for each new process, and this thread executes code in the application. This includes message handling, dialog box display, and window repainting.

You can create additional threads to perform tasks in your application. Because Windows CE is a multitasking operating system, these threads appear to execute in parallel with other threads.

Threads are of the following two types:

- **Worker Threads:** These threads don't create windows or dialog boxes and don't handle messages. Note that you can display message boxes in a worker thread.
- **User Interface Threads:** These threads create windows or display dialog boxes and have special calls to enable message handling.

Creating User Interface Threads is much more complex than creating Worker Threads. Until you get used to managing multiple threads, I suggest that you keep all window creation, dialog box display, and message handling in your primary thread, and only create worker threads.

Here are some of the reasons that you may want to create additional threads:

- You need to facilitate background communications and transfer of data.
- Your applications needs to wait for another process to complete without your user interface being hung.
- Your applications needs to perform background processing (for example, calculations that take a long time to complete).

Go easy on creating threads! Your application's complexity increases dramatically as you add more threads, and a whole host of new potential problems arises! Keep your use of threads simple.

Threads have the following characteristics:

✔ Each thread has its own stack for local variables and function calls.

✔ Threads share global (static) data with all other threads in the application.

✔ Threads can be assigned different execution priorities (such as background or high priority).

✔ A process terminates automatically when the last thread is terminated.

Creating a thread

Creating a thread involves two steps:

1. Create a thread function to be executed by the thread.

2. Create the new thread by calling `CreateThread`.

A thread function has the form in Code Listing 13-6.

Code Listing 13-6

```
DWORD WINAPI ThreadFunc( LPVOID lpParam)
{
        // code to be executed by the thread
        return 0;       // thread will now terminate
}
```

When you create a thread, Windows CE calls this function through the new thread. The thread continues to execute until this function performs a return. Remember that creating a thread is more than a simple function call; the code in the thread function executes in parallel with the other threads in the application.

The `CreateThread` function is called to create the new thread. Windows CE requires only a single parameter — the address of the thread function (for example, `ThreadFunc` in the previous code). The function returns a thread kernel object handle (see Code Listing 13-7).

Code Listing 13-7

```
HANDLE hThread;
hThread = CreateThread(NULL, 0, ThreadFunc, NULL, 0, NULL);
CloseHandle(hThread);
// thread now executing!
```

Remember to close the thread kernel object handle after the thread is created!

Making the thread do something

Typically, a thread function performs one of the following tasks:

- ✔ Creates a loop and processes, for example, multiple records in a database or multiple reads from a communications device
- ✔ Waits for something to happen (such as a process to terminate)

A thread function can call any other function in the application in the usual way, or it can create C++ class objects or allocate dynamic memory. In this respect, thread functions are no different from standard functions.

Waiting for something to happen takes a little more care. The natural temptation is to write a loop like this (Code Listing 13-8).

Code Listing 13-8

```
while (something hasn't happened)
      {
      // do nothing
      }
// it's happened now!
```

The problem is that this loop executes continuously and takes up valuable processing time. To reduce the processing time, put the thread to sleep in the loop. The Sleep function allows you to put the current thread to sleep for the specified number of milliseconds (Code Listing 13-9).

Code Listing 13-9

```
while (something hasn't happened)
      {
      Sleep(100);      // sleep for 1/10th Second
      }
// it's happened now!
```

A sleeping thread does not take up any processing time.

In Windows CE 2, you can use the WaitForSingleObject function to wait until a process or thread terminates. For example, you can run an application then call WaitForSingleObject to wait until the application has finished executing. This function takes a handle to the process or thread and the amount of time the function should wait. The value `INFINITE` specifies that the call to `WaitForSingleObject` should wait for ever (see Code Listing 13-10).

Code Listing 13-10

```
WaitForSingleObject(pi.hProcess, INFINITE);
CloseHandle(pi.hProcess);
CloseHandle(pi.hThread);
```

Notice how you must call `WaitForSingleObject` before you close the process handle.

Pulling a thread

A thread can terminate itself immediately without returning from the thread function by calling `ExitThread`. This function takes a single argument — the thread's exit code:

```
ExitThread(1000);
```

This is useful if the thread needs to be terminated in a long function-calling sequence.

As a last resort, a thread can terminate another thread by calling `TerminateThread`. Don't call this function as a matter of course, because the thread being terminated does not have the opportunity to execute termination code, and resources may not be freed. The function requires the thread's kernel object handle and a thread exit code:

```
TerminateThread(hThread, 1000);
```

Signaling danger ahead — global data and threads

Global data presents particular dangers for multithreaded applications because of the way threads are scheduled.

For example, consider the situation illustrated in Figure 13-3, in which an application has a `LONG` global variable called `g_lNum` that is accessed by code in two separate threads.

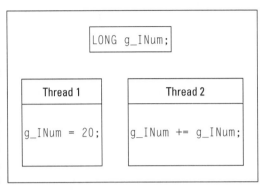

Figure 13-3:
Two
threads
accessing
a global
variable.

In this situation, code in both threads is accessing the same global variable. First, notice that you can't predict the order in which the statements in the two threads will execute. The order of execution depends on how the threads are scheduled.

The next problem is more dangerous and not nearly so obvious. Because Windows CE supports only a single processor, only one thread can be executing at any time, even though this single processing appears to the user to be parallel processing.

Single processing means that the thread schedule starts a thread executing for a short period of time, and then it transfers the processor to the next thread before starting the process again. The threads don't know when they're about to be swapped.

Remember that the processor executes the binary codes generated by the compiler and does not directly execute the lines of code you write. One line of code can result in several binary codes being generated. A thread can be swapped out after *any* binary code has executed, which means that a line of code you've written may only be partially executed when the thread is swapped.

If you assume that the statement g_lNum += g_lNum takes four op codes to execute, the thread could be swapped out after the execution of any of these four op codes. Therefore, the statement may be only partly complete when the next thread continues executing. If this other thread attempts to access g_lNum, it may find that g_lNum contains a strange value.

Although this happens only infrequently, it leads to bugs that are difficult to reproduce and find.

You should always protect access to global data in a multithreaded application by creating a critical section. A critical section ensures that a thread can execute a section of code without being interrupted, which protects access to global data. In the previous example, you would want to ensure that the two statements `g_lNum = 20` and `g_lNum += g_lNum` were marked as critical.

Only when all such critical sections have been identified and protected can you describe your application as *thread safe!*

Going critical

To create a critical section, you must follow these requirements:

- Declare a `CRITICAL_SECTION` structure. This is generally a global variable.

  ```
  CRITICAL_SECTION g_CriticalSection;
  ```

- Create the critical section object from this structure by calling `InitializeCriticalSection` in your application's initialization code:

  ```
  InitializeCriticalSection(&g_CriticalSection);
  ```

- A thread marks a section of code as critical by calling `EnterCriticalSection` at the start and `LeaveCriticalSection` at the end. This should be done for all code that accesses the global data (see Code Listing 13-11).

Code Listing 13-11

```
// for thread 1
EnterCriticalSection(&g_CriticalSection);
g_lNum = 20;        // this is critical
LeaveCriticalSection(&g_CriticalSection);
// for thread 2
EnterCriticalSection(&g_CriticalSection);
g_lNum += g_lNum;   // this is critical
LeaveCriticalSection(&g_CriticalSection);
```

- Call `DeleteCriticalSection` when the critical section is no longer required (for example, in your application's termination code).

  ```
  DeleteCriticalSection(&g_CriticalSection);
  ```

You can place multiple lines of code between the EnterCriticalSection and LeaveCriticalSection calls. You want to be careful not to do too much processing in a critical section; otherwise, one thread holds up the execution of another.

When you use the CRITICAL_SECTION structure, Windows CE checks to see whether another thread is in a critical section when EnterCritical Section is called. If this is the case, the thread calling EnterCritical Section is suspended until the first thread calls LeaveCriticalSection.

Although you can create multiple CRITICAL_SECTION structures to protect separate global variables, I recommend that you have only one and limit the amount of processing performed in the critical sections.

Avoiding deadlocks

If you use multiple critical sections, you run the risk of a deadlock, which is illustrated in Figure 13-4.

In this situation, thread 1 becomes critical using Critical Section 1, and thread 2 becomes critical using Critical Section 2. Thread 1 now has to become critical using Critical Section 2, but it can't because another thread is critical already with Critical Section 2. Thread 2 has to become critical using Critical Section 1, but it can't because another thread is critical already using Critical Section 1.

Both threads wait until the other exits the critical section. Therefore, they wait forever. Deadlocks can occur when shared resources can be *locked* (that is, accessed so another thread cannot use the resource until it is unlocked).

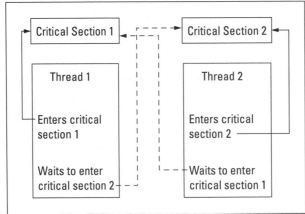

Figure 13-4:
Deadlock!

Whenever possible, lock resources in the same order in all parts of code —
by doing so, you can avoid most deadlock situations.

Prioritizing threads

Not all threads have to be created equally. Often, you want some processing
to be done, but it need not be done quickly. At other times, though, you may
need particular processing to take priority over other activities.

In these situations, you can change the thread's priority using the
SetThreadPriority function, which takes a thread kernel object handle
and a priority constant value from the list in Table 13-1. Here is an example:

```
SetThreadPriority(hThread, THREAD_PRIORITY_IDLE);
```

In this case, the thread identified by the thread kernel object handle
hThread has its priority set to idle. Therefore, it executes in the background.

Table 13-1	Thread Priority Constants
Priority	*Meaning*
THREAD_PRIORITY_ABOVE_NORMAL	1 point above normal priority
THREAD_PRIORITY_BELOW_NORMAL	1 point below normal priority
THREAD_PRIORITY_HIGHEST	2 points above normal priority
THREAD_PRIORITY_IDLE	Background processing priority
THREAD_PRIORITY_LOWEST	2 points below normal priority
THREAD_PRIORITY_NORMAL	Normal priority
THREAD_PRIORITY_TIME_CRITICAL	Highest possible priority

You can use a thread's current priority by using the GetThreadPriority
function, as in Code Listing 13-12.

Code Listing 13-12

```
int nThreadPri;
nThreadPri = GetThreadPriority(hThread);
```

Avoid using THREAD_PRIORITY_TIME_CRITICAL unless you are writing a
real-time system. If you choose this priority, your thread may try to run
faster than parts of the operating system!

Chapter 14

Managing Power

. . . .

In This Chapter

▶ Exploring power management states

▶ Changing power management states

▶ Determining battery state

. . . .

*A*rmed with only a couple of AA batteries, valiant Windows CE users can go to the corners of the world and take computing where it hasn't gone before. As a programmer, one of your tasks is to ensure that Windows CE conserves as much power as possible. To live up to this responsibility, you need to understand the different power-management states and how they affect your application.

Assuming Power

Windows CE makes the following assumptions about typical use when adopting a power-management strategy:

▸ Typical use is less than two hours per day in bursts from five minutes to one hour at a time.

▸ The display is on 100 percent of the time during use.

▸ The CPU is on less than ten percent of the time during typical use.

In a way, Windows CE assumes that the user spends most of his or her time doing nothing!

You also need to consider the impact of using PCMCIA cards (such as modems and network adapter cards) on battery usage. For example, a modem will quickly drain batteries (often in as little as 3 to 5 minutes).

Understanding Power-Management States

Windows CE automatically selects the appropriate power management state for a device, depending on how the device is being used. Applications don't have much control over the change from one state to another. Windows CE can run in one of the following power-management states:

- ✔ **Dead:** The Windows CE device has no batteries (either primary or backup), and no data is maintained. Windows CE devices are delivered in the dead state, but hopefully they don't return to that state.

- ✔ **On:** Windows CE and its applications are operating in the normal full-speed state.

- ✔ **Idle:** Windows CE decreases power consumption by reducing the processor speed. The change from On to Idle is transparent to the user and to applications.

- ✔ **Suspend:** This is the minimum power mode in Windows CE. The display is turned off, and everything except memory maintenance is suspended.

Your applications must allow Windows CE to change from On to Idle and from Idle to Suspend as appropriate to minimize battery use. Be sure to follow the rules for changing states that are covered in the next two sections of this chapter.

Changing from On to Idle State

Windows CE switches to Idle state when all applications are idle. An application is considered to be *idle* when it has returned control to Windows CE (that is, when it has finished processing a message) or when a thread is suspended or sleeping. The switch from On to Idle occurs very quickly — in about ten microseconds.

Try to avoid using loops that do not relinquish control in your applications, because these loops stop Windows CE from entering Idle state and, hence, do not allow good power management. The following sample uses the GetTickCount function (which returns the number of milliseconds that has elapsed since Windows CE started) to pause the application for five seconds. In doing so, your application uses valuable processing time and stops Windows CE from entering the Idle state (see Code Listing 14-1).

Code Listing 14-1
```
DWORD dwTime = GetTickCount();
while(GetTickCount() - dwTime < 5000)
{
}
```

Instead of using the GetTickCount function, use the Sleep function, which I describe in Chapter 13. To pause the application for 5 seconds, use the following code:

```
Sleep(5000);    /sleep for 5000 milliseconds.
```

An application does not know when Windows CE changes from the On to the Idle state or vice versa. However, if the application needs to be executing code, Windows CE must be in the On state (obviously!).

Remember, if any application is currently executing code, the Windows CE device must be in the On state.

Changing from Idle to Suspend State

Applications enter the Suspend state in the following situations:

- ✔ When the user turns off the computer
- ✔ When the user selects the Start⇨Suspend menu
- ✔ When the computer detects a critically low power condition
- ✔ When the activity timer times out

The activity timer monitors the time since the last key press or stylus tap event. When Windows CE detects a key press or tap event, the timer is reset to the value that's specified by the user in the Control Panel's Power section; this value is typically 2 or 3 minutes.

The activity timer constantly counts down the time since the last key press or tap event occurred, and when the timer reaches 0, Windows CE enters the Suspend state. Note that applications are not notified when Windows CE enters this state.

Applications are frozen and don't execute when Windows CE is in the Suspend state. They resume execution when the state switches from Suspend to On.

Most applications are not affected by entering the Suspend state. The exceptions are those applications that use the Sleep function to pause the current thread for a specified number of milliseconds. Note that the sleep counter does not increment when Windows CE is in Suspend mode, so the thread does not continue executing until Windows CE returns to the On mode.

Monitoring Battery Status

Windows CE provides the GetSystemPowerStatusEx function to obtain information about the current state of the backup and main batteries.

This function returns the information to a SYSTEM_POWER_STATUS_EX structure. The function takes a second parameter that, when set to TRUE, asks Windows CE to obtain the most up-to-date battery information, as shown in Figure 14-1. If you set this second parameter to FALSE, Windows CE returns cached information. It is faster to use cached information, but this information may be a few seconds out-of-date.

Figure 14-1: Sample output from pmgmt.exe showing the battery status.

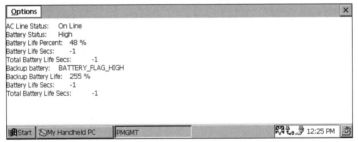

Code Listing 14-2 shows a simple example of calling the GetSystemPowerStatusEx function.

Code Listing 14-2

```
SYSTEM_POWER_STATUS_EX sStatus;

GetSystemPowerStatusEx(
    &sStatus, // structure in which power status is returned
    TRUE);    // get most up-to-date information
```

You can find the sample code for this chapter in the \samples\pmgmt\ pmgmt.dsw folder on the enclosed CD-ROM. This application displays the current power-management settings when the application window receives the WM_PAINT message. Select <u>O</u>ptions⇨<u>B</u>attery State to update the display.

The SYSTEM_POWER_STATUS_EX structure returns information for the following items:

- ✔ The status of the AC line connection
- ✔ The state of the primary batteries (typically two AA batteries in an H/PC)
- ✔ The state of the backup battery (typically a Lithium -cell battery)

The ACLineStatus member of the SYSTEM_POWER_STATUS_EX structure can contain one of the following values:

Value	*Meaning*
0	OffLine (not connected)
1	OnLine (connected to mains)
255	Unknown status

Table 14-1 shows the SYSTEM_POWER_STATUS_EX members that return information about the primary batteries. Note that BatteryLifeTime and BatteryFullLifeTime often return *unknown* values (as in Figure 14-1) and should not be relied on.

Table 14-1	Primary Battery Status Members for SYSTEM_POWER_STATUS_EX
Member	*Description*
BatteryFlag	This BYTE member returns the battery charge status. It can be a combination of the following values (although not all combinations have sensible meanings): 1: High, 2: Low, 4: Critical, 8: Charging, 128: No system battery, and 255: Unknown status.
BatteryLifePercent	The percentage of the full battery charge remaining, returned in a BYTE. Returns 255 if the status is unknown. Most Windows CE devices return 255.
BatteryLifeTime	The number of seconds of battery life remaining, returned as a DWORD. Returns -1 if unknown.
BatteryFullLifeTime	The number of seconds of total battery life when fully charged, returned as a DWORD. Returns -1 if unknown.

The `BatteryFlag` member uses individual bits to signify each of the legal values. Therefore, you need to use a bitwise AND operator (&) to test whether a particular bit is set. For example, to determine whether the battery is charging, write code shown in Code Listing 14-3.

Code Listing 14-3

```
if(sStatus.BatteryFlag & 8)
{
    // charging
}
```

`Unknown status` has all bits set — therefore, you should test for `Unknown status` *before* testing the other states by using code shown in Code Listing 14-4.

Code Listing 14-4

```
if(sStatus.BatteryFlag == 255)
{
    // no status to report
}
```

Table 14-2 shows the values that Windows CE returns for the backup battery. These values are similar to those for the primary batteries, except that constants are provided for the `BatteryBackupFlag` member.

Table 14-2   **Backup Battery Status Members for SYSTEM_POWER_STATUS_EX**

Member	*Description*
BackupBatteryFlag	Returns one of the following values: BATTERY_FLAG_HIGH, BATTERY_FLAG_CRITICAL, BATTERY_FLAG_CHARGING, BATTERY_FLAG_NO_BATTERY, BATTERY_FLAG_UNKNOWN, BATTERY_FLAG_LOW.
BackupBatteryLifePercent	The percentage of the full battery charge remaining, returned in a BYTE. Returns 255 if the status is unknown.
BackupBatteryLifeTime	The number of seconds of battery life remaining, returned as a DWORD. Returns -1 (0xFFFFFFFF) if unknown.
BackupBatteryFullLifeTime	The number of seconds of total battery life when fully charged, returned as a DWORD. Returns -1 (0xFFFFFFFF) if unknown.

Check the current state of the primary battery before you attempt a long operation, such as communicating through the serial port or a PCMCIA card. Communications can quickly exhaust the batteries. Make sure that your application warns the user or disables the option if primary battery power is low before commencing communications. You don't want Windows CE to issue a low-battery warning in the middle of an international phone call in which you are downloading valuable information!

Chapter 15

Dynamic Link Libraries

● ●

In This Chapter

▶ Introducing dynamic link libraries (DLLs)

▶ Benefiting from DLLs

▶ Understanding how to write a DLL

▶ Calling a DLL from your application

● ●

A natural temptation for programmers is to write application (.exe) files that contain all the code they need. After all, most applications start small and grow organically! Applications grow *organically* when new features are added over a period of time without a proper structure being created for the organization of the application's code. However, you can find advantages in breaking an application into smaller units. Breaking up an application helps code maintenance and can speed development.

You can break up an application by placing some of the code into dynamic link libraries (DLLs) and then calling the DLL code from your application. It's important to design the structure of your application to use DLLs *before* you start writing code; otherwise, you may never get around to using DLLs!

Defining Dynamic Link Libraries

A DLL, in many respects, is just like an application, except that it cannot be run in a stand-alone mode. You must always call a DLL from an application.

A DLL can contain the following shareable elements:

✔ Code contained in C functions or C++ classes

✔ Global (static) data

✔ Resources (such as strings, dialog box definitions, and menus)

You build a DLL in much the same way as you do an application. First, you create a project in Visual Studio and then add source files and resources. The DLL is then compiled to generate a file with a DLL extension.

At some stage, an application that uses code in a DLL must bind to the DLL so that functions in the DLL can be called. You can specify the binding when the application is built (which is easy) or as the application is executing (which is more difficult).

Realizing the Benefits of DLLs

Initially, creating DLLs requires more effort than simply creating a large, self-contained .exe file. So why expend the extra effort? Some reasons are as follows:

- ✔ **You can reuse code in a DLL in many applications:** You save memory, because the code is only written once, regardless of how many applications use it.

- ✔ **You can develop applications faster:** When you change code in the DLL, you only have to compile the DLL, not necessarily the application that uses it. Furthermore, if you only change the DLL, only that DLL needs to be downloaded to the Windows CE machine for testing.

- ✔ **Multi-programmer developments are easier:** If you have more than one developer on your project, one programmer can work on the DLL while another works on the EXE file.

Don't go crazy creating DLLs! Consider writing just a few useful DLLs that perform self-contained functionality rather than creating many small, DLLs that call each other.

Writing DLLs

In order to create a DLL and call it from an application, you need to follow several steps. Broadly, the steps can be grouped into these three stages:

1. **Design the function interface that the DLL is going to present to an application.**

   You should first be sure that you clearly design the DLL's function interface. Making changes after the DLL is implemented is time consuming, as you need to change both the DLL and the application that calls the DLL.

2. **Implement the DLL.**

   Create a project for the DLL, and then implement a function that all DLLs require, called *DllMain*.

   Next, you need to implement the functions that form the DLLs interface and any other functions that you need in the DLL.

3. **Add code to the application to call functions in the DLL.**

   After you write the DLL, you then call the DLL's functions from an application.

Designing the DLL interface

The DLL interface defines the functions that the DLL presents to the world at large. This interface typically consists of some C functions, and perhaps some structures, that you use to pass data.

You can use C++ classes to create DLL interfaces, but this can be difficult. I suggest that you only use C functions. You can, however, use C++ classes for the code that is used within the DLL.

The DLL and the application that uses the DLL must both use the same function definitions (for example, they must both define the same arguments and return types for the functions). For this reason, you should create a header (H) file that contains the function definitions that form the DLL interface. You then use this header file when building the DLL and when building any application that uses the DLL.

In this chapter, I show you how to build a simple DLL with a function that converts inches to centimeters.

Creating a DLL project

The simplest way to write a DLL in Visual Studio is to create another project within the workspace in which the application itself is built. Visual Studio then ensures that the application and DLL are both rebuilt correctly as modifications are made.

You can find the completed project, with the source code shown in this chapter, in the \samples\dllapp\dllapp.dsw folder on the enclosed CD-ROM. To work through the steps that are outlined in this chapter, copy the contents of the samples\dllapp\start\ folder and follow the steps listed below.

To add a DLL to a workspace, follow these steps:

1. **Open the workspace (dllapp.dsw) in Visual Studio.**

2. **Select File⇨New.**

3. **Select the Projects tab.**

4. **Choose Win32 Dynamic Link Library from the list of project types.**

5. **Type** TestDLL **in the Project Name edit box.**

6. Leave the Location option at its default value.

This is a folder called TestDLL, which is a subfolder under the main project folder.

7. Click the Add to Current Workspace button.

8. Select the Dependency Of check box.

9. Check the platforms that you need to build for (typically all but Win32).

10. Click OK.

Figure 15-1 shows how the dialog box should look just before you click the OK button.

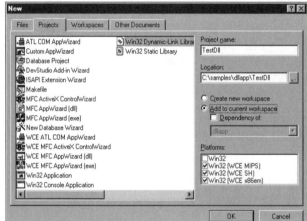

Figure 15-1:
Adding a
DLL project
to an
existing
workspace.

Notice that two projects are now displayed in the ClassView tab of the Project Workspace window (shown in Figure 15-2); the one shown in bold is the active project. Selecting any Project menu command (such as Build) applies to the active project. You can change the active project by right-clicking another project and selecting the Set as Active Project menu from the pop-up menu.

Writing the DllMain function

You must write a function called `DllMain` for each DLL. Windows CE calls this function when the DLL is loaded by an application and again when the application has finished with the DLL. In some respects, it's like the function `WinMain` in a standard Windows application.

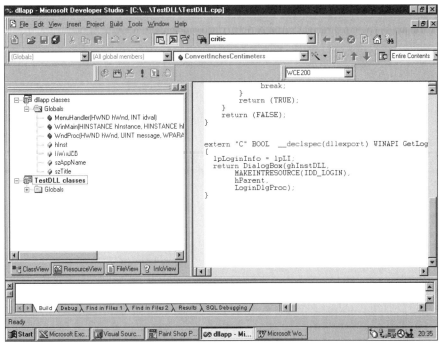

Figure 15-2:
The active
project is
shown
in bold.

First, you create a source file for the D11Main code as follows:

1. Select File⇨New, and ensure that File tab is selected.

This displays the New dialog box. Click the File tab, as you are adding a new file to the project.

2. Select C++ Source file.

3. Enter TestDLL.cpp **as the filename.**

4. Click OK.

Notice that the Add To Project box is checked — Visual Studio automatically adds this file to the project (TestDLL) that's displayed in the combo box (drop down list box).

The code in Code Listing 15-1 is required to implement the D11Main function for this DLL.

Code Listing 15-1

```
#include <windows.h>
HINSTANCE ghInstDLL;

BOOL WINAPI DllMain(HINSTANCE hInstDLL, DWORD dwReason,
          LPVOID lpvReserved)
{
  switch (dwReason)
  {
    case DLL_PROCESS_ATTACH:
      ghInstDLL = hInstDLL;
      break;
    case DLL_PROCESS_DETACH:
      break;
  }
  return TRUE;
}
```

Windows CE calls the DllMain function when a process loads the DLL ("attaches" to the DLL) and when the application unloads the DLL ("detaches" from the DLL). Windows CE passes a value in dwReason that specifies which event is occurring. In response, the DLL can perform any initialization or cleanup that is necessary.

When dwReason is set to DLL_PROCESS_ATTACH, the function can return TRUE to indicate that it initialized correctly or FALSE if it failed. If a DLL fails to load (and returns FALSE), the application using that DLL also fails to load.

A DLL has its own instance handle (just like an application), and this handle is passed by Windows CE to the DLL through DllMain. Because DLLs can have their own resources (such as dialog boxes and strings), Windows CE requires the instance handle to access these resources. Note how this is saved in a global variable for future use.

The DllMain function is also called when a thread is created or destroyed in the application. The reason codes are DLL_THREAD_ATTACH and DLL_THREAD_DETACH.

Writing interface functions

The interface function that I show you converts inches to centimeters.

First, you need to write the function prototype. You place the function prototype in the interface header file. (Remember, the header file is shared between the DLL and the application calling the DLL.) The steps are as follows:

1. **Create a new file called TestDLL.h, and add it to the project.**

2. **Include the file TestDLL.h in TestDLL.cpp by adding the boldface line in Code Listing 15-2.**

Code Listing 15-2

```
#include <windows.h>
#include "TestDLL.h"

HINSTANCE ghInstDLL;
```

3. **Add the function prototype to TestDLL.h as follows (see Code Listing 15-3).**

Code Listing 15-3

```
// TestDLL.h - Interface header file for TestDLL.DLL

// convert inches to centimeters
extern "C" float __declspec(dllexport) WINAPI
ConvertInchesCentimeters(float fInches);
```

This example shows you differences from a standard C or C++ function. These differences are as follows:

- ✔ **You mark the function as** `extern "C"`. This specifies that the name of the function should be retained and not changed by the compiler (as happens with C++ functions). This makes the function much easier to call from non-C++ applications.

- ✔ `__declspec(dllexport)` **exports the function.**

  This specifies that the function is to be exported. This means that information about the function should be written into the compiled DLL so that applications can call it.

- ✔ **You declare the function** `WINAPI`. This is the standard function-calling convention that's used by DLLs.

Be sure that you always export the functions correctly. Otherwise, you can't call them from applications. Note that there are *two* underscores before `declspec`.

At this point, you can write the function `ConvertInchesCentimeters`. This function can be added to TestDLL.cpp, or you can create a new source file. It's best to keep all the interface functions in the same location.

Always include the interface header file (TestDLL.h) in any source file that uses or implements the interface functions.

Code Listing 15-4 is the function's implementation; it should be added to the file TestDLL.cpp after `DllMain`.

Code Listing 15-4

```
extern "C" float __declspec(dllexport) WINAPI
ConvertInchesCentimeters(float fInches)
{
    return fInches * 2.54f;
}
```

Building the DLL

Use the following steps to build the DLL:

1. **Select <u>B</u>uild⇨Select Active <u>C</u>onfiguration, and be sure that the correct target is selected (either x86em or the target chip, such as SH3).**

2. **Select <u>B</u>uild⇨<u>B</u>uild TestDLL.dll.**

You cannot run the DLL! If you try to, you are prompted to specify the name of an application that calls the DLL.

Calling a DLL function

Now that you have built a DLL, the following steps show you how to call a DLL function from an application:

1. **Change the active project to dllApp by right-clicking dllApp Classes in the ClassView or dllApp Files in the File View tab, and select Set as Active Project in the pop-up menu.**

   You can leave the application's project (in this case, dllApp) as the active project. You can still modify the DLL's files even if the DLL project is not the active project. Then, when you run your application, Visual Studio ensures that the DLL is rebuilt if it has been modified.

2. **Include the DLL's interface header file (TestDLL.h) in any source file that calls an interface function.**

   In this case, the header file TestDLL.h should be included in the file dllApp.cpp. You should add the single line shown in boldface to dllApp.cpp, as shown in Code Listing 15-5.

Code Listing 15-5

```
#include <windows.h>
#include <commctrl.h>
#include <string.h>
#include "resource.h"
#include ".\\TestDLL\\TestDLL.h"
```

Note that the file TestDLL.h is not in the same folder as dllApp.cpp. In fact, it's in the subfolder TestDLL. I could have used a full qualified path name to the header file (for example, c:\samples\dllApp\TestDLL\TestDLL.h), but if the project was then moved, the build fails. Using a relative path as I've shown is much safer. A relative path uses the current folder (specified by the special name) as the starting point for the name of the folder. So, the filename .\\TestDll\\TestDll.h specifies that the file TestDll.h is located in the folder TestDll which is a subfolder of the current folder.

3. **Now make the call to the function as follows in Code Listing 15-6.**

Code Listing 15-6

```
float fI, fC;
fI = 20.5;
fC = ConvertInchesCentimeters(fI);
```

Building the application

You can build the application in the normal way. When you execute the application, Visual Studio downloads the DLL and EXE file to the target machine. These two files are then placed in the same folder (the root, by default). The DLL is loaded automatically when the application executes.

Windows CE searches the following folders for a DLL that's used by an application:

- The root folder of the PCMCIA RAM expansion card, if one exists
- The windows folder (\Windows)
- The root folder (\)

The application fails to load if the DLL cannot be found in one of these locations.

An application is unable to load a DLL that's located in the same folder unless the folder is one that is shown in the previous list.

Part IV

Working with the Shell and the Object Store

In this part . . .

No, this part doesn't have any thing to do with a trip to the beach — it's a look at the features that the Windows CE user interface provides and how you can use those shell features in your applications. In this part, I show you how to create shortcuts to your applications on the desktop and how to access the registry.

As you work with Windows CE, you'll find that you can't use standard C or C++ functions for creating, reading, and writing to files. Instead, you need to use Windows CE API functions; so in this part, I also show you how these work.

Chapter 16

Using the Shell Features

● ●

In This Chapter

▶ Managing shortcuts

▶ Adding icons

▶ Using common dialog boxes

▶ Executing applications with the shell functions

▶ Using common dialog boxes

▶ Notifying applications with notification functions

● ●

*T*he Windows CE shell consists of the desktop and taskbar, together with a set of functions for managing shortcuts, files and folders, and event notifications. The shell is designed to make accessing applications and managing files and folders much easier. The Windows CE shell has many of the same features found in the Windows NT and Windows 95 shells. You can use the shell functions to fully integrate your application with Windows CE. By adding a few simple function calls, you can

✔ Add a shortcut on the desktop to your application so that your application can run quickly and easily.

✔ Add icons to the Taskbar Status Area (just like the Power Properties and PC Link applications).

✔ Receive notification of an event (such as the Windows CE device being connected to a PC), so you can carry out specific tasks when these events occur.

Not all Windows CE devices have a shell, or even a user interface at all!

All of the source code that's described in this chapter is located in the \samples\shelleg\shelleg.dsw workspace on the enclosed CD-ROM. You can copy the code from this sample to your own applications to add shell functions, create common dialog boxes, and write notification routines.

Not all of the functions in this sample application work correctly under emulation. This is because emulation does not implement certain functions (for example, RS-232 notification) or Windows CE applications such as Pocket Word are not present. See Chapter 2 for more on emulation.

Getting to Know the Shortcuts

Shortcuts are icons that appear on the desktop or in other folders, that allow an application or document to be run by simply double-clicking the icon. Note that the application or document itself may reside in a directory other than that in which the shortcut is located.

A shortcut is a file with an LNK extension whose contents contain all the information that's needed to represent the application or document and to execute it.

When you know how to create shortcut files, you can use standard file-manipulation techniques to copy, rename, and delete them.

Creating a shortcut

Many Windows CE applications have a File menu command that, when selected by the user, places a shortcut to your application on the desktop. After creating the shortcut, the user can run your applications from the desktop by double-tapping the shortcut icon.

You create a shortcut by using the SHCreateShortcut function. This function requires the following two pieces of information:

✔ A pointer to the name of the new shortcut.

✔ A pointer to the path name of the application or document that the shortcut represents. This name can be up to 255 characters long, but cannot include the following characters: \ / : * ? " < > |.

Note that the SHCreateShortcut function is not supported in Windows 95 or Windows NT.

Code Listing 16-1 is an example of calling SHCreateShortcut. This code creates a shortcut on the Desktop for the application ShellEg.exe.

Code Listing 16-1

```
if(!SHCreateShortcut(
    TEXT("\\windows\\Desktop\\Shortcut to ShellEG.lnk"),
    TEXT("\\ShellEg.exe")))
  MessageBox(hWnd, TEXT("Could not create shortcut!"),
    szTitle, MB_OK);
```

You must include two backslashes in the path name, because the backslash is treated as an escape character in C++.

While this code works, it contains the following problems:

- **It assumes that the user has not renamed the Windows and Desktop folders:** The function SHGetSpecialFolderLocation can be used to determine the new folder name for any of the standard folders such as the Desktop or Recycle bin.

- **It assumes that shellEg.exe is located in the root directory:** You can pass the full pathname to the EXE in the second argument (that is, replace \\ShellEg.exe with a full pathname).

Always use the LNK extension in the shortcut's filename. Otherwise, the shortcut appears to be created correctly, but it is not recognized by Windows CE as a true shortcut file.

Finding your own identity

When creating shortcuts to your application, you need to know where the .exe file is located — it may have been moved from its setup location.

The function GetModuleFileName returns the location of the EXE file. You need to provide a buffer into which the path and filename are returned. The following is an example of how to obtain this information:

```
TCHAR szTarget[MAX_PATH + 1];
GetModuleFileName(NULL, szTarget, MAX_PATH);
```

You can then pass the buffer szTarget as the second argument in SHCreateShortcut so that the pathname for your shortcut is no longer in your code as a string constant. See Code Listing 16-2.

Code Listing 16-2

```
SHCreateShortcut(
    TEXT("\\windows\\Desktop\\Shortcut to ShellEG.lnk"),
    szTarget);
```

The first argument in `GetModuleFileName` is a handle to the process whose EXE file pathname is to be found. If you pass `NULL`, Windows CE returns the path for the currently executing application (yours!). You can pass a handle to any process that you know about.

Checking where the shortcut cuts to

You can check the target that a shortcut refers to by using the `SHGet ShortcutTarget` function. You specify the name of the shortcut file (`TEXT("\\windows\\Desktop\\Shortcut to ShellEG.lnk")`), a buffer (`szTarget`) into which the target is to be returned, and the maximum number of characters that can be copied into the buffer (`MAX_PATH`), as Code Listing 16-3 shows.

Code Listing 16-3

```
TCHAR szTarget[MAX_PATH + 1];
SHGetShortcutTarget(
        TEXT("\\windows\\Desktop\\Shortcut to ShellEG.lnk"),
        szTarget,
        MAX_PATH);
```

Shortcutting documents

You can also create shortcuts to documents. The technique is the same as that used for applications, except that you specify the name of a document, not an application.

For example, Windows CE devices often have a file called Alarm2.wav that's located in the windows folder. This is the sound file that you may hear early one morning! I use Alarm2.wav for creating a shortcut, because the file is present on all H/PC devices. You can use this technique to create shortcuts to documents that your application creates. After creating the shortcut, your users can open the document by double clicking the icon. Code Listing 16-4 shows how you can create a shortcut on the Desktop to this WAV file.

Code Listing 16-4

```
if(!SHCreateShortcut(
        TEXT("\\windows\\Desktop\\Alarm!.lnk"),
        TEXT("\\windows\\Alarm2.wav")))
    MessageBox(hWnd,
        TEXT("Could not create shortcut!"),
        szTitle, MB_OK);
```

Of course, Windows CE needs to be able to map documents to the application that is used to play or edit them. This information is based on the file extension that's used by the document. The file extension is WAV in the case of a sound file.

When the shortcut is double-tapped, Windows CE looks in the Registry and, using the extension, attempts to find the application that's associated with the extension.

Adding to the Document menu

If your application is document based, you should add the documents that are opened by the user to the Document menu. The `SHAddToRecentDocs` function performs this task. The following is an example of adding the file Alarm2.wav to the recent document menu:

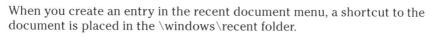

```
SHAddToRecentDocs(SHARD_PATH,
        TEXT("\\windows\\Alarm2.wav"));
```

The first argument specifies how the document is to be identified. In this case, `SHARD_PATH` indicates that the second argument contains a pathname to the document. This is the easiest way of specifying the document.

Documents can be identified by either their pathname or by a unique document identifier. A number of shell functions allow you to determine information about the document through this identifier.

When you create an entry in the recent document menu, a shortcut to the document is placed in the \windows\recent folder.

You can have a maximum of ten documents on the recent document menu at any time.

Performing an action on a file

You can perform a shell action on a document (such as opening it) or run an application by using the `ShellExecuteEx` function.

In ShellEG.cpp, the `OpenBitmap` function is called when you select File⇨ Open Bitmap. This selection opens the default.bmp file in the Explorer application.

First, you declare a SHELLEXECUTEINFO structure. This structure specifies all the information that's required to perform the action on the file. As usual, the first member specifies the number of bytes in this structure. See the following example:

```
SHELLEXECUTEINFO exinf;
exinf.cbSize = sizeof(exinf);
```

The fMask member specifies options that are used when calling the function. For example, you can get a handle to the icon that represents the document. In this case, fMask is set to the default of 0, indicating that an action is to be performed on a document or application, as follows:

```
exinf.fMask = 0;
```

Next, you specify the verb (which indicates the action that is to be performed). Which verbs are legal depends on the nature of the document and its capabilities. Most documents support an "Open" verb, and this is the default. See the following example:

```
exinf.lpVerb = TEXT("Open"); // verb to be performed
```

Because Open is the default, you could simply set lpVerb to be NULL, but in this case, I show you how to explicitly specify a verb.

You use the lpFile member to specify the name of the document or application that is to be opened, as follows:

```
exinf.lpFile = TEXT("\\windows\\Default.bmp");
```

The ShellExecuteEx function displays error messages if the document cannot be opened, so the function ShellExecuteEx needs a handle to a window that can act as a parent window, as follows:

```
exinf.hwnd = hWnd; // handle for error message dialogs
```

You can now call the ShellExecuteEx function to perform the specified action, as shown in Code Listing 16-5.

Code Listing 16-5

```
if(!ShellExecuteEx(&exinf))
{
    MessageBox(hWnd, TEXT("Could not open bitmap"),
        szTitle, MB_OK);
}
```

If the call fails, you can use the hInstApp member to determine the nature of the error. The hInstApp member contains one of the following constant values in the event of an error, as Table 16-1 shows.

Table 16-1	Detecting Errors
Constant	*Meaning*
SE_ERR_FNF	File not found
SE_ERR_PNF	Path not found
SE_ERR_ACCESSDENIED	Access denied
SE_ERR_OOM	Out of memory
SE_ERR_DLLNOTFOUND	Dynamic link library not found
SE_ERR_SHARE	Cannot share open file
SE_ERR_ASSOCINCOMPLETE	File association information not complete
SE_ERR_DDETIMEOUT	DDE operation timed out
SE_ERR_DDEFAIL	DDE operation failed
SE_ERR_DDEBUSY	DDE operation busy
SE_ERR_NOASSOC	File association not available

Using the shell to run an application

The ShellExecuteEx function provides an easy way to run an application. This function can be easier to use than the CreateProcess function that's described in Chapter 13.

You can use the ExecutePWord function in ShellEG.cpp to make a call to ShellExecuteEx to run Pocket Word and to make Pocket Word open the file Letter.pwd. Use Code Listing 16-6.

Code Listing 16-6

```
void ExecutePWord(HWND hWnd)
{
    SHELLEXECUTEINFO exinf;

    exinf.cbSize = sizeof(exinf);
    exinf.fMask = 0
    exinf.lpVerb = NULL; // default verb
    exinf.lpFile = TEXT("\\windows\\PWord.exe");
```

(continued)

(continued)

```
        exinf.hwnd = hWnd;
        exinf.lpParameters = TEXT("\\windows\\Letter.pwd");
        exinf.lpDirectory = NULL;
        exinf.nShow = SW_SHOWNORMAL;
        if(!ShellExecuteEx(&exinf))
        {
            MessageBox(hWnd,
                TEXT("Could not run Pocket Word!"),
                szTitle, MB_OK);
        }
    }
```

The following list gives you a breakdown of the preceding code:

- ✔ lpVerb is set to NULL — the default verb is to execute an application.
- ✔ lpFile points to the name of the executable file that you want to run.
- ✔ lpParameters points to the command line parameters that you pass to Pocket Word. You can specify NULL if there are none.
- ✔ nShow specifies how the application is to appear. You can use the constants that are specified in the ShowWindow function to hide or minimize the application if required.

Again, you can use the hInstApp member to determine why an application failed to run.

The file Letter.pwd is marked for read-only access, so you receive a message telling you this fact.

Adding Icons to the Taskbar Status Area

The taskbar status area provides a convenient place for access to utility-type applications that don't warrant a standard taskbar application. Figure 16-1 shows a number of these icons in the taskbar status area.

Take a look at Chapter 3, which shows how to ensure that your application has a taskbar icon when you build an API application.

You use the Shell_NotifyIcon function to add or remove an icon from the taskbar status area, and to specify how the application receives notifications of when the icon is accessed by the user.

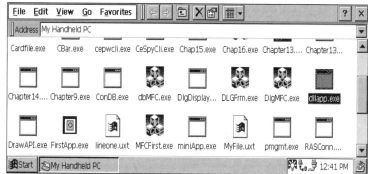

Figure 16-1:
Icons in the taskbar status area.

The taskbar status area is sometimes known as the *taskbar notification area* or the *tray notification area.*

Adding the icon

First, I show you how to add an icon to the taskbar status area. The code is taken from the sample application ShellEG.dsw. This application has a menu command Options⇨Taskbar Status Icon, which causes the application to hide its main window and add the icon. The application window is toggled between being displayed and being hidden as the taskbar status area button is pressed. Note that the application removes the icon when the application terminates.

The file ShellEG.cpp in the \samples\shelleg\shelleg.dsw workspace on the enclosed CD-ROM contains the functions `TaskNotify`, `SetTaskBarIcon`, and `DestroyTaskBarIcon`. These functions contain all the code that you need for managing taskbar status icons. You can copy the code from this sample to your own applications to manage your own taskbar status icons.

First, you create an icon in the project. The icon should be 16 x 16 pixels in size, because it is to be displayed in the taskbar. You can create a 16- or 256-color bitmap and rely on the system to reduce the number of colors on a monochrome display. Alternatively, you can create individual bitmaps for each resolution that your application supports.

Try creating a 16-color icon, and design it so that it still looks good when displayed in monochrome and on 256-color displays.

Follow these steps to create the icon:

1. **Select the Resource View.**

2. **Right-click and select Insert.**

3. **Click Icon and click New.**

4. **Choose Image⇨New Device Image, and select the appropriate target image from the list.**

5. **Set the ID for the icon (**IDI_TBAR **in the sample code).**

You can now design the image to the best of your artistic talents!

Loading the icon

You must load the icon before calling the Shell_NotifyIcon function. Because you're dealing with a 16-x-16-pixel icon, you need to call LoadImage rather than LoadIcon.

I suggest that you create a global variable to hold the icon handle, because the icon needs to be unloaded later. Use the following code.

```
HICON ghIcon = NULL;  // global variable
```

Use the call in Code Listing 16-7 to load the icon:

Code Listing 16-7

```
ghIcon = (HICON)LoadImage(hInst,
    MAKEINTRESOURCE(IDI_TBAR),
    IMAGE_ICON, 16, 16, LR_DEFAULTCOLOR);
```

Note the following items about this call:

✔ The return result from LoadImage must be cast to a HICON, because the function can also return handles to other images, such as bitmaps.

✔ hInst is the instance handle of the application from whose EXE file the image is to be loaded.

✔ MAKEINTRESOURCE is called, as usual, to convert an ID (numeric value) to a string name.

✔ IMAGE_ICON specifies the type of image to be loaded.

✔ The values 16 and 16 specify the size of the image to be loaded (16 x 16 pixels). This allows you to specify a particular device image size.

✔ LR_DEFAULTCOLOR requests that the default color device image be selected.

Setting the icon in the taskbar status area

The `Shell_NotifyIcon` function requires that a `NOTIFYICONDATA` structure be initialized with information specifying the characteristics of the icon that's being added. First, you declare the structure as follows:

```
NOTIFYICONDATA nid;
```

In this case, you must set the size of the structure into the `cbSize` member as follows:

```
nid.cbSize = sizeof(nid);
```

When setting the icon, you need to specify the following four items:

✔ **The identifier of the icon for the taskbar:** An application should specify an identifier for each icon that it adds to the taskbar status area. The number itself is not important, but it should be unique for all icons that you add, as follows (Code Listing 16-8).

Code Listing 16-8

```
#define ID_SHELLEG 3000
nid.uID = ID_SHELLEG;        // our task bar id
```

✔ **The handle to the icon being added:** You do this by initializing the `hIcon` member, as follows:

```
nid.hIcon = ghIcon;        // icon to display
```

✔ **How notification is to be done:** (By this, I mean when the user interacts with the icon, how is the application told about it.) This requires you to specify the handle of a window to receive notification and to specify a value to be used for the message, as shown in Code Listing 16-9.

Code Listing 16-9

```
#define WM_TASKSTATUSNOTIFY   (WM_USER + 1)
nid.hWnd = hWnd;  // window to receive notifications
nid.uCallbackMessage = WM_TASKSTATUSNOTIFY;
```

Notice how the new message is created: You use a `#define` statement with the value being set to one greater than `WM_USER`. The constant `WM_USER` is defined in the Windows.h file and represents the value at which programmers can start defining their own messages.

✔ **What exactly is being specified in the structure:** You can use this structure to modify as well as to add an icon — in this case, the icon and notification information is being specified, as follows:

```
nid.uFlags =  // what to change/add
      NIF_MESSAGE | NIF_ICON;
```

After you have specified all this information, `Shell_NotifyIcon` can be called to add the icon.

You use Code Listing 16-10 to load the icon and to set the icon into the taskbar status area. The `#define` statement would normally be placed in a header file or at the start of the source file.

Code Listing 16-10

```c
#define WM_TASKSTATUSNOTIFY  (WM_USER + 1)
#define IDI_SHELLEG 3000

void SetTaskBarIcon(HWND hWnd)
{
    NOTIFYICONDATA nid;

    if(ghIcon == NULL)
        ghIcon = (HICON)LoadImage(hInst,
            MAKEINTRESOURCE(IDI_TBAR),
            IMAGE_ICON, 16, 16, LR_DEFAULTCOLOR);

    if(ghIcon == NULL)
        MessageBox(hWnd, TEXT("Could not load icon"),
            szTitle, MB_OK);

    nid.cbSize = sizeof(nid);
    nid.uID = IDI_SHELLEG;  // our task bar id
    nid.hWnd = hWnd;      // window to receive notifications
    nid.uFlags = NIF_MESSAGE | NIF_ICON;
    nid.hIcon = ghIcon; // icon to display
    nid.uCallbackMessage = WM_TASKSTATUSNOTIFY;

    if(!Shell_NotifyIcon(
        NIM_ADD,   // we're adding the icon
        &nid))  // structure specifying options
    {
        MessageBox(hWnd, TEXT("Could not add icon!"),
            szTitle, MB_OK);
        return;
```

```
    }
    ShowWindow(hWnd, SW_HIDE);
}
```

In ShellEG.cpp, the function `SetTaskBarIcon` is called in response to the Options⇨Taskbar Status Icon menu item that's being selected. Notice how the main application window is hidden by a call to `ShowWindow` after the icon has been installed.

Notifying in the taskbar status area

Windows CE notifies your application when the icon is double-tapped by the user. The window handle that's specified in `nid.hWnd` receives the `WM_TASKSTATUSNOTIFY` message when, for example, the user double-clicks the icon.

In ShellEG.cpp, the `TaskNotify` function is called in response to the message in Code Listing 16-11 in the main window's message processing function.

Code Listing 16-11

```
case WM_TASKSTATUSNOTIFY:
        TaskNotify(hWnd, uParam, lParam);
        break;
```

The `TaskNotify` function is shown in Code Listing 16-12.

Code Listing 16-12

```
void TaskNotify(HWND hWnd, WPARAM wParam, LPARAM lParam)
{
    UINT uID = (UINT)wParam;
    UINT uMouseMsg = (UINT)lParam;

    if(uMouseMsg == WM_LBUTTONUP)
    {
        if(IsWindowVisible(hWnd))
            ShowWindow(hWnd, SW_HIDE);
        else
            ShowWindow(hWnd, SW_SHOWNORMAL);
    }
}
```

The wParam value contains the idenifier of the status bar icon that's generating the message (IDI_SHELLEG in this code). The lParam message data indicates the type of interaction and is one of the standard mouse messages. WM_LBUTTONUP indicates the end of a tap. In response to this message, the code changes how the main application window appears.

Removing a taskbar status area icon

You can remove the taskbar status area icon at any time, but it should always be removed when the application terminates.

In the sample code shown in ShellEG.cpp, the DestroyTaskBarIcon function is called in response to the WM_DESTROY message for the main application window, as follows (Code Listing 16-13).

Code Listing 16-13

```
void DestroyTaskBarIcon(HWND hWnd)
{
  NOTIFYICONDATA nid;

  if(ghIcon != NULL)
  {
      DestroyIcon(ghIcon);
      ghIcon = NULL;
      nid.cbSize = sizeof(nid);
      nid.uID = IDI_SHELLEG;   // our task bar id
      nid.hWnd = hWnd;  // window receiving notifications
      nid.uFlags = NIF_MESSAGE | NIF_ICON;
      nid.hIcon = ghIcon;   // icon to display
      nid.uCallbackMessage = WM_TASKSTATUSNOTIFY;

      if(!Shell_NotifyIcon(
          NIM_DELETE,  // deleting the icon
          &nid))         // structure specifying options
      {
          MessageBox(hWnd, TEXT("Could not delete icon!"),
              szTitle, MB_OK);
      }
  }
}
```

This function performs the following tasks:

- ✔ Checks to see if the icon has been loaded. If the icon has not been loaded, there is no icon in the taskbar status area to remove.

- ✔ Initializes a NOTIFYICONDATA structure with the same information as when the icon was added.

- ✔ Calls Shell_NotifyIcon with the flag NIM_DELETE to remove the icon.

Modifying a taskbar status area icon

You can change the icon or the notifications specification for a taskbar status area icon at any time by doing the following things:

1. **Initializing a** NOTIFYICONDATA **with the new information but with the same** uID **(which is** IDI_SHELLEG **in this code).**

2. **Calling** Shell_NotifyIcon **with the** NIM_MODIFY **flag.**

Saving Time by Using Common Dialog Boxes

Common dialog box functions provide a quick and easy way to display dialog boxes for the following common tasks:

- ✔ Selecting a filename to open
- ✔ Selecting a filename for saving to
- ✔ Selecting a color
- ✔ Specifying print job options and starting printing

You must include the statement #include <commdlg.h> to all source files that are going to use common dialog boxes.

Next, I show you how to use the File Open and File Save As dialog boxes as examples of common dialog boxes.

The File Open common dialog box

Don't even consider trying to write your own File Open dialog box — life's too short! Always use the GetOpenFileName function to create this common dialog box. This function does all the file and folder navigation for you, as shown in Figure 16-2.

Figure 16-2:
The
standard
File Open
common
dialog box.

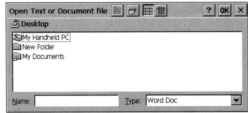

The ShowFileOpenDlg function in ShellEG.cpp shows a call to create a File Open common dialog. Calling GetOpenFileName requires careful programming, so I suggest that you copy the function ShowFileOpenDlg into your own application to avoid errors.

Initializing OPENFILENAME

The GetOpenFileName function takes an OPENFILENAME structure that specifies how the dialog box should be displayed. This structure has myriad members that must be initialized, even if they are not used. For this reason, you should initialize the whole structure to zeros. You can do this by using the memset function.

Your application may hang (stop responding to user input) or fail in some way if you fail to initialize OPENFILENAME correctly.

You declare and initialize the structure using the code in Code Listing 16-14.

Code Listing 16-14

```
OPENFILENAME ofn;
memset(&ofn, 0, sizeof(ofn));
ofn.1StructSize = sizeof(ofn);
```

Specifying the file and path string buffer

The OPENFILENAME member lpstrFile points to a character buffer that has the following characteristics:

- ✔ It specifies the default filename to be displayed when the File Open dialog is displayed.

- ✔ It is used to return the pathname and filename that are selected by the user.

The code in Code Listing 16-15 declares the buffer variable and initializes the structure member variables.

Code Listing 16-15

```
TCHAR szFilePath[MAX_PATH + 1];
szFilePath[0] = '\0';
ofn.lpstrFile = szFilePath;
ofn.nMaxFile = MAX_PATH;
```

If you don't use the buffer pointed to be szFilePath to specify the default filename, the first byte in the buffer should be set to a '\0' character, and the open dialog box will not display a default filename. If you don't do this, your application may hang!

Notice how I use the nMaxFile member to specify the maximum number of bytes available in the szFilePath buffer.

Setting file filters

File filters allow the user to quickly select the type of file (based on file extensions) that is displayed. For example, you could specify two filters — Pocket Word documents, with a PWD extension, and text files with a TXT extension. These file types are displayed in the Type combo (drop-down list) box.

You use the following OPENFILENAME members to specify file filters:

- ✔ lpStrFilter points to a character string that specifies the file type descriptions and extensions.
- ✔ nFilterIndex specifies the file extension that is used when the dialog box is first displayed. The number 1 refers to the first filter, 2 refers to the second, and so on.

Using memset for structure initialization

You can use the function memset (which is declared in the file memory.h or string.h) to initialize all structure members to 0 or NULL pointers as appropriate. This is useful for complex structures where, if not set to 0 or NULL, Windows CE attempts to use members as legitimate values or valid pointers. The result is that, sooner or later, your application is going to fail.

You should pass the following arguments to memset:

- ✔ A pointer to the structure that is being initialized
- ✔ The byte code value to initialize to (use 0)
- ✔ The number of bytes to initialize (use the sizeof operator to specify the size of the structure)

Code Listing 16-16 initializes these two members.

Code Listing 16-16

```
ofn.lpstrFilter =
    TEXT("Text Files\0*.txt\0Word Doc\0*.pwd\0");
ofn.nFilterIndex = 2;
```

Formatting the filter specification takes a bit of care — as usual, if it's not formatted correctly, your dialog box may fail dramatically! Each file filter consists of the following items:

- ✔ A textual description (for example, text files)
- ✔ The extension, in the form *.txt

You should separate these strings by a NULL character \0. The filter specifications (the two strings) are separated from each other with a NULL character as well. The whole string is terminated with *two* NULL characters. You need only place one NULL character at the end of a string constant, because the constant already has a NULL character at its end. If you build up the filters in a string buffer, you must remember to place the two NULLs manually.

You can create more complex file filters using any legal filename characters. For example, you could create a filter that only specifies documents starting with the letter *M* by specifying M*.pwd.

Using other initializations

Finally, you initialize the following additional members:

- ✔ hwndOwner specifies a window handle that is the parent of the dialog box.
- ✔ lpstrTitle points to a string buffer that contains the title for the dialog box. This is optional.
- ✔ Flags specifies that the selected file and path must exist.

Code Listing 16-17 is the remainder of the initialization code.

Code Listing 16-17

```
ofn.hwndOwner = hWnd;
ofn.lpstrTitle = TEXT("Open Text or Document file");
ofn.Flags = OFN_FILEMUSTEXIST | OFN_PATHMUSTEXIST;
```

Putting all the code together

Code Listing 16-18 is the entire code that's used to display the File Open dialog box in the `ShowFileOpenDlg` function in ShellEG.cpp.

Code Listing 16-18

```
void ShowFileOpenDlg(HWND hWnd)
{
    OPENFILENAME ofn;
    TCHAR szFilePath[MAX_PATH + 1];

    szFilePath[0] = '\0';
    memset(&ofn, 0, sizeof(ofn));
    ofn.lStructSize = sizeof(ofn);
    ofn.lpstrFile = szFilePath;
    ofn.nMaxFile = MAX_PATH;
    ofn.lpstrFilter =
        TEXT("Text Files\0*.txt\0Word Doc\0*.pwd\0");
    ofn.nFilterIndex = 2;
    ofn.hwndOwner = hWnd;
    ofn.lpstrTitle =
        TEXT("Open Text or Document file");
    ofn.Flags = OFN_FILEMUSTEXIST | OFN_PATHMUSTEXIST;
    if(GetOpenFileName(&ofn))
    {
        MessageBox(hWnd, ofn.lpstrFile, szTitle, MB_OK);
    }
}
```

The `lpstrFile` member contains the full path and filename for the selected file — this is displayed in a message box if the function `GetOpenFileName` returns `TRUE`. The function returns `FALSE` if the user clicks Cancel or if an error occurs.

The File Save As common dialog box

Using the File Save As dialog box is very similar to using the File Open dialog box, but note the following important exceptions:

✔ **You should specify a default extension using the** `lpstrDefExt` **member:** If you don't do this, the common dialog box doesn't add an extension by default (even if a filter has been specified).

✔ **Don't use the** `OFN_FILEMUSTEXIST` **and** `OFN_PATHMUSTEXIST` **flags:** Instead, use `OFN_OVERWRITEPROMPT` (which prompts the user about overwriting existing files before the dialog box is closed).

Code Listing 16-19 demonstrates the ShowFileSaveAsDlg function from ShellEG.cpp file, showing how you can create a File Save As dialog box to save a file with a default extension of PWD and a single filter for PWD files.

Code Listing 16-19

```
void ShowFileSaveAsDlg(HWND hWnd)
{
    OPENFILENAME ofn;
    TCHAR szFilePath[MAX_PATH + 1];

    szFilePath[0] = '\0';
    memset(&ofn, 0, sizeof(ofn));
    ofn.lStructSize = sizeof(ofn);
    ofn.lpstrFile = szFilePath;
    ofn.nMaxFile = MAX_PATH;
    ofn.lpstrFilter = TEXT("Word Doc\0*.pwd\0");
    ofn.nFilterIndex = 1;
    ofn.hwndOwner = hWnd;
    ofn.lpstrTitle =
        TEXT("Save As Text or Document file");
    ofn.Flags = OFN_OVERWRITEPROMPT;
    ofn.lpstrDefExt = TEXT("pwd");
    if(GetSaveFileName(&ofn))
    {
        MessageBox(hWnd, ofn.lpstrFile, szTitle, MB_OK);
    }
}
```

Controlling Future Events with Notification Functions

Here's the part that drives desktop programmers wild with envy! Windows CE provides a set of functions that allows you to specify tasks to occur in the future in response to events or at a specified time.

You can write notifications to perform the following tasks:

✔ Run an application at a particular time.

✔ Run an application when a particular event occurs.

✔ Notify the user at a particular time. Windows CE notifies the user through the user-configured notification method, such as playing a sound.

The notification functions and associated constants are defined in the file notify.h.

Starting applications at a specified time

You can use the `CeRunAppAtTime` function to start an application at a time that's specified by your application. This function takes the following arguments:

- ✔ A pointer to a string buffer holding the name of the application to run
- ✔ The local time at which the application is to be run

Code Listing 16-20 is an example.

Code Listing 16-20

```
SYSTEMTIME sysTime;

GetLocalTime(&sysTime);
sysTime.wHour= 17;
sysTime.wMinute = 0;

if(!CeRunAppAtTime(TEXT("\\windows\\pword.exe"), &sysTime))
    MessageBox(hWnd,
        TEXT("Cannot set application to run"),
        szTitle, MB_OK);
else
    MessageBox(hWnd,
        TEXT("To run at 17:00 (5:00PM) today!"),
        szTitle, MB_OK);
```

You use the `GetLocalTime` function to fill `sysTime` with the current local date and time. The members `wHour` and `wMinute` are set to 1700 hours (5:00 p.m.), and this structure is then passed to `CeRunAppAtTime`.

If you specify a time before the current time, the application runs immediately.

A strange thing happens at 5:00! Pocket Word displays the message box that appears in Figure 16-3. I didn't ask Pocket Word to open the file AppRunAtTime.pwd!

Figure 16-3:
Message box displayed when `CeRunApp AtTime` function is called.

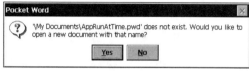

For this reason, you usually don't run standard applications using this technique. Generally, you run miniapplications, with no user interfaces, to perform specific tasks. In this way, the application being run doesn't distract the user, who may otherwise be surprised when the applications appear from nowhere!

Writing applications with no user interface

Writing applications without a user interface is easy — the following is a simple example (Code Listing 16-21).

Code Listing 16-21

```
#include <windows.h>

int WINAPI WinMain(HINSTANCE hInstance,
    HINSTANCE hPrevInstance,
    LPTSTR lpCmdLine, int nCmdShow )
{

    MessageBox(NULL, lpCmdLine,
        TEXT("Small App. Command Line"), MB_OK);
    return 0;

}
```

Notice that the miniapplication has the usual `WinMain` entry point but does not register a window class or create a window. The application simply displays a message box that shows the command line and then quits by returning from the function.

Windows CE passes any application a command-line parameter when run from a notification function that specifies why it was run. Pocket Word recognizes this as a file that should be opened and appends the PWD extension.

Time pieces

The `GetLocalTime` function returns the current local time (as displayed in the taskbar notification area). The notification function `CeRunAppAtTime` uses local time.

Coordinated Universal Time (CUT) is the current time at Greenwich, London, and can be obtained using the `GetSystemTime` function. This was formerly known as Greenwich Mean Time (GMT).

You can use the `GetTimeZoneInformation` function to return the current time zone name and to determine whether daylight savings time is in effect.

You can place virtually any code in `WinMain`. You can loop continuously, performing some sort of processing, or use the Sleep function to suspend the application for a period of time. Remember, the application stops when you return from `WinMain`.

The source code for this miniapplication is included as a subproject called miniApp in the ShellEG.dsw workspace on the enclosed CD-ROM.

You can now run this miniapplication at a particular time using `CeRunAppAtTime` as follows:

```
if(!CeRunAppAtTime(TEXT("\\miniApp.exe"), &sysTime))
```

If necessary, this miniapplication can run other applications (such as Pocket Word) and need not pass the command-line notification string. This avoids dialog boxes like those shown in Figure 16-4.

Starting an application on an event

You can have an application run when any of the following events occur:

- ✔ Data synchronization is completed (`NOTIFICATION_EVENT_SYNC_END`)

- ✔ A PCMCIA device is changed (`NOTIFICATION_EVENT_DEVICE_CHANGE`)

- ✔ An RS-232 connection is made (`NOTIFICATION_EVENT_RS232_DETECTED`)

- ✔ The system time is changed (`NOTIFICATION_EVENT_TIME_CHANGE`)

- ✔ A full device data restore is completed (`NOTIFICATION_EVENT_RESTORE_END`)

You use the CeRunAppAtEvent function in much the same way as you use CeRunAppAtTime, except that the second parameter is one of the constants shown in the preceding list.

As with CeRunAppAtTime, the application is passed a string on the command line that informs the application that it is being run in response to a particular event.

Code Listing 16-22 (from ShellEG.cpp) shows how the miniapplication that I created in the previous section can be run when Windows CE detects a connection through the RS-232 serial port.

Code Listing 16-22

```
void NotifyRS232(HWND hWnd)
{
  if(!CeRunAppAtEvent (TEXT("\\MiniApp.exe"),
       NOTIFICATION_EVENT_RS232_DETECTED))
    MessageBox(hWnd,
       TEXT("Cannot set application to run"),
       szTitle, MB_OK);
}
```

After the NotifyRS232 function is executed, MiniApp.exe is run whenever a connection is made through the RS-232 port. Figure 16-4 shows the message box displayed by MiniApp.exe when an RS-232 connection is made.

After the notification event is set up (by calling the function NotifyRS232), the application (MiniApp.exe) is run whenever the event (a connection is made through the RS-232 port) occurs, even if the application that set up the event (Shelleg.exe in this case) was terminated. You must remember to cancel the event notification when appropriate (generally, this is when your application terminates or is uninstalled), by calling CeRunAppAtEvent with the option NOTIFICATION_EVENT_NONE. Note that the event is associated with the application that is to be run, not with the application that set the event. Therefore, to clear the RS-232 connection event that I previously set up, you could write the following code (shown in Code Listing 16-23).

Code Listing 16-23

```
if(!CeRunAppAtEvent (TEXT("\\MiniApp.exe"),
     NOTIFICATION_EVENT_NONE ))
  MessageBox(hWnd,
     TEXT("Cannot clear notification for application"),
     szTitle, MB_OK);
```

Figure 16-4:
MiniApp
message
box
displayed in
response to
an event.

Calling `CeRunAppAtEvent` with `NOTIFICATION_EVENT_NONE` results in the cancellation of *all* events that are associated with the application.

Notifying the user

Your application can set up a notification that notifies the user with one of the following techniques (depending on the hardware that's present):

- ✔ Plays a sound (which can be repeated every 15 seconds)
- ✔ Flashes an LED
- ✔ Vibrates the device
- ✔ Displays the user notification dialog box (the title and text for the dialog box must be specified)

You use the `CeSetUserNotification` function to set up the notification, and this is passed a `CE_USER_NOTIFICATION` structure. This structure specifies the type of notification and additional information (such as the name of the sound file to play).

Windows CE places an annunciator icon in the taskbar notification area when the notification occurs. Windows CE selects the primary icon from the application that is associated with the notification. The user can double-click this icon, and the application that's associated with the notification (typically yours!) is run. This annunciator must be removed at some stage, and this is done by calling the `CeHandleAppNotifications` function.

Setting a sound notification

The code in this section is an example of a call that plays a sound at a particular time and sets an annunciator icon.

The function `UserNotification` in shelleg.cpp from workspace \samples\ shelleg\shelleg.dsw contains the code in Code Listing 16-24 to set a user notification. You can copy this code directly into your application, and simply change the time for the notification, the action to be performed and the document and application associated with the event.

Code Listing 16-24

```
HANDLE hNotify;
SYSTEMTIME sysTime;
CE_USER_NOTIFICATION ceNot;

GetLocalTime(&sysTime);
sysTime.wHour= 23;
sysTime.wMinute = 06;

ceNot.ActionFlags = PUN_SOUND;
ceNot.pwszSound = TEXT("\\windows\\Alarm2.wav");
hNotify = CeSetUserNotification(
    NULL,    // not modifying an existing notification
    TEXT("\\ShellEG.exe"),
    &sysTime,
    &ceNot);
```

This code does the following things:

- Gets the local time and stores this in a SYSTEMTIME structure

- Sets the time to 2306 hours (11:06 p.m.) for the current day

- Initializes a CE_USER_NOTIFICATION structure to play a sound (using the PUN_SOUND constant in the ActionFlags member)

- Calls CeSetUserNotification, passing the name of the application that is associated with the notification, the time for the notification (2306), and the CE_USER_NOTIFICATION structure

The call to CeSetUserNotification returns a handle that represents the notification, and this is stored in the hNotify variable. You can use this handle to modify the notification by passing this handle as the first argument. In the previous code, passing NULL specifies that a new notification is being created.

After the notification has been set up, things continue as normal. The user can terminate the application, and the notification remains in place.

At the time specified, the notification technique is activated — in this case, the WAV file is played. At the same time, the annunciator icon appears in the taskbar notification area. The user can double-click this icon, and the application that's referred to when CeSetUserNotification was called is run.

The application, when run, is passed the string AppRunToHandle Notification, a space, and then the notification handle as a decimal number in text format.

The annunciator icon remains in the taskbar notification area even after the user has double-tapped it to start the application.

Setting a dialog box notification

You can notify the user by displaying a dialog box — you can specify the dialog box's title and body text (see Figure 16-5).

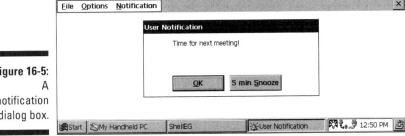

Figure 16-5:
A notification dialog box.

The function UserNotificationDlg in shelleg.cpp from workspace \samples\shelleg\shelleg.dsw contains the code shown here to set a user notification. You can copy this code directly into your application, and simply change the dialog text and title, and the name of the application.

Making the call to CeSetUserNotification is very similar to setting a sound notification. See Code Listing 16-25.

Code Listing 16-25

```
ceNot.ActionFlags = PUN_DIALOG;
ceNot.pwszDialogTitle = TEXT("User Notification");
ceNot.pwszDialogText - TEXT("Time for next meeting!");
hNotify = CeSetUserNotification(
    NULL,// not modifying an existing notification
    TEXT("\\ShellEG.exe"),
    &sysTime,
    &ceNot);
```

Notice that you use PUN_DIALOG for the ActionFlags value. The members pwszDialogTitle and pwszDialogText are initialized with the dialog box's title and body text, respectively.

Removing the annunciator icon

The annunciator icon should generally be removed by the application that is run when the icon is double-tapped by the user.

This icon can determine if the string `AppRunToHandleNotification` is passed on the command line, and if it is, the application calls `CeHandleApp Notifications` to cancel the icon.

The following is an example of calling the function `CeHandleApp Notifications` from ShellEG.cpp. The function is called in `WinMain` to remove the icon if the application was run when the user double-taps the icon (see Code Listing 16-26).

Code Listing 16-26

```
TCHAR szAppRun[] = TEXT("AppRunToHandleNotification");
if(wcsncmp(lpCmdLine, szAppRun, wcslen(szAppRun)) == 0)
{
    CeHandleAppNotifications(TEXT("\\ShellEG.exe"));
}
```

You use the `wcsncmp` function to compare the first part of the command line with the string `AppRunToHandleNotification`. Remember that Windows CE also passes the notification handle in the command line. If the string is present, `CeHandleAppNotifications` is called, indicating that the notification that's associated with the application ShellEG.exe has been handled.

Remembering user notification preferences

Users may have a preference about how they want to be notified. Your application can call the `CeGetUserNotificationPreferences` function to display a dialog box that allows the user to specify his or her preferences (see Figure 16-6). This function is passed a window handle that is the parent to the dialog box and an initialized `CE_USER_NOTIFICATION` structure. This structure defines the default values that are used when the dialog box is displayed, as in Code Listing 16-27.

Code Listing 16-27

```
CE_USER_NOTIFICATION ceNot;
ceNot.ActionFlags = PUN_SOUND;
ceNot.pwszSound = TEXT("\\windows\\Alarm2.wav");
CeGetUserNotificationPreferences(hWnd, &ceNot);
```

Figure 16-6: Setting user notification preferences.

Chapter 17

The Object Store

In This Chapter

▶ Defining the object store

▶ Using files and folders

▶ Creating lists of databases

▶ Experimenting with the Registry

▶ Working with handles and Registry keys

S ooner or later, you'll probably want to store data that is accessible after your application terminates. This is called *persistent data,* and it is placed in a file system called the *object store.* You must decide the best way of storing your data, because the object store allows data to be stored in files, databases, or the Registry. In this chapter, I show you how to determine the appropriate location for your data. I also discuss how to list the files and databases in the object store, and how to find out information about them.

On the CD-ROM that accompanies this book, you can find the sample code for this chapter in the \samples\objstr.dsw workspace. All the code from this chapter is included in this workspace, and you can copy the code directly into your own applications to use the object store functions, including the common registry operations.

Entering the Object Store

The object store is used by applications to save data. Your applications can use the object store to save documents and other data so that the data is available the next time the user runs the application. The *object store* is a file system, but it is different from the file allocation table (FAT) and NT File System (NTFS) that are used by Windows 95 and Windows NT. For a start, the object store is not stored on a hard disk! The object store is implemented using "structured storage" techniques, which are available in Windows NT and Windows 95 and are used to create file systems within files.

Chapter 13 covers memory management and describes how the memory in a Windows CE machine is divided between program memory (used for storing the data used by the application as it runs) and the object store. The user can decide on the amount of physical memory that's configured for each.

Data that is owned by an application in the program memory area is lost when the application terminates and when the Windows CE machine is reset. On the other hand, data in the object store is maintained during a reset. The data is only lost when the backup battery is removed for more than a short period of time.

Choosing a Storage Technique

The object store enables you to use files, databases, and a registry for storage. You can store data using any of these three techniques — the following list shows the individual benefits of each:

- **Files** allow reading, writing, and random file access. Use files where the data is unstructured and doesn't benefit from indexing. For example, you would use files to store data for your application's documents. See Chapter 18 for information on using files.

- **Databases** allow you to quickly and efficiently store and retrieve records of structured data. Databases allow data to be retrieved using indexes that are created on specific bits of information. For example, you would use a database to store information on addresses and other contact data. See Chapter 11 for details about creating and using databases.

- **The Registry** allows you to store configuration and other small pieces of data. You should use the Registry when you want to store and retrieve string or numeric data. For example, you would use the registry to save the options and preferences set by the user for your application.

Whichever technique you use, always remember that storage space is in short supply! If Windows CE runs out of storage space, it attempts to clear the Recycle Bin, and then it's stuck! The user must then delete files to make more space.

Determining the Amount of Space in the Object Store

Users can configure the amount of the total RAM that is set aside for the object store. This is typically around half the RAM, so on a 4MB Windows CE device, about 2MB is used by the object store. You use the GetStore Information function to determine the overall amount of memory allocated to the object store and how much of it is currently available. The function takes a pointer to a STORE_INFORMATION structure, as shown in Code Listing 17-1.

Code Listing 17-1

```
STORE_INFORMATION si;
TCHAR szBuffer[100];
GetStoreInformation(&si);
wsprintf(szBuffer,
    TEXT("Object store %d KBytes, Free Space %d KBytes"),
        si.dwStoreSize / 1024,
        si.dwFreeSize / 1024);
MessageBox(hWnd, szBuffer, szTitle, MB_OK);
```

This code calls GetStoreInformation and passes a pointer to a STORE_INFORMATION variable called si. The members dwStoreSize and dwFreeSize contain the total and available storage space (in bytes) when the function returns. These values are converted to kilobytes and then formatted into a string buffer using wsprintf. Finally, the results are displayed to the user in a message box.

You should check for sufficient free storage space before attempting to save large amounts of data to the object store.

Organizing Files and Folders

Files and folders are organized in the same way as they are with NTFS and FAT systems, although the files and folders are actually part of the object store. From the programmer's standpoint, though, you find the following significant differences:

- ✔ There is no concept of the current directory.
- ✔ There are no environment variables and, therefore, no path.

Windows CE provides functions that enable you to easily perform typical types of file operations, such as moving, copying, and so on. (See Table 17-1.) I describe operations on individual files (such as creating, opening, writing, and reading) in Chapter 18.

Table 17-1 Functions for Performing Common File Operations

Function	Operation
CopyFile	Copy a file from one location to another
CreateDirectory	Create a new directory (folder)
DeleteFile	Remove a file from a folder
FindFirstFile FindNextFile FindClose	List files and folders that match a file specification, such as *.txt
GetFileAttributes SetFileAttributes	Get or set attributes for a file or folder, such as read-only status
MoveFile	Move a file from one folder to another, or rename a file or folder
RemoveDirectory	Delete an existing, empty directory

Most of the functions in Table 17-1 are very straightforward. The exception is using the FindFirstFile, FindNextFile, and FindClose functions to get a list of files and/or folders that match a file specification. Follow these steps to do that:

1. **Call** FindFirstFile**, passing the file specification to use and a pointer to a** WIN32_FIND_DATA **structure, in which file information for the first file is returned.**

   This function returns a handle that is used in subsequent function calls.

2. **Call** FindNextFile **repeatedly until the function returns** FALSE.

   This indicates that no more files match the specification. The function is passed the handle that is returned by the call to FindFirstFile and, once again, a pointer to a WIN32_FIND_DATA structure.

3. **Call** FindClose **when the search is complete, passing the handle that is returned by** FindFirstFile.

The example application ObjStr on the CD-ROM has a menu command Object Store⇨List Files, which displays a dialog box containing a list box. The WM_INITDIALOG message handler fills the list box with the files and folders that are located in the root directory of the object store. The code in the function FileDlgProc can be copied in your applications wherever you need to list files in a directory.

The following source code from ObjStr.cpp fills the list box with the list of files and folders. The list box has the indentifier IDC_FILES, and the SendMessage function is used to add the string to the list box using the LB_ADDSTRING message, as shown in Code Listing 17-2.

Code Listing 17-2

```
case WM_INITDIALOG:
// load list of files / directories in root directory
    HANDLE hFindFile;
    WIN32_FIND_DATA fd;

    hFindFile = FindFirstFile(TEXT("\\*.*"), &fd);
    SendMessage(GetDlgItem(hDlg, IDC_FILES),
            LB_ADDSTRING, 0, (LPARAM)fd.cFileName);
    while(FindNextFile(hFindFile, &fd))
    {
        SendMessage(GetDlgItem(hDlg, IDC_FILES),
            LB_ADDSTRING, 0, (LPARAM)fd.cFileName);
    }
    FindClose(hFindFile); // Always do this!
    return (TRUE); // from dialog message handler
```

Always remember to call FindClose on the handle! Memory is lost if you don't do this.

As well as giving the name of the file, the structure WIN32_FIND_DATA contains other important information about the file. These items are listed in Table 17-2.

Table 17-2	WIN32_FIND_DATA Structure Members
Member	*Description*
dwFileAttributes	File attribute flags, such as read-only status
ftCreationTime	A FILETIME structure containing the time that the file was created
ftLastAccessTime	A FILETIME structure containing the time that the file was last accessed
ftLastWriteTime	A FILETIME structure containing the time that the file was last written to
nFileSizeHigh	Two DWORDs that, when combined, show the file size nFileSizeLow in bytes. In Windows CE, you can use just nFileSizeLow to determine the file size
cFileName	The filename (without the path)

The `WIN32_FIND_DATA` structure has the member `cAlternateFileName` in Windows 95/NT; this member is used to return the 8.3-style short filename. Windows CE does not constrain you to 8.3 filenames — all filenames are stored as long filenames. Therefore, the `cAlternateFileName` member is not needed.

Understanding Object Identifiers

Everything in the object store (files, directories, databases, and database records) has a unique number that is associated with it, known as an *object identifier*. You use the data type `CEOID` to store these values, which is actually a `DWORD` data type.

If you know an object's identifier, you can use the `CeOidGetInfo` function to return information about the object. You pass this function the `CEOID` of the object, and information about the object is returned in a `CEOIDINFO` structure.

You probably won't use this function to get information about files and directories, because no convenient mechanism exists for finding the `CEOID` for these objects. Object identifiers are, though, particularly important when dealing with databases.

It just so happens that the root folder has a `CEOID` of 0, so I use this identifier to show you some code for calling this function, as in Code Listing 17-3.

Code Listing 17-3

```
CEOIDINFO ceObjInfo;
CeOidGetInfo(0,    // CEOID - 0 for root directory
    &ceObjInfo); // information returned in structure
```

You use the `CEODINFO` structure to return different information for files, directories, databases, and database records. Therefore, the structure uses the `wObjType` member to indicate the type of object that the `CeOidGetInfo` function returned information on. The `wObjType` member can have one of the values shown in Table 17-3.

Table 17-3	wObjType Member Values
Value	*Meaning*
OBJTYPE_INVALID	The object identifier is invalid.
OBJTYPE_FILE	The object identifier refers to a file.
OBJTYPE_DIRECTORY	The object identifier refers to a directory (folder).
OBJTYPE_DATABASE	The object is a database.
OBJTYPE_RECORD	The object is a record in a database.

The CEODINFO structure contains four union members (which are them-selves structures), one for each of the object types. The structure in Code Listing 17-4 shows the members in the CEODINFO including the union members.

Code Listing 17-4

```
typedef struct _CEOIDINFO {
    WORD wObjType;
    WORD wPad;
    union {
        CEFILEINFO      infFile;
        CEDIRINFO       infDirectory;
        CEDBASEINFO     infDatabase;
        CERECORDINFO    infRecord;
    };
} CEOIDINFO;
```

Using CeOidGetInfo on files and directories is not particularly useful, because it's easier to get the information using the standard file functions. In the next section, I show you how knowing about object indentifiers is essential to accessing information about databases.

Part of the union

The next few paragraphs may be useful if you're rusty on unions. A *union* defines two or more members in a structure that are to occupy the same memory. In the case of CEOIDINFO, the structure stores data on files or directories or databases or records. It would be wasteful if the structure contained members to store the different types of data for all these objects, because only one object's information is stored at any given time.

So, unions step in! In this case, the same memory is used to store CEFILEINFO, CEDIRINFO, CEDBASEINFO, and CERECORDINFO structures. It's important that

I know which of these structures I use to reference the information. For example, if the structure contained information on a data-base, I could (by mistake) access the data using CEDIRINFO. I would then get invalid data back.

If I know that the structure contains informa-tion on a directory (because wObjType contains the value OBJTYPE_DIRECTORY), I can access the directory's name by writing the following code:

```
ceObjInfo.infDirectory.szDirName
```

Listing Databases

The object store provides databases to allow structured data (that is, data that can be organized into rows) to be stored. In Chapter 11, I show you how to create databases and how to add, delete, and update records. Chapter 11 also explains how Windows CE databases are not like standard relational databases that use SQL (Structured Query Language).

In this section, I discuss how to find out information about databases that are installed on a Windows CE machine.

Using the ObjStr application to produce a list of databases

Look at the example application ObjStr on the enclosed CD-ROM. This application contains the menu command Object Store⇨List Databases, which displays a dialog box with a list box. This list box contains the names of all the databases in the object store.

You use the following steps to produce the list of databases that is displayed in the dialog box in the ObjStr sample application:

1. **Declare the variables that are to be used in the listing.**

   Use the variables in Code Listing 17-5.

Code Listing 17-5

```
HANDLE hEnumDB;
CEOID WceObjID;
CEOIDINFO WceObjInfo;
```

2. **Use** `CeFindFirstDatabase` **to get a handle to search for databases.**

   You pass the `CeFindFirstDatabase` function a 0, indicating that all databases should be listed. Information on databases is not returned at this stage. Check to see if the handle is valid using Code Listing 17-6.

Code Listing 17-6

```
hEnumDB = CeFindFirstDatabase(0);
if (INVALID_HANDLE_VALUE == hEnumDB)
{
      return TRUE;
}
```

3. **Continue calling** `CeFindNextDatabase`.

The `CeFindNextDatabase` function returns the object identifier of the next database in the list, or it returns 0 if the end of the list is reached. Use the following code:

```
while( (WceObjID = CeFindNextDatabase(hEnumDB)) != 0)
{
```

4. **For each loop, call** `CeOidGetInfo` **to get information on the database.**

You pass the `CeOidGetInfo` function the object identifier that you obtained in Step 3. If the call to `CeOidGetInfo` fails, you close the handle from `CeFindFirstDatabase` by calling `CloseHandle`. If the call succeeds, the database name is added to the list box by a call to `SendMessage`, as follows in Code Listing 17-7.

Code Listing 17-7

```
if (!CeOidGetInfo(WceObjID, &WceObjInfo) )
{
    CloseHandle(hEnumDB);
    return TRUE;
}
else { // add database name to listbox
    SendMessage(GetDlgItem(hDlg, IDC_DBS),
        LB_ADDSTRING, 0,
        LPARAM(WceObjInfo.infDatabase.szDbaseName));
}
```

5. **Call** `CloseHandle`, **after all the databases have been added to the list box, by using the following code:**

```
CloseHandle(hEnumDB);
```

Breaking down the CEDBASEINFO structure

In the previous section, the name of the database was added to a list box using the `szDatabaseName` member of the `CeOidGetInfo` structure. You can find out more information about databases using the `infDatabase` union member, which is a `CEDBASEINFO` structure variable. You can, for example, find out the size of the database in bytes, or the number of records the database contains.

I show some of the members that provide useful information on databases in the Table 17-4.

Table 17-4	Useful Database Information
Member	*Description*
szDbaseName	The name of the database. Most databases are placed in the Databases folder. You use the database name when you open the database to access records. Chapter 11 describes how to access records in a database.
wNumRecords	The number of records in this database. The number of records in the database gives users a good idea of how big the database is.
dwSize	The storage space, in bytes, that's occupied by the database. As the object store has only a limited size, you should monitor carefully how big your databases are.
ftLastModified	A FILETIME structure containing the time that the database was last modified. This can be useful when determining the last time the user changed the contents of the database.

Getting to Know the Windows CE Registry

The Registry is the best place to store application configuration information. For example, you would store the list of most recently opened files or the user preference settings in the Registry. While Windows CE supports functions for searching the Registry for particular data, I concentrate on the three basic operations that an application needs to perform — adding, deleting, and retrieving values from the Registry. These operations are described later in this chapter, in the sections "Saving and updating values in a key," "Deleting keys," and "Retrieving values from keys." But first, I tell you about how the Registry is organized and some techniques that you must use to access data in the Registry.

Understanding the elements of the Registry

The Registry consists of *keys,* and these keys can have data or other keys associated with them. This arrangement creates a hierarchical structure in which data can be stored.

The Registry has the following predefined keys:

- ✓ HKEY_LOCAL_MACHINE: This key stores information about the machine's hardware configuration and installed software.

- ✓ HKEY_CLASSES_ROOT: This key stores information on the Component Object Model (COM) and ActiveX components that are installed on the machine. It also includes mappings between file extensions and applications.

- ✓ HKEY_CURRENT_USER: This key stores the current user's preferences and configurations.

Place application configuration information that applies to all users in HKEY_LOCAL_MACHINE\Software, while preferences that are specific to individual users should be placed in HKEY_CURRENT_USER\Software. Of course, on a Windows CE device, only one user exists, so the distinction is a bit arbitrary.

Viewing and editing the Registry

You can use the Windows CE Remote Registry Editor to view and edit the Registry in the emulation environment and for Windows CE devices. The Editor also lets you view your desktop PC's Registry. Use Windows CE Remote Registry Editor to check that the data you're adding to the Registry in your applications is being written to the correct location and in the correct format.

You run the Registry Editor by selecting Tools➪Remote Registry Editor in Visual Studio. Figure 17-1 shows the Registry Viewer with the Pocket IE (Pocket Internet Explorer) entry expanded to display the values that are associated with the key.

Keep in mind the following points when working with the Remote Registry Viewer:

- ✓ Each folder icon represents a key.

- ✓ A key can contain more than one key.

- ✓ A key can contain values that have names (for example, EnableWarning0).

- ✓ Each key can have a value that uses the default name.

- ✓ Values have different data types, such as numeric (for example, EnablePCT) or string (for example, StartPage).

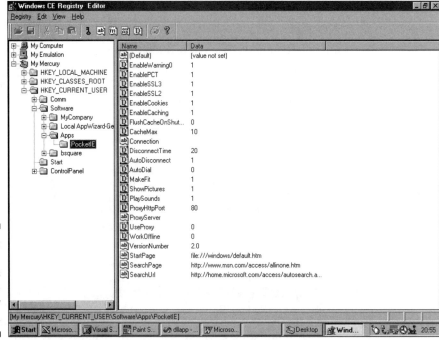

Figure 17-1:
The
Windows
CE Remote
Registry
Viewer.

Obtaining handles to keys

Each data item in the Registry is saved under a key. Before a key can be accessed, however, you must first open it to obtain a handle. It sounds like you need to be a confused locksmith rather than a programmer to access the Registry, huh?

Predefined handles exist for `HKEY_LOCAL_MACHINE`, `HKEY_CLASSES_ROOT`, and `HKEY_CURRENT_USER` so that you can access the Registry without having to open keys. However, in many situations, it is easier to open keys yourself, as discussed in the following steps:

1. **Define a variable to store the key's handle, as follows:**

   ```
   HKEY hKey;
   ```

2. **Declare a variable that holds the key's name, as follows:**

   ```
   TCHAR szRegKey[] = TEXT("Software\\MyCompany\\ObjStr");
   ```

   This specifies a key called `ObjStr`, which is a subkey of `MyCompany`, which is itself a subkey of `Software`. Notice how the key hierarchy is specified like a path to a file, with each key being separated by a backslash.

Remember, the backslash character \ is special in C/C++. You must include *two* backslashes wherever you need to place a single backslash in a string constant.

3. **Place your application-specific Registry entries in the Software key in either** HKEY_LOCAL_MACHINE **(for application-specific settings) or** HKEY_CURRENT_USER **(for user-specific settings).**

   Also, create a subkey that is the name of your company (MyCompany) and a subkey under that using the name of your application (ObjStr).

4. **Call the** RegOpenKeyEx **function to open a specific key.**

   Keys are always referenced through other keys. The predefined handles, such as HKEY_CURRENT_USER, are the starting point to the hierarchies.

So, the call in Code Listing 17-8 requests that a key handle be returned in the variable hKey for the key that is specified in the string szRegKey, which is located under the key HKEY_CURRENT_USER. The two 0 parameters can be ignored.

Code Listing 17-8

```
if(RegOpenKeyEx(
   HKEY_CURRENT_USER,
   szRegKey,
   0,
   0,
   &hKey) !=  ERROR_SUCCESS)
{
   MessageBox(hWnd, TEXT("Could not open key"),szTitle,
      MB_OK | MB_ICONEXCLAMATION);
}
```

The handle that is stored in the hKey can now be used to add, update, or retrieve Registry settings. When you're finished, remember to call RegCloseKey on the handle, as follows in Code Listing 17-9.

Code Listing 17-9

```
if(RegCloseKey(hKey) != ERROR_SUCCESS)
   MessageBox(hWnd, TEXT("Could not close key!"),
      szTitle, MB_OK);
```

Creating a Registry key

You create new Registry keys by calling the function `RegCreateKeyEx`, and this requires the following information:

- ✔ **The starting-point key:** For example, this may be `HKEY_CURRENT_USER` or a handle that you've obtained through calling `RegOpenKeyEx`.

- ✔ **The name of the key to be created:** This is `szRegKey`, which is declared in the previous section. Note that you can create a whole hierarchy at one time — you don't have to create each individual key and subkey.

- ✔ **A pointer to an** `HKEY` **variable:** This is `hKey`, in which a handle to the new key is returned.

- ✔ **A pointer to a** `DWORD` **variable:** This is `dwDisp`. The value placed here by the function can be used to see if the key was created (`REG_CREATED_NEW_KEY`) or whether the key already existed and was simply opened by the function call (`REG_OPENED_EXISTING_KEY`).

You can use Code Listing 17-10 to create your own keys. Just change the key name in `szRegKey`.

Code Listing 17-10

```
HKEY hKey;
DWORD dwDisp;
if(RegCreateKeyEx(
      HKEY_CURRENT_USER,
      szRegKey,
      0,NULL,0,0,NULL,
      &hKey,
      &dwDisp) !=  ERROR_SUCCESS)
{
   MessageBox(hWnd, TEXT("Could not create key"), szTitle,
   MB_OK | MB_ICONEXCLAMATION);
}
```

After the key has been created, you can do the following things:

- ✔ Set data into the default value for this key.
- ✔ Add one or more named values for the key to store data.
- ✔ Create subkeys.

Don't forget to close the key handle in `hKey` when you're done by calling `RegCloseKey`!

Saving and updating values in a key

You can save data into the registry by creating a new key or opening an existing key and updating the current value. Data can be saved in a key using the RegSetValueEx function using a key handle obtained either by opening (RegOpenKeyEx) or creating a new key (RegCreateKeyEx).

For starters, I discuss how to add string data to the default value for the key that I created in the previous section. You use the following string declaration to specify the value to be saved:

```
TCHAR szKeyValue[] = TEXT("Preference Data");
```

The call to RegSetValueEx requires the following items:

✔ The key handle for which the value is to be added.

✔ The data type — REG_SZ specifies string data.

✔ A pointer to the data, cast to a BYTE * pointer. This is necessary because the function can be passed data in many different formats.

✔ The number of *bytes* of data to write. You use the wcslen function to determine the length of the string szKeyValue, with 1 added to allow for the terminating \0 character. The result is multiplied by 2 because szKeyValue is a Unicode string, and each character occupies 2 bytes.

You can use Code Listing 17-11 to set the value into the key.

Code Listing 17-11

```
if(RegSetValueEx(hKey,
     NULL, 0,
     REG_SZ,
     (BYTE *)szKeyValue,
     (wcslen(szKeyValue) + 1)* 2) != ERROR_SUCCESS)
```

After making this call, you should use the Registry Editor to check that the data was saved correctly. Figure 17-2 shows how the key looks with the strings that I've declared. Note that the data was added to the default value for the ObjStr key.

Figure 17-2:
The contents of the Software key after adding the key and a default value.

You can save data as named values in a key, too — this allows multiple pieces of data to be saved under a single key. As usual, you need to obtain a handle to the key and then call `RegSetValueEx` multiple times, specifying a value name as the second parameter. The results are shown in Figure 17-3 after executing Code Listing 17-12.

Code Listing 17-12

```
if(RegSetValueEx(hKey,
    TEXT("Pref2"), // value name
    0,
    REG_SZ,
    (BYTE *)TEXT("Pref 2 data"),
    (wcslen(szKeyValue) + 1)* 2) != ERROR_SUCCESS)
```

You can save data in other formats as well as string (`REG_SZ`). The two most useful formats are `REG_DWORD` (for `DWORD` unsigned integer values) and `REG_BINARY` (for binary data, such as structures or arrays).

You can use Code Listing 17-13 to add a `DWORD` data value to a key. Note how a pointer to `dwData` is passed and that the `sizeof` operator is used to specify the number of bytes being saved.

Figure 17-3:
Software
key after
adding
a named
value.

Code Listing 17-13

```
DWORD dwData = 123;
RegSetValueEx(hKey,
      TEXT("dwPref"), // value name
      0,
      REG_DWORD,
      (BYTE *)&dwData,
      sizeof(dwData));
```

Updating key values is easy! Just call RegSetValueEx again, passing a
handle to the key and the same value name.

Retrieving values from keys

You retrieve key values using the RegQueryValueEx function. You need to
do the following things:

✔ Get a handle to the key (hKey), and specify the value name.

✔ Provide a variable in which the data is to be returned (szBuffer).

✔ Provide a variable that is initialized with the size of this variable in
bytes (dwSize).

✔ Pass a pointer to a variable (dwType) in which the function returns the data type of the value returned. In this case, this variable contains the value REG_SZ.

Code Listing 17-14 retrieves the string data that is saved under the value name Pref2.

Code Listing 17-14

```
TCHAR szBuffer[100];
DWORD dwType;
DWORD dwSize = sizeof(szBuffer);
if(RegQueryValueEx(hKey,
     TEXT("Pref2"),
     0,
     &dwType,
     (BYTE *)szBuffer,
     &dwSize) != ERROR_SUCCESS)
   MessageBox(hWnd, TEXT("Could not retrieve key!"),
     szTitle, MB_OK);
```

Deleting keys

Windows CE allows a key, and the subkeys and values they contain, to be deleted through a single call to RegDeleteKey. The code in Code Listing 17-15 deletes the MyCompany key and all its subkeys and data.

Code Listing 17-15

```
if(RegDeleteKey(HKEY_CURRENT_USER,
     TEXT("Software\\MyCompany")) != ERROR_SUCCESS)
   MessageBox(hWnd, TEXT("Could not delete key!"), szTitle,
     MB_OK);
```

The RegDeleteKey function uses the first two arguments to specify which key to delete. The first key is the starting-point key in the hierarchy, and the second key is assumed to be a subkey of this starting-point key.

You can open a key using the RegOpenKeyEx function, passing this key as the first argument and NULL as the second, as follows:

```
if(RegDeleteKey(hKey, NULL);
```

You must delete all the Registry keys that are created by your application when uninstalling it! Chapter 9 shows how to create setup programs to install and uninstall applications.

Chapter 18

The File System API

- -

In This Chapter

▶ Opening, creating, writing to, and reading from files

▶ Finding errors

▶ Using an MFC archive object to read and write data

- -

*W*indows CE doesn't support the standard C or C++ library file input/output (I/O) functions, such as `fopen` (which opens files), `fread` and `fwrite` (which read and write files), and `fclose` (which closes files). Instead, files are created and accessed through API functions. Windows CE uses `CreateFile` to create new files and open existing ones, uses `ReadFile` and `WriteFile` to read and write to files, and uses `CloseHandle` to close files. The functions provide binary — not text — file access, so you don't have functions to read and lines of text to write. In this chapter, I show you how to use these functions to manage file I/O.

Similar limitations apply if you're programming using Microsoft Foundation Classes (MFC). I also discuss how to use the MFC archive method for saving and loading files, and show you the `CFile` class, which provides the same file I/O functionality as `CreateFile` and related functions. You can find more information on the MFC in Chapter 4.

On the CD-ROM that accompanies this book, you can find the sample code for this chapter in the \samples\fileio.dsw workspace. This application implements a simple Notepad text editor. This code shows you how to read and write files using the Windows CE API and MFC archive functions. You can use this code as the starting point for any file I/O your application requires.

Examining the Windows CE File System API

Windows CE File System API functions are used to open, create, read, write, and close files. The files that are created using the File System API functions are all placed in the object store, which I describe in Chapter 17.

Remember that these files are stored in RAM, so the size of the files is limited. Reading and writing files is fast, so file I/O is a good technique to use for storing data in your applications.

Opening and creating files

Strangely enough, you use the CreateFile function to create new files *and* to open existing files! The *Create* part of this function name refers not to creating files but to creating a file kernel object. The *file kernel object* is used by Windows CE to maintain and manage information about an open file. At some stage, you must close this object by calling the CloseHandle function. Refer to "What's in a Process?" in Chapter 13 for more detail on kernel objects.

The file kernel object that is returned by calling CreateFile is a different type of handle from the handle that's returned by calling the standard C/C++ fopen function.

You can specify the following options when calling CreateFile to create or open a file:

- ✔ **The filename:** This name can include a path that's used to open or create a file.

- ✔ **Access options:** These options determine whether the file can be read, written, or both. You can use the following values:

  - GENERIC_READ: Provides read-only access.

  - GENERIC_WRITE: Provides write-only access.

  - GENERIC_READ | GENERIC_WRITE: Provides read/write access. Remember that | is the C and C++ OR operator.

- ✔ **Sharing options:** These options specify whether other applications can read or write the file while you have it open. The valid options are as follows:

  - 0: All other file-open attempts on this file are going to fail; the file is opened exclusively.

- FILE_SHARE_READ: Other file-open attempts on this file can succeed only if read access is requested.

- FILE_SHARE_WRITE: Other file-open attempts on this file can succeed only if write access is requested.

✔ **Creation options:** These options specify whether the file is to be created or opened. When creating a file, you specify what should happen if the file already exists (for example, when truncating all existing content or appending to it). The valid options are as follows:

- CREATE_NEW: Creates a new file. The call to CreateFile fails if the file exists.

- CREATE_ALWAYS: Creates a new file. The call to CreateFile results in an existing file being overwritten.

- OPEN_EXISTING: Opens an existing file. The call to CreateFile fails if the file does not exist.

- OPEN_ALWAYS: Opens the file if it exists. If the file does not exist, it is created as if the CREATE_NEW option were specified.

- TRUNCATE_EXISTING: Opens an existing file (which must exist) and truncates the contents. You must open the file for writing with GENERIC_WRITE.

✔ **The file attributes:** These attributes are applied to a file when it is created. Attributes can be combined, and the common attributes are as follows:

- FILE_ATTRIBUTE_HIDDEN: The file is hidden from ordinary file lists unless the user specifies that hidden files should be displayed.

- FILE_ATTRIBUTE_NORMAL: The file has normal file characteristics. This attribute cannot be combined with other attributes.

- FILE_ATTRIBUTE_ARCHIVE: The file is marked to be archived (backed up).

- FILE_ATTRIBUTE_READONLY: The file can only be opened for read access.

- FILE_ATTRIBUTE_SYSTEM: The file is one of the operating-system files.

You can use Code Listing 18-1 to open an existing file for reading only.

Code Listing 18-1

```
HANDLE hFile;
hFile = CreateFile(
    TEXT("file.txt"),      // name of file to open
    GENERIC_READ,          // Access Options
    FILE_SHARE_READ,       // Sharing Options
    NULL,                  // ignored
    OPEN_EXISTING,         // Creation Options
    0,                     // File Attributes
    NULL);                 // ignored
```

Code Listing 18-2 shows you how to create a new file and open it for reading and writing.

Code Listing 18-2

```
hFile = CreateFile(
    TEXT("\\MyFile.txt"),  // name of file to create
    GENERIC_READ | GENERIC_WRITE, // Access Options
    FILE_SHARE_READ,           // Sharing Options
    NULL,                      // ignored
    CREATE_NEW,                // Creation Options
    FILE_ATTRIBUTE_NORMAL,     // File Attributes
    NULL);                     // ignored
```

Note that this call fails if the file already exists, because the CREATE_NEW creation option is used. If you want this function to succeed even if the file you are opening exists, use CREATE_ALWAYS. Take care, though, because this option deletes the contents of the file that you are opening.

Checking for errors

Many things can go wrong when writing file I/O code, so it's essential that you check each call for an error.

The CreateFile function returns INVALID_HANDLE_VALUE if the call fails. If this happens, call GetLastError to retrieve the error code. All the error codes and their meanings are listed in the header file winerror.h. This file, which is part of the Windows CE Toolkit for Visual C++, is generally located in the Program Files\DevStudio\WCE\Include\WCE200 directory (on the CD that comes with the toolkit — not the one that comes with this book!). Code Listing 18-3 uses the GetLastError function to find the last error number and displays the value in a message box.

Code Listing 18-3

```
TCHAR szBuffer[100];
wsprintf(szBuffer, TEXT("Error code %d"), GetLastError());
MessageBox(hWnd, szBuffer,
    TEXT("File I/O Application"), MB_OK);
```

Table 18-1 shows some of the common values that are returned by GetLastError for file I/O.

Table 18-1	Values Returned by GetLastError	
Constant	*Value*	*Meaning*
ERROR_FILE_NOT_FOUND	2	The specified file does not exist.
ERROR_PATH_NOT_FOUND	3	The specified path does not exist.
ERROR_TOO_MANY_OPEN_FILES	4	Windows CE does not have enough resources to open another file.
ERROR_ACCESS_DENIED	5	You tried to perform an operation that is illegal for the way that the file was opened. For example, you attempted to write to a file that was opened as read only.
ERROR_INVALID_HANDLE	6	You attempted to perform a file I/O operation using an invalid handle.

If you encounter an error number that's not listed in this table, open winerror.h and search for the error number.

Writing to a file

You use the WriteFile function to write data to a file that was previously opened or created through a call to CreateFile. You need to provide the following information when calling this function:

> ✔ A file handle that is returned from calling CreateFile

> ✔ A pointer to a buffer that contains the information to write to the file

✔ The number of bytes of data to write

✔ A pointer to a DWORD variable in which the number of bytes written to the file is returned

The function returns TRUE if the write succeeds or FALSE if it fails. As with all file I/O operations, you must check that the call to WriteFile succeeds. Code Listing 18-4 writes out the text that szBuffer points to.

Code Listing 18-4

```
TCHAR szBuffer[] = TEXT("String contents of the file!");
DWORD dwBytesWritten;
if(!WriteFile(hFile,      // file handle
    szBuffer,             // pointer to data to write
    wcslen(szBuffer),     // number of bytes to write
    &dwBytesWritten,      // number of bytes written
    NULL)                 // ignored
{
    // report file write error
}
```

Notice that the number of bytes is calculated by finding the length of the string by calling wcslen and multiplying this number by 2. This is necessary because all strings in Windows CE are Unicode, and each character occupies 2 bytes.

You can make multiple calls to WriteFile to write multiple buffers of data to the same file — each write is placed after the last write that is performed on the file.

Reading from a file

You read data from an open file using the ReadFile function. This function takes the same arguments as WriteFile, except that you specify the maximum number of bytes to be read rather than the number of bytes to be written. This is usually the size of the buffer into which you place the data.

You can use Code Listing 18-5 to read data from a file into a string buffer.

Code Listing 18-5

```
TCHAR szBuffer[100];
DWORD dwRead;
if(!ReadFile(hFile,      // file handle
    szBuffer,            // buffer to receive bytes
    200,                 // max. number of bytes to read
```

```
        &dwRead,        // actual number of bytes read
        NULL))          // ignored.
{
  // report file write error
}
```

The number of bytes read from the file (which is returned in dwRead) may be less than the maximum number of bytes that you specified to be read. This happens if the end of the file is reached before all the bytes could be read. In this case, your buffer contains dwRead bytes.

If you perform multiple reads on an open file, the next read begins where the last read finished.

Performing random file I/O

The techniques that I describe earlier in this section for reading from and writing to a file always start at the beginning of the file and read or write to the end of the file. This is called *sequential I/O*. In many situations, it is convenient to be able to jump around in the file, reading and writing as you go; this is called *random I/O*.

When you open a file, Windows CE maintains a *current file pointer* variable. This contains the byte offset from the beginning of the file where the next read or write is to take place. The current file pointer is updated automatically by WriteFile and ReadFile.

You can take control of the current file pointer by using the SetFilePointer function. This function moves the current file pointer relative to the start of the file, the current file pointer, or the end of the file. You can therefore specify where the next read or write is to take place.

SetFilePointer requires the following pieces of information:

  ✔ A handle to an open file that is returned by CreateFile.

  ✔ Knowledge about whether you're moving the current file pointer relative to the start of the file, the current file pointer position, or the end of the file. The allowed values are FILE_BEGIN, FILE_CURRENT, and FILE_END.

  ✔ The number of bytes to move.

Code Listing 18-6 shows an example of calling SetFilePointer to move the current file pointer to the position 20 bytes from the start of the file.

Code Listing 18-6

```
if(!SetFilePointer(hFile,    // file handle
    20,                      // number of bytes to move
    NULL,                    // ignored
    FILE_BEGIN))             // where to move from
{
  // Report error
}
```

You can specify negative values for the number of bytes to move. You can therefore move backward from the current file pointer or from the end of file.

The following example shows you how to move to the end of file:

```
SetFilePointer(hFile, 0, NULL, FILE_END);
```

Calls made to `ReadFile` and `WriteFile` after calling `SetFilePointer` use the new current file pointer, but they update the current file pointer after performing the I/O operation.

Using file I/O with the MFC

You have more choices when using the MFC for performing file I/O. You can use the Windows CE API functions to perform I/O operations, but it is more convenient to use the MFC class `CFile`. This class provides a similar set of functions, but it has the advantage of being a C++ class. The `CFile` class has member functions for opening and creating files, reading and writing files, and performing random file I/O by moving the current file pointer. Some of the member functions are shown in Table 18-2.

Table 18-2	CFile Member Functions
Member Function	*Purpose*
Open	Opens or creates the specified file. This is equivalent to calling `CreateFile`.
Close	Closes an open file. The file closes automatically when the CFile object is destroyed, so you don't always have to call this member function. This is equivalent to calling `CloseHandle`.
Read	Reads a specified number of bytes from an open file, starting at the current file pointer. This is equivalent to calling `ReadFile`.

Member Function	Purpose
Write	Writes a specified number of bytes to an open file, starting at the current file pointer. This is equivalent to calling `WriteFile`.
Seek	Moves the current file pointer to the specified location. This is equivalent to calling `SetFilePointer`.
SeekToBegin	Moves the current file pointer to the beginning of the file.
SeekToEnd	Moves the current file pointer to the end of the file.

Archiving with the MFC

The MFC provides an additional mechanism for reading and writing files that requires much less effort for you, the programmer. When you create an MFC application, all the code that is necessary for displaying File Open and File Save dialog boxes is created for you as part of your `CDocument` class. This class contains a single method called `Serialize`, which is shown in the Code Listing 18-7.

Code Listing 18-7

```
void CFileIO::Serialize(CArchive& ar)
{
  if (ar.IsStoring())
  {
    // code to write data to file
  }
  else
  {
    // code to read data from file
  }
}
```

The MFC calls the `Serialize` method whenever the data in the document needs to be saved to a file or read back from a file. This typically occurs as a result of the user selecting one of the following commands: File⇨Save, File⇨Save As, or File⇨Open. The method is passed a `CArchive` object called `ar`, and this is used to write or read the data. The `CArchive` object has opened the file already, so you don't need to do this.

Writing or reading with serialization

You must determine whether you need to write the data out or read it in. The CArchive method called IsStoring returns TRUE if you are requested to save the data. IsStoring returns FALSE if you need to read the data.

You can use the CArchive << operator to write data to the file that is associated with the archive or use the >> operator to read the data in. The data must be stored in one of the following data types: CString, BYTE, WORD, int, LONG, DWORD, float, or double.

For example, if your document has two variables that need to be saved to the file called m_lNumPoints (a LONG variable) and m_sString (a CString variable), use the following code in the Serialize method (Code Listing 18-8) to save and load the data.

Code Listing 18-8

```
if (ar.IsStoring())
    {       // saving data to file
    ar << m_lNumPoints;
    ar << m_sString;
    }
    else
    {       // loading data from file
    ar >> m_lNumPoints;
    ar >> m_sString;
    }
```

The data must be read in and written out using the same order. The data is written out as a series of bytes, and if the data is not read back in using the same order, the variables end up containing the wrong data.

You can use the CArchive Write and Read functions to read and write data using other formats, including buffers and structures. The CArchive WriteString and ReadString functions are similar; these functions allow text to be written to and read from an archive.

Finding errors when archiving

Be sure to check for errors when performing file I/O, and this includes using the CArchive object. To add error checking, you should use exception handling. *Exception handling* is a coding technique that allows you to trap errors that occur in your application while the application is running (so that you can write code to recover from those errors). This allows one or more lines of code to be executed and permits a block of code to be jumped to in the event of an error.

Implementing exception handling requires you to do the following:

1. **Add a** TRY **block around the code that may cause the errors.**

2. **Add a** CATCH **block after this** TRY **block that contains the code that is to be executed if an error is detected.**

3. **Define the type of exception that is to be caught in the** CATCH **block.**

   You provide the type of exception that is to be caught by specifying one of the standard MFC exception classes, such as CFileException for file I/O errors, and a variable name (e) in which a pointer to a class object is returned. See the following code:

   ```
   CATCH (CFileException, e)
   ```

4. **Delete the exception class object that is passed to you in the** CATCH **block when you're finished using it, as follows:**

   ```
   e->Delete();
   ```

5. **Mark the end of the exception handler with** END_CATCH**.**

In Code Listing 18-9, two lines that write data out to an archive file are enclosed in a TRY block. The CATCH block specifies that CFileException errors are to be caught and that a pointer to a CFileException object containing details on the error are to be placed in the variable e by the MFC.

Code Listing 18-9

```
TRY
{
    ar << m_lNumPoints;
    ar << m_sString;
}
CATCH (CFileException, e)
{
    TCHAR szBuffer[10];
    wsprintf(szBuffer, _T("%d"), e->m_cause);
    AfxMessageBox(_T("Error archiving to ") +
        e->m_strFileName + _T(" Code: ")
        + szBuffer);
    e->Delete();
}
END_CATCH
```

The `CFileException` class contains the following useful members for determining the type of error:

- ✔ `m_strFileName`, which contains the name of the open file
- ✔ `m_cause`, which is an integer value that contains an error code

The `CFileException` class contains constant values for all the errors that can be caught, and you can use these constants to test for the particular type of error that has occurred. For example, you can write the following code to see if the error that was generated was caused by the object store running out of space:

```
if(e->m_cause == CFileException::diskFull)
```

These error constants are documented in the Windows CE online help under `m_cause`.

Part V
Improving Desktop Connectivity and Communications

The 5th Wave   By Rich Tennant

"YOU KNOW, IF WE CAN ALL KEEP THE TITTERING DOWN, I, FOR ONE, WOULD LIKE TO HEAR MORE ABOUT KEN'S NEW POINTING DEVICE FOR HANDHELD PCs."

In this part . . .

No Windows CE application is an island — connectivity is essential. Windows CE provides an extremely rich set of connectivity options, ranging from serial communications to infrared connections, network support to Windows sockets. Each has its own place, and in this part, I explain how and when to use the most commonly used communications facilities, so that you can communicate with the world from *anywhere!*

Chapter 19

Serial Communications Programming

• •

• •

*N*early all Windows CE devices have a serial port that allows communications with a wide range of devices and operating systems. For
example, you can use serial communications to transfer data to and from
the following types of computers and peripherals:

- ✔ Computers running Windows 3.1, Windows 95, Windows NT, Unix,
  Linux, OS/2, and other operating systems, such as Hewlett Packard's
  MPE and Digital's VMS

- ✔ Printers and plotters with serial ports

- ✔ External and internal modems, and internal PCMCIA modem cards

Using the Windows CE serial communications functions, you can write
programs that implement the following protocols:

- ✔ **Terminal emulation:** The Windows CE device can act as if it were a true
  data terminal.

- ✔ **File transfer:** The Windows CE device can transfer files using standard
  file transfer protocols such as Kermit and zmodem.

- ✔ **Data transfer:** The Windows CE device can send or receive data from
  devices such as global positioning system (GPS) navigational devices.

In this chapter, I show you how to communicate using the Windows CE serial
port, so that you can open the communications port, send and receive data,
and then close the communications port.

Usually, a Windows CE device connects to a desktop PC that runs Windows 95 or Windows NT by using the serial ports on the Windows CE device and Windows 95 or Windows NT PCs. This connection allows the Windows CE Explorer and Windows CE synchronization programs to transfer data between the two computers. In this case, the Windows CE is connecting through *Remote Access Services* (RAS), so the applications are communicating using network protocols and not serial communications. These network protocols are described in Chapters 20 and 21. You should use serial communications when connecting to computers that don't support RAS.

Understanding Serial Communications Basics

In this section, I show you the basics of serial communications — how data is communicated through a serial cable, how serial communication ensures that the data is received reliably, and how to configure a serial port. As you become familiar with these concepts, you can attempt to add serial communication functions to your application.

Okay, here goes: Any form of data communication needs to transfer bytes of information between two devices as a series of *bits*. In *serial communications,* each bit is sent down a single wire — one bit after another. With *parallel connections,* on the other hand, each bit in a byte has its own wire through which the bits travel. (You may have come across parallel communications before. For example, the typical printer generally communicates with a PC through a parallel connection.)

The advantage of serial communications is that a serial connection requires fewer wires to connect the two devices (which makes the connectors much smaller). Although parallel communications is generally much faster, the connector would be too big for most Windows CE devices.

The serial communications standard most commonly in use is *RS-232C.* The RS-232C protocol defines how data is transferred through a serial cable, including how each wire is used in the cable and how the bits of data are sent between the serial ports. While several different standards are in use (such as RS-232C and RS-232), they are usually referred to collectively as RS-232.

Making the connection

You use a *multicore cable* (which is a cable containing many separate wires) to make a serial connection between two computers. Each wire in the cable is attached to a pin on a connector, and each pin is given a number. *Pins* are small gold-plated pegs that fit into corresponding holes in the computer. The pins are located in a *connector,* which is usually made of plastic, and is attached to the multicore cable. Normally you push the connector into a *port,* which has sockets for each of the pins in the connector, and is usually located on the back or side of the device.

Windows CE devices generally use one of three types of serial connectors:

✔ **25-pin connector:** This type of connector (shown in Figure 19-1) has all the pins defined by the RS-232 standard. This type of connector is found frequently on modems, which may require all the functionality provided by RS-232.

✔ **9-pin connector:** This connector (shown in Figure 19-2) is the most common type used with PCs.

✔ **Mini-connector:** The serial port on a Windows CE device is generally much smaller and a different shape than the 9-pin connector found on PCs. Mini-connectors tend to be specific to each manufacturer. Mini-connectors typically have the same pins as the 9-pin connector.

Figure 19-1:
25-pin connectors offer the full range of RS-232 pins.

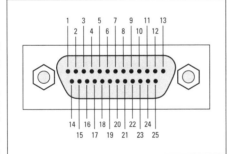

Figure 19-2:
Pins on a 9-pin connector.

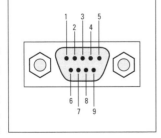

If you need to connect your Windows CE device to a non-PC device (such as a computer other than a PC), you may need to get a special cable made up by an electronics store (the documentation that comes with your device should specify what pins are required). If you need to get a special cable made, get a *male* 9-pin connector at the Windows CE device end. This connector can then be attached to the *female* 9-pin connector on the serial cable supplied with most Windows CE devices. Your connection is then: Windows CE device⇨Standard Serial Cable⇨Custom Made Cable⇨non-PC device.

The 9- and 25-pin connectors are known as *male* (when pins are present) and *female* (when holes are present). In computing, male connectors can only be joined with female connectors.

While each pin is given a number, these numbers are different on the 25-pin and 9-pin connectors. For example, pin 4 on a 25-pin connector is numbered 7 on a 9-pin connector. Table 19-1 lists the pins commonly used on 9-pin and 25-pin connectors.

Table 19-1		Commonly Used Pin Numbers	
25-Pin	*9-Pin*	*Name*	*Description*
2	3	TD	Transmit data. Data is sent along this wire to the other device.
3	2	RD	Receive data. Data is received from the other device along this wire.
4	7	RTS	Ready to send. This device is ready to send data.
5	8	CTS	Clear to send. This device is ready to accept data.
6	6	DSR	Data set ready. The data receiving device is connected and is ready to communicate.
7	5	GND	Signal Ground. Ensures that both devices are using the same voltages for transmitting data.
20	4	DTR	Data terminal ready. The data terminal device is ready.

DSR and DTR are used by RS-232 to indicate that the two devices at either end of the cable are ready to communicate. When you connect two devices with a serial connection, you nominate one device to be the terminal (the Data Terminal Equipment, or DTE) and the other the host (the Data Computer Equipment, or DCE).

CTS and RTS are used by RS-232 to indicate whether a device is ready to send or receive data. These pins provide *hardware handshaking*. Handshaking ensures that one device does not transfer data until the other device is ready to receive the data, and that a device stops sending data when the other device can no longer receive data — basically, handshaking makes sure that data is not lost. Handshaking can either be controlled by hardware (for example, using the CTS and RTS pins), or by software (where special data is sent between the two devices to control the transfer of data).

Configuring a port

Before attempting to communicate through an RS-232 serial connection, you must ensure that the serial port is properly configured at each end of the connection, and that you use compatible configurations. The section "Programming Serial Communications," later in this chapter, shows you how to write code to configure the serial port. The most important configuration options, however, are as follows:

- **Communications speed:** This is the rate at which data is transferred between the two devices.

- **Handshaking:** This is how the flow of data between the two devices is controlled.

- **Bit settings:** This specifies how the data is sent as a series of bits (1's or 0's). Parity and the number of stop bits are used to specify the bit settings.

It is essential that both devices are transmitting and receiving characters at the same speed. Remember that data is transmitted as a series of bits (which are translated into electrical pulses). The communication speed determines the duration of each electrical pulse, and the time interval between each byte. The baud rate is used to specify communication speeds for serial connections. Common baud rates are 1200, 2400, 4800, 9600, 14400, 19200, and 56000 electrical pulses per second. See the sidebar called "Baudy bytes and other technical trivia" for more information.

Baudy bytes and other technical trivia

The *baud rate* — the number of electrical pulses that can be transmitted per second — specifies the communication speed between two serial devices. For slow transmission rates (below about 1200 baud), each bit is transmitted as a single electrical pulse. Each byte of data must be proceeded by a start bit and followed by an end bit. Because 10 bits in total are required to transfer each byte, the effective transmission rate (in characters) equals the *baud rate divided by 10*. At higher communication speeds, more than one bit can be encoded in a single pulse, so the relationship between baud rate and transmission rate (in number of characters) does not hold. For this reason, transmission rates at higher speeds are often quoted as *characters per second* (cps).

Serial communication devices use two forms of handshaking:

- **Software handshaking:** Special characters are sent in with the data that starts or stops the data transmission. XON/XOFF is the most common software handshaking technique. A receiver sends an XOFF (by default, Ctrl+S) character when it cannot receive more characters, and an XON (by default, Ctrl+Q) character when it is ready to receive more characters. This handshaking protocol is commonly used in terminals talking to minicomputers and other host computers.

- **Hardware handshaking:** The CTS and RTS pins are used to control the flow of data. This handshaking technique is commonly used with Windows CE devices. (Refer to Table 19-1.)

You typically use either software handshaking or hardware handshaking, but not both. After you implement one form of handshaking, the other is redundant.

Not using handshaking is dangerous — your application is very likely to lose data.

A byte is always preceded by a *start bit* — a single bit of data that precedes the actual byte of data being sent. The byte (which contains eight bits) is then transmitted, and is followed by one or more *stop bits*. A stop bit is another bit of data that marks the end of the data in the byte being sent. These days, nearly everyone uses a single stop bit, which means that each byte is actually sent as a total of 10 bits.

Parity is a primitive technique for detecting transmission errors. Rather than using all 8 bits in the byte for representing data, the eighth bit is used to check that the other 7 data bits are correct. For example, when *even parity* is used, the number of 1's in the 7 data bits is counted — if this number is even, the eighth bit is set to 1; if the number of 1's in the 7 data bits is odd, the eighth bit is set to 0.

Parity is not generally used (except in some older terminal systems) because:

- ✔ Binary data and the full range of ANSI characters cannot be easily transmitted.
- ✔ The error detection is primitive, and errors can often go undetected.

Programming Serial Communications

Writing code for communicating through a serial port requires the following general steps:

1. **Open the communications port.**

2. **Configure the port to match the configuration of the device you're communicating to.**

3. **Read and write data to the port, as appropriate.**

4. **Close the port.**

Ports are accessed, believe it or not, through the same functions as are used for file I/O. The port is opened by calling `CreateFile`, and closed by calling `CloseHandle`. Some important differences do exist, though:

- ✔ **Port configuration:** You must configure the port after opening it to ensure the correct settings.

- ✔ **Timing issues:** Reading and writing to a port require special programming because of timing issues. For example, how long should you wait for data to arrive at the port? How do you know when data has arrived at the port? See the sections "Reading from the port" and "Writing to the port" later in this chapter, for more information.

You can refer to Chapter 18 for more information on the file I/O functions used in Windows CE.

The workspace \samples\sercom\sercom.dsw (which you can find on the CD-ROM at the back of this book) contains code for a simple serial communications application. This application contains code for all the basic communications techniques. The application allows the user to enter text and then send this text to the host computer. Choosing Comms⇨Send Buffer sends the text to the host. Any text returned from the host is displayed in the lower (read only) edit box (as shown in Figure 19-3). You can actually use this code in your applications.

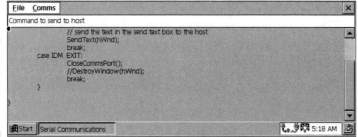

Figure 19-3:
Sample
serial
commu-
nications.

Microsoft Visual C++ for Windows CE ships with a sample application and code called TTY. This application shows you how to implement a simple terminal application for Windows CE. You can find this application located in the folder \Program Files\DevStudio\WCE\SAMPLES\WIN32\TTY.

Opening the port

The port is opened by calling the function CreateFile. The first argument you pass to CreateFile is the name of the port that you want to open; for example, COM1:. Code Listing 19-1 shows the parameters you should pass to CreateFile to open the port.

Code Listing 19-1

```
hCommPort = CreateFile (TEXT("COM1:"),
    GENERIC_READ | GENERIC_WRITE,
    0,
    NULL,
    OPEN_EXISTING,
    0,
    NULL);
```

You *must* include the colon at the end of the port name on Windows CE. (This is optional on Windows NT and Windows 95, so it may take a bit of getting used to.)

If the call to CreateFile results in an error, the value INVALID_HANDLE_VALUE is returned. You should call GetLastError to get the error code associated with the error.

One of the most common error codes returned from create file is 55, indicating that the port is already open. In this case, you should prompt the user to close down the application that has the communications port open.

Closing the port

Call the function `CloseHandle` to close the port when you finish using it. This function takes a single argument, which is the handle returned from `CreateFile` when the port was opened:

```
CloseHandle(hCommPort);
```

Configuring the port

Windows CE uses the default port settings when you call the function `CreateFile`. You generally need to set the port settings (such as baud rate and parity) to match the host you're communicating to. The `DCB` structure contains members for all the configurable port settings. The functions `GetCommState` and `SetCommState` use the `DCB` structure to retrieve or set port settings.

Be sure to set the timeout values using the `COMMTIMEOUTS` structure. These values specify how much time must elapse before a read or write operation will timeout. An error is returned to your application when a timeout occurs.

You should configure the port after opening it but before reading or writing to it. If you try to read or write before you correctly configure the port, default settings are used. These default settings are unlikely to be correct for the device that you're communicating with, so your attempt to read or write data will fail.

The function `OpenCommsPort` in sercom.cpp in the sample workspace \samples\sercom\sercom.dsw contains all the code necessary to open and configure a communications port on a Windows CE machine, suitable for communicating with a PC running Windows NT or Windows 95. Note that the baud rate is hard coded at 19200 — you probably want to change this to one of the values shown in the section called "The DCB structure" if you use this code in your applications.

The DCB structure

The DCB structure has about 30 different members that are used to configure the communications port. Luckily, only a few of these are frequently used, and they are:

  ✔ `DCBlength`: This member should be set to the length of the DCB structure before passing the variable to *any* function, as Code Listing 19-2 shows.

Code Listing 19-2

```
DCB dcb;
dcb.DCBlength = sizeof(DCB);
```

✔ BaudRate: The required baud rate should be assigned to this member either as a numeric (for example, 9600) or as a constant (for example, CBR_9600).

For example, you can set the baud rate to 19200 by writing:

```
dcb.BaudRate = CBR_19200;
```

✔ ByteSize, Parity, and StopBits: These members are used collectively to specify the number of bits that are transmitted and their meaning. These days, hardly anyone uses parity, so you can nearly always use Code Listing 19-3 to initialize the members.

Code Listing 19-3

```
dcb.ByteSize      = 8;
dcb.Parity        = NOPARITY;
dcb.StopBits      = ONESTOPBIT;
```

✔ fOutX and fInX: These members are used to specify whether XON/XOFF software flow control is to be used. Although you can specify XON/XOFF in only one direction (for example, when sending), it is usual to configure XON/XOFF for both sending and receiving.

Code Listing 19-4 turns off XON/XOFF flow control. You can assign TRUE to both members to turn XON/XOFF flow control on.

Code Listing 19-4

```
dcb.fOutX      = FALSE;
dcb.fInX       = FALSE;
```

You should use either hardware flow control or software flow control, but not both at the same time. It is very dangerous not to use any flow control, because this will result in data loss. Hardware and software flow control are described in the section "Making the connection," earlier in this chapter.

✔ fRtsControl and fOutxCtsFlow: Ready to send (RTS) and Clear to send flow (CTS) control is the most common form of hardware hand-shaking. Code Listing 19-5 turns on RTS/CTS handshaking.

Code Listing 19-5

```
dcb.fOutxCtsFlow = TRUE;
dcb.fRtsControl = RTS_CONTROL_HANDSHAKE;
```

You can assign the value TRUE to the member to enable CTS handshaking or FALSE to disable. RTS handshaking is a little more complex, because several options exist other than simply setting RTS handshaking to TRUE or FALSE. The following values can be assigned to fRtsControl:

- RTS_CONTROL_HANDSHAKE: Enables RTS handshaking. This implements flow control.

- RTS_CONTROL_DISABLE: Turns off the RTS line when the port is opened. Use this if you're not using RTS flow control and the host device ignores the state of the RTS line.

- RTS_CONTROL_ENABLE: Turns on the RTS line when the port is opened. Some hosts require that the RTS line be on for the entire time that the connection remains open.

✔ fOutxDsrFlow and fDtrControl: Data Set Read (DSR) and Data Terminal Ready (DTR) can be used for flow control, although it's much less common than CTS/RTS. More commonly, hosts require that the DTR line is turned on for the entire time the connection remains open. I recommend that you turn on the DTR line. Code Listing 19-6 turns on the DTR line when the connection is opened and disables DSR flow control.

Code Listing 19-6

```
dcb.fDtrControl = DTR_CONTROL_ENABLE;
dcb.fOutxDsrFlow = FALSE;
```

Getting and setting DCB settings

After opening a port, you can call the function GetCommState to obtain the default DCB settings from Windows CE. The function SetCommState is used to change the current settings based on the values in a DCB structure.

You should call GetCommState to get the current communications settings and then modify the structure. You can then call SetCommState to set the new values. This is much easier than trying to configure a DCB structure from scratch.

Code Listing 19-7 shows how to get the current settings. The hCommPort handle (obtained when you call CreateFile) is passed to specify the port to return the values for. In this code, they are returned in the DCB structure.

Code Listing 19-7

```
DCB dcb;
dcb.DCBlength = sizeof(DCB);
GetCommState(hCommPort, &dcb);
```

It's most important that you initialize the DCBlength member before calling GetCommState. If you don't do this, the call to GetCommState fails or returns incorrect data.

After modifying the DCB members (as described in the previous section), you can call SetCommState to set the new values. This reconfigures the port with the settings that you need to communicate:

```
SetCommState(hCommPort, &dcb)
```

The COMMTIMEOUTS Structure

The COMMTIMEOUTS structure contains values that specify the timeout values when reading from a port using ReadFile and writing to a port using WriteFile. If a call to ReadFile or WriteFile times out, the number of characters successfully read or written are returned.

When communications programs don't work

Serial communications programs often don't work for a variety of different reasons. The following are some of the most common problems:

✔ **No communication at all:** The cable perhaps has incorrect pin connections for the device you're trying to connect to. Try using some standard communications packages (such as terminal emulators) to test the connection before developing your own applications.

✔ **Garbage is received:** If the characters appear as garbage, or as white or black boxes, then you probably have different baud rate or parity settings on the two devices you're trying to have communicate. Check the settings used when opening the port.

✔ **Characters are lost:** This indicates that you're not using flow control (for example, XON/XOFF or CTS/RTS), or you're not using the correct one for the device you're communicating with.

The following members can be set for read operations (all timings are in milliseconds):

- ReadIntervalTimeout: The maximum time that can elapse between two characters arriving at the port without a timeout occurring. The value 0 specifies that no timeout is used.

- ReadTotalTimeoutMultiplier: The timeout period for a read operation is calculated by taking the number of characters to be read multiplied by the ReadTotalTimeoutMultiplier.

- ReadTotalTimeoutConstant: The ReadTotalTimeoutConstant value is added to the result of multiplying the number of bytes to be read by ReadTotalTimeoutMultiplier to give the overall timeout for a single read operation.

For multitasking reasons, it is often preferable that a call to ReadFile return immediately with the characters waiting to be read. This is the technique used in the sample workspace \samples\sercom\sercom.dsw (which you can find on the CD-ROM at the back of this book). The following code assigns special values to a COMMTIMEOUT structure to cause ReadFile to return immediately with any characters waiting to be read (see Code Listing 19-8).

Code Listing 19-8

```
COMMTIMEOUTS ct;
ct.ReadIntervalTimeout = MAXDWORD;
ct.ReadTotalTimeoutMultiplier = 0;
ct.ReadTotalTimeoutConstant = 0;
```

MAXDWORD is the maximum value that can be stored in a DWORD variable. This is a very large number, and one that you would not normally pass to ReadIntervalimeout.

You can use two members to configure timeouts for writing, using WriteFile:

- WriteTotalTimeoutMultiplier: The timeout period for a write operation is calculated by taking the number of characters to read multiplied by the WriteTotalTimeoutMultiplier.

- WriteTotalTimeoutConstant: The WriteTotalTimeoutConstant value is added to the result of multiplying the number of bytes to write by WriteTotalTimeoutMultiplier, to give the overall timeout for a single write operation.

Code Listing 19-9 sets values for the members used to configure timeouts for writing.

Code Listing 19-9

```
ct.WriteTotalTimeoutMultiplier = 10;
ct.WriteTotalTimeoutConstant = 1000;
```

With these settings, a write of 50 bytes will timeout after (10*50) + 1,000 milliseconds, which is 1,500 milliseconds, or about 1.5 seconds.

Getting and setting COMMTIMEOUTS settings

The current COMMTIMEOUT settings can be obtained by calling the GetCommTimeouts and SetCommTimeouts functions. Because COMMTIMEOUT has only a few members, programmers often initialize the structure from scratch (Code Listing 19-10), and pass it to SetCommTimeouts.

Code Listing 19-10

```
COMMTIMEOUTS ct;
ct.ReadIntervalTimeout = MAXDWORD;
ct.ReadTotalTimeoutMultiplier = 0;
ct.ReadTotalTimeoutConstant = 0;
ct.WriteTotalTimeoutMultiplier = 10;
ct.WriteTotalTimeoutConstant = 1000;
SetCommTimeouts(hCommPort, &ct);
```

Writing to the port

After opening and configuring the port, you can write data to the port using the WriteFile function. This is how you transfer data with the device at the other end of the serial cable.

While WriteFile allows you to write multiple bytes of data to a port in one go, you probably find it easier to write single bytes, because you need to convert Unicode characters to ANSI characters when transferring text data.

When calling WriteFile, you must pass the following arguments:

✔ **Open port handle (returned from** CreateFile**):** For example, hCommPort.

✔ **A pointer to the data to be written:** This is typically an array of characters or pointer to binary data.

✔ **The number of bytes to be written out:** This is the number of bytes in the array of characters or the pointer to binary data.

✔ **A pointer to a** DWORD **variable:** This is filled with the number of bytes actually written and allows you to check exactly how much of the data was transferred.

✔ NULL: Overlapped I/O is not supported under Windows CE.

Code Listing 19-11 takes the text contained in a text box (with the window handle hSendBox) and sends it character-by-character to the port, using WriteFile. Use the function GetWindowTextLength to determine the number of characters to send, and the function GetWindowText to fill the array szBuffer with the text from the text box.

Code Listing 19-11

```
DWORD dwBytesToWrite = GetWindowTextLength(hSendBox);
DWORD dwBytesWritten;

TCHAR szBuffer[256];
GetWindowText(hSendBox, szBuffer, 255);

for(DWORD i = 0; i < dwBytesToWrite; i++)
{
  if(!WriteFile(hCommPort,
      &szBuffer[i],
      1,   // bytes to write to port
      &dwBytesWritten,
      NULL))
  {
      DWORD dwErr = GetLastError();
      // report error
  }
}
```

In this code, szBuffer is declared as a TCHAR array, which means that each array element has two bytes. Most serial connections do not use Unicode characters — they use single byte ANSI characters. Therefore, the first byte in each character in the buffer szBuffer is sent — and this contains the ANSI code version of the Unicode character.

Reading from the port

Data coming from a host computer is read from the port when you call the ReadFile function. This function takes the same arguments as WriteFile, which is described in the previous section called "Writing to the port."

You can read data from a port whenever you expect the data to arrive. For example, you may write to a port (say, send a command to a host computer), and then attempt to read characters coming back from the host computer (the results of executing the command on the host computer).

For many communications applications, you may find it more convenient to create another thread and have this thread constantly waiting for data to arrive at the port — as the data arrives, it is processed.

Refer to Chapter 13 for more information on creating and managing threads.

The sample application in \samples\sercom\sercom.dsw uses this technique of creating a thread to read data (displayed in a read-only text box) coming from the host. The thread function is called `CommReadThreadFunc`, and the thread is created after the port is opened and configured in the function `OpenCommsPort`. This code can form the basis of your own communications applications.

Communications events

With Windows CE, you can't read and write data to the port at the same time. If you call `ReadFile` with a long timeout, any calls to `WriteFile` wait until the `ReadFile` completes or a timeout occurs. This can disrupt the transfer of data. Instead of calling `ReadFile` and waiting for data to arrive, you should use communications events. A *communications event* is a notification received by your application from Windows CE, indicating that something significant has occurred — for example, data has been received. To use a communications event, you should:

- ✔ **Call** `SetCommMask`: The call to this function specifies the event or events that you're interested in responding to. In the following call, the single event `EV_RXCHAR` is specified, which means that the application is interested in the event called "characters received:"

  ```
  SetCommMask (hCommPort, EV_RXCHAR);
  ```

- ✔ **Call** `WaitCommEvent`: The call to this function won't return until the specified event (for example, `EV_RXCHAR`) has occurred. You can specify multiple events when `SetCommMask` is called, so the call to `WaitCommEvent` returns the actual event that happened in the variable called `fdwCommMask`. The last parameter in this call is an overlapped I/O option that is not supported under Windows CE:

  ```
  WaitCommEvent (hCommPort, &fdwCommMask, 0);
  ```

- ✔ **Call** `SetCommMask`: When `WaitCommEvent` returns, you know that the event you're interested in has occurred (that is, characters have been received). Before calling `WaitCommEvent` again (to wait for more characters), you must call `SetCommMask` again with the same arguments to again specify the events that you're interested in responding to.

After WaitCommEvent returns, there is now data waiting to be read from the port. You should call ReadFile to receive this data, and this is described in the next section, "Reading data from the port."

The function call to WaitCommEvent does not return until data has arrived at the port. You can now see why applications often create a thread to read incoming data — you don't want your main thread to be held up with calls to WaitCommEvent. If your main thread is held up, your application cannot redraw the application window or respond to the user selecting menus.

The thread function generally has a loop that performs the following tasks repeatedly:

- ✔ Call SetCommEvent
- ✔ Call WaitCommEvent
- ✔ Call ReadFile multiple times to read the data one byte at a time
- ✔ Start again by calling SetCommEvent

Reading data from the port

After you know that data is available to be read, you can call ReadFile. The arguments are the same as required for WriteFile: the port handle, a pointer to a variable to receive the data, the number of bytes to read, and a pointer to a DWORD variable to receive the actual number of bytes read (Code Listing 19-12).

Code Listing 19-12

```
TCHAR cChar;
DWORD dwBytesRead;
ReadFile(hCommPort,
     &cChar,
     1,
     &dwBytesRead,
     NULL))
```

As with WriteFile, it is easiest to read the characters one at a time. You need to take care with ANSI to Unicode conversions, and this conversion is easiest with single character reads.

After you know that data is available to be read, you should call ReadFile repeatedly, reading one byte at a time. If you specify the timeout values shown in Code Listing 19-10, the call to ReadFile returns immediately, with dwBytesRead set to 1 if a byte is read, or set to 0 if no more data is waiting to be read.

After all the data has been read, you go back in the loop to calling `WaitCommEvent` to wait for the next characters to be received at the port.

Code Listing 19-13 shows a thread function that reads data from the port.

Code Listing 19-13

```
DWORD WINAPI CommReadThreadFunc(LPVOID lpParam)
{
  TCHAR cChar;
  DWORD dwBytesRead;
  DWORD fdwCommMask;

  SetCommMask (hCommPort, EV_RXCHAR);
  while(hCommPort != INVALID_HANDLE_VALUE)
  {
      WaitCommEvent (hCommPort, &fdwCommMask, 0);
      SetCommMask (hCommPort, EV_RXCHAR);
      do
      {
          if(!ReadFile(hCommPort, //(the open comm port)
                  &cChar, 1, &dwBytesRead, NULL))
              {
                  // report error
                  return 0;  // terminate thread
              }
          if(dwBytesRead > 0)
              {
              // deal with the data
              }
      } while(dwBytesRead == 1);
  }
  return 0;
}
```

Notice in Code Listing 19-13, that the while loop continues looping while `hCommPort` is not equal to `INVALID_HANDLE_VALUE`. When the main thread closes the port, it sets `hCommPort` to `INVALID_HANDLE_VALUE`. `WaitCommEvent` returns immediately when the port is closed with an error, and this while loop then completes.

Testing serial communications

More than likely, you'll test serial communications on a Windows CE device that's connected to the PC that runs Microsoft Visual C++. So, the serial port on the Windows CE device is being used as a RAS connection to transfer the application down onto the Windows CE device. When your application runs under Windows CE, the application fails to open the port, because the RAS connection already has the port open.

In this section, I show you how to close the RAS connection so that you can use the serial ports on both the desktop PC and Windows CE device.

When writing an application that uses serial communications to a device other than your desktop PC, you need to close down the RAS connection on the Windows CE machine, disconnect the serial connection from the desktop machine, and reconnect the serial connection on the target device. You can then run your application on the Windows CE device.

Closing the RAS connection

After Visual C++ downloads your application to the Windows CE device, you must close the RAS connection by following these steps on your PC:

1. **Choose Start⇨Microsoft Windows CE Services⇨Mobile Devices.**

   This action opens the Mobile Devices window, which contains a list of all the Windows CE devices that are connected, or have been connected in the past, to your desktop PC.

2. **Choose File⇨Communications.**

   This action opens the Windows CE Services Properties dialog box, as shown in Figure 19-4. This dialog box allows you to change the Windows CE communication options, and lets you control how and when a Windows CE device can connect to the desktop PC. Figure 19-4 shows how the dialog box looks when automatic connections are allowed by the desktop PC (the first Enabled check box is checked).

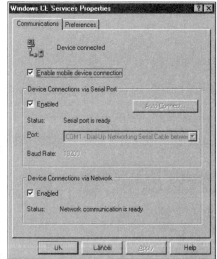

Figure 19-4: The Windows CE Services Properties dialog box.

If the Windows CE Devices icon appears in the taskbar status area (which is also known as the taskbar notification area — it's on the right-hand side of the taskbar) of your desktop PC, you can simply right-click the icon, and choose Communications to display this dialog box.

3. **Uncheck the Enabled check box in the Device Connections Via Serial Port group box.**

   This check box disables connections via the serial connection and closes any existing connections.

4. **Click OK.**

   This action closes the port on the desktop PC and Windows CE device.

After you carry out these steps, your PC and Windows CE devices are no longer communicating (the RAS connection has been broken) and the serial ports on the PC and Windows CE device can now be opened by other applications.

Testing a Windows CE application's serial communications

After you close the RAS connection, you can run your Windows CE application (which can now open the port on the Windows CE device).

When you first start writing serial communications software, I suggest that you use a *terminal emulation package* that tests the basic communications of your application. Windows NT is supplied with HyperTerminal, which works well for this purpose.

You can use HyperTerminal to test communications with the sample application called sercom, located in the workspace \samples\sercom\sercom.dsw on the CD-ROM, by following these steps:

1. **Compile and download sercom.exe to your Windows CE device.**

   You can find instructions for compiling the sample applications in the Appendix.

   Don't try to run sercom.exe at this stage (if you do, you'll see a message box displaying an error 55 on the Windows CE device, which means the port is already open).

2. **Disconnect RAS.**

   Follow the steps outlined in the section called "Closing the RAS connection" to disconnect the RAS connection.

3. **Run sercom.exe on the Windows CE device.**

   This program should be located in the root folder by default. This should display the user interface shown in Figure 19-3, but without the text in the text boxes.

4. **Choose Start↪Programs↪Accessories↪HyperTerminal↪ HyperTerminal on the desktop PC.**

This action starts HyperTerminal on the desktop PC. HyperTerminal displays a dialog box that prompts you for a name for the connection.

5. **Enter** HPC **for the Connection Name, and then click OK.**

The settings you configure are saved under this name. You can reuse these settings when you run HyperTerminal again — the name H/PC appears on the HyperTerminal menu.

Clicking OK then displays the Connect To dialog box.

6. **Choose COM1 from the Connect Using combo box (drop-down list box).**

If your Windows CE device is not connected via COM1, select the appropriate device name.

7. **Click OK.**

This displays the Port Settings dialog box.

8. **Choose the appropriate port settings (Figure 19-5), and then click OK.**

Figure 19-5 shows the settings that you should use for connecting to sercom.exe. The application sercom.exe hard-codes various communications options, so it's important to match exactly these options in HyperTerminal.

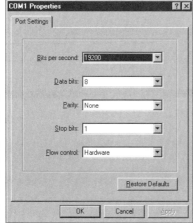

Figure 19-5:
Hyper-
Terminal
settings to
communicate
with
sercom.exe.

9. **Try sending text from HyperTerminal to sercom.exe.**

Any characters that you type into HyperTerminal appear in the lower of the two edit boxes in sercom.exe.

10. **Try sending text from sercom.exe to HyperTerminal.**

Enter text into the upper of the two edit boxes in sercom.exe, and choose Comms⇨SendBuffer.

11. Close down HyperTerminal and sercom.exe

Don't do this until you finish testing the communications!

The next section, "Reopening the RAS connection," shows you how to re-establish the RAS connection. You may need to modify your communications application, so the RAS connection is required to download a new version of your application to the Windows CE device.

Reopening the RAS connection

Before reopening the RAS connection, be sure that your communication applications on the Windows CE device and desktop PC have been closed down.

To reopen the RAS connection, open the Windows CE Services Properties dialog box (as described above in the section "Closing the RAS connection"), check the Enabled check box in the Device Connections Via Serial Port box, and click OK.

Using the Infrared Port

The infrared port can be used for serial communications to other devices such as PC's or printers with infrared ports.

The following are the steps you need to set up communications through the infrared port:

1. Open the infrared port.

Use the CreateFile function as I described in the section "Opening the port". Obtain the port number from the registry key \HKEY_LOCAL_ MACHINE\Comm\IrDA\Port. The port number may not be the same on all devices. You can refer to the section "Getting to Know the Windows CE Registry" in Chapter 17 to find out how to open the Windows CE Registry and find keys.

2. Place the port into IR mode.

Call the function EscapeCommFunction passing SETIR as the function value:

```
EscapeCommFunction(hCommPort, SETIR);
```

After this, use the standard serial communications functions.

While infrared port communication speeds are faster than serial ports, they are often unreliable. In particular, infrared ports cannot send and receive data at the same time.

Chapter 20

Programming Windows Sockets

. . . .

In This Chapter

▶ Understanding socket communications

▶ Writing a socket client application

▶ Writing a socket server application

. . . .

*S*ockets provide a reliable mechanism for Windows CE applications
to communicate with other computers on a Transmission Control
Protocol/Internet Protocol (TCP/IP) network. TCP/IP is a network protocol
that specifies how data can be put into packets and sent across the network
to another computer. You can connect your Windows CE device configured
for TCP/IP to a desktop PC that uses Remote Access Services (RAS) or to
another computer that uses Point to Point Protocol (PPP). You can also
connect with a modem that uses PPP to an Internet Service Provider (ISP),
so you can use Windows sockets to communicate with other computers on
the Internet.

You can take the code directly from the code listings in this chapter and
implement socket communications in your own applications.

Refer to *TCP/IP for Dummies,* 2nd Edition, by Candace Leiden and Marshall
Wilensky (IDG Books Worldwide, Inc.), for complete information on the
TCP/IP protocol and TCP/IP networks.

What's a Socket, Anyway?

Think of a *socket* as a black box on a computer that a socket on another
computer can be connected to. The *connection* is the network on which the
computers reside. (The two sockets that are communicating can reside on
the same computer.)

You need to provide two pieces of information to connect to a socket:

- ✔ **The Internet Protocol (IP) address of the computer on which the socket resides:** The IP address can be specified using the standard numeric format (for example, 192.168.55.100) or as a URL (say, www.dummies.com).

- ✔ **The port number:** A computer can have several different sockets that you can connect to that serve different purposes. Each different socket has a unique number. Standard protocols (such as HTTP) have standard port numbers (80 in the case of HTTP). You can use port numbers above 1024 for your own purposes.

Using Client and Server Sockets

An application that can act as a *server* (and so provide information to other applications) allows other applications (the *clients*) to connect to it. The client application then requests information from the server, and this information is returned to the client application.

After a socket connection is made between two applications, the sockets are actually *peers* — that is, a two-way data communication is formed, with neither socket necessarily acting as a server or client. However, in many cases, one socket acts as a server and the other acts as a client. This makes the design and implementation of your applications easier.

An application that allows other applications to connect to it through the use of sockets must create a listening socket. The *listening socket* is a special type of socket in that it waits for another socket to connect to it, thereby creating a connection. This listening socket is created by the application for a specified IP address and port number.

The IP address must always be the IP address used by the computer on which the listening socket is created. Usually, the listening socket defaults to the IP address of the computer on which it is created. Sometimes, a computer has several IP addresses, and in this situation, you must specify which IP address to use.

You can only create one listening socket with a particular IP address and port number. An attempt to create another listening socket with the same IP address and port number will fail.

After a listening socket is created, it waits for another application to connect to it. An application can connect to a listening socket by creating its own socket and then connecting to the listening socket. The IP address and port number of the listening socket must be specified.

When a listening socket receives a request to connect, it creates an ordinary socket for the application that owns the listening socket. This new socket is set up to communicate to the socket that makes the connection request. The listening socket then goes back to listening for another connection request.

If the connection between the two applications is maintained for a significant amount of time (say, for more than a second or two), the application with the listening socket must be multithreaded. The listening socket requires a thread on which to listen, and each connection needs its own thread so that one connection doesn't block another connection.

Either of the two applications can send text or binary data through the socket connection. Typically, one application acts as the server and the other as the client. The client sends a request to the server for data, and the server responds with the data. If you write both the client and server applications, you can make up your own protocols, deciding on the format of the request that the client makes and how the data will be returned.

The connection can be closed at any time by either of the applications. The other application will be notified of the closure.

Writing Socket Applications

You can write socket applications using two techniques:

- ✔ **Standard socket functions:** Using these functions is not the easiest way because the order of bytes used for sending data is different from that used on Windows CE.

- ✔ **MFC socket classes:** These classes make using sockets much easier and more reliable. I use the MFC classes in this chapter.

I use two applications as an example of how to write a simple client/server application that uses sockets to communicate. The client application (called *sockcli,* that runs on Windows CE) connects to the server application (called *socksrv,* that runs on Windows NT or Windows 95). The *sockcli* application sends a filename and the *socksrv* application returns the contents of the file (which exists on the Windows NT or Windows 95 PC). This is illustrated in Figure 20-1. The socket connection is then closed.

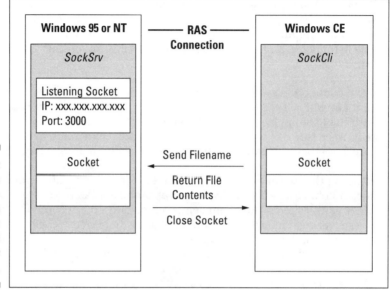

Figure 20-1:
The communications between the sockcli and socksrv applications.

Understanding the MFC Socket Classes

The MFC classes that you're likely to use when writing Windows CE applications are CCeSocket (on Windows CE devices), CSocket (on Windows NT and Windows 95 PCs), CSocketFile, and CArchive (both of which are available in Windows CE, Windows NT, and Windows 95). These classes give you member functions that allow you to read and write from sockets as if they were ordinary files. This makes your job of creating socket applications much easier, because you're dealing with familiar techniques.

CSocket and CCeSocket

You use CSocket in Windows 95 and Windows NT applications, and CCeSocket in Windows CE applications to create sockets, read data from the sockets, and write data to the sockets.

CSocket is available on Windows CE, but you should always use CCeSocket instead. CSocket attempts to use features for controlling communications (such as waiting for data to arrive at a socket) that are not present in Windows CE, and should only be used with Windows 95 and Windows NT. CCeSocket uses Windows CE features to implement features such as waiting for data to arrive at the socket.

When using the CCeSocket class, you may need to include wcesock.h in your source code. This includes the class declarations and other definitions.

The CCeSocket and CSocket classes provide the following functionality:

- **Create a socket:** A socket is created by calling the Create member function.

- **Connect to a socket:** The Connect member allows you to connect to a socket on another machine.

- **Create a listening socket:** You can create a listening socket by calling the Listen member function. When another socket attempts to connect, the Accept member function is called, and this returns another CSocket or CCeSocket class object that is connected and ready to communicate.

- **Sending and receiving data:** You can call the member functions Send and Receive to send data to and receive data from a connected socket.

- **Closing a socket:** The member function Close closes a socket connection. Close is called in the CCeSocket or CSocket destructor, so you don't need to call it yourself.

CArchive and CSocketFile

You may already use the CArchive class for reading and writing files from within MFC — this process is called *serialization*. Classes are generally expected to be serializable so that they can write or read their data content to an archive. You can also serialize simple data types, such as WORD or DWORD data values. The CArchive class can be used with sockets in place of files. Therefore, any class that can serialize itself to a file can serialize itself to a socket.

After you create a CSocket or CCeSocket class object, a CSocketFile class object can be created based on the socket. Then, you can create a CArchive object based on the CSocketFile, and so the CArchive object can read or write to the socket. This is illustrated in Figure 20-2.

Archives, which are implemented using the CArchive class, are described in Chapter 18.

A CArchive object can only write or read through a socket. You must create a CArchive object for writing and another for reading if you want two-way communication through the socket.

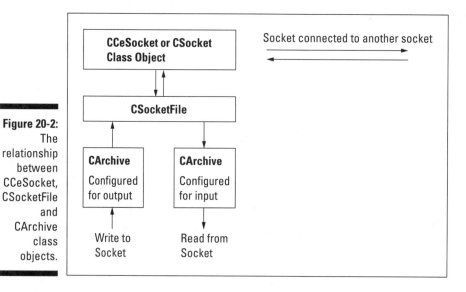

Figure 20-2:
The relationship between CCeSocket, CSocketFile and CArchive class objects.

Using the sockcli Application

You can copy the source code off the CD-ROM from the \samples\socksrv directory and compile this application using the instructions in the Appendix. This produces a file called socksrv.exe that you can execute on either Windows NT or Windows 95.

You should run the sockcli application on the same PC that your Windows CE device is connected to. The socksrv application displays a status dialog box with the message Waiting for Connection, as shown in Figure 20-3. This is updated when sockcli connects.

Figure 20-3:
When run, the socksrv application displays a status dialog box.

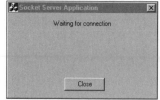

The application socksrv creates a listening socket, and it uses the default IP address for the computer on which it runs. See the section entitled "Using the socksrv Application," later in this chapter.

Connecting to the correct IP address

When you run sockcli.exe, the application prompts for the IP address of where socksrv is running. You can enter either:

- ✔ **A host name** (for example, dummies.com) if your TCP/IP network has a Domain Name Server (DNS).

- ✔ **An IP Address** (for example, 192.168.55.99).

If you don't know the IP address of the computer running socksrv, you can follow these steps:

1. **Run the Control Panel application, and click the Networks icon.**

    The Network dialog box appears. Be sure to note the contents of the field called Computer Name — you use it in Step 3. I assume (for the purposes of this example) that your computer has the name Mary.

Note: You should run the Control Panel on the same machine that you're running socksrv (that is, a Windows 95 or Windows NT PC).

2. **Run a command shell.**

    You can run command.com on a Windows 95 PC or cmd.com on a Windows NT PC.

3. **Type the ping and the information from the Computer Name field (in the Network dialog box) in the command shell:**

    ping *Mary*

    This command executes the ping application that attempts to connect to the specified computer. Take note of the IP address that ping gets a reply from.

You can use the WCE MFC AppWizard to create a Windows CE application that uses sockets. You must be sure that the Windows sockets check box is selected in the Step 2 dialog box in the AppWizard.

Where to put the socket code

In the document/view architecture used by MFC, the document is responsible for loading and saving the data used by the application. Because sockets are also used to load and save data associated with the application, the document should manage the sockets — the only difference is that sockets don't read and write to *files,* but to other *applications.*

Creating a socket class

One of the most difficult tasks in programming is to figure out when data is waiting to be read from the socket. If you try to read data from a socket, you may have to wait for quite some time before the data is available for reading.

During this time your application is *blocked* — that is, unable to complete any other tasks. (An application is blocked when it is waiting for something to happen, such as data arriving at the socket, during which time the application cannot perform tasks such as painting windows or handling input from the user.)

The CCeSocket class has the member function OnReceive, which you can override if you create a new class that inherits from CCeSocket. Your override is called whenever data is available for reading.

In the sockcli application, I created a new class called CCliSocket that inherits from CCeSocket. This class has two member functions: a new constructor and an override of OnReceive.

CCliSocket constructor

The document class CSockCliDoc in sockcli is responsible for managing the socket and the communications that go along with it. Therefore, this new class, CCliSocket, must be able to call member functions in the class CSockCliDoc. For this reason, the CCliSocket class has a constructor with an argument that is a pointer to the CSockCliDoc document class with which it is associated. This CSockCliDoc pointer is saved in a CCliSocket member variable called pDoc, as shown in Code Listing 20-1.

Code Listing 20-1

```
CCliSocket::CCliSocket(CSockCliDoc *pInDoc)
{
    pDoc = pInDoc;
}
```

OnReceive override

The CCliSocket also overrides the CCeSocket::OnReceive member function. The OnReceive member function is called whenever data is ready to be read from the socket. The CSockCliDoc class has three functions that are called by OnReceive:

- MoreToRead: Returns TRUE if more characters can be read from the socket.

- GetLine: Returns a line of text from the socket — the new line and carriage return characters are not returned.

- AppendText: Appends (concatenates) a CString class object onto the text currently being stored in the document. This text is placed in the edit box in the view when all of the file has been received.

If terms like "inherits," "appends," and "concatenates" don't sound familiar to you, check out *C For Dummies,* Volumes I and II, by Dan Gookin and *C++ For Dummies,* 2nd Edition, by Steven R. Davis (both by IDG Books Worldwide, Inc.).

You may notice that while this code is being executed in a class inherited from CCeSocket class, it does not access the socket directly. This is because the document class uses CArchive class objects for reading and writing through the socket. See Code Listing 20-2 for the OnRecieve member function.

Code Listing 20-2

```
void CCliSocket::OnReceive(int nErrorCode)
{
    CString s;
    while(pDoc->MoreToRead())
    {
        s = pDoc->GetLine();
        pDoc->AppendText(s + "\r\n");
    }
}
```

Remember that all strings in Windows CE are Unicode. This application assumes that the strings being received from the socket are Unicode strings. The socksrv application (running on Windows NT or Windows 95) converts ANSI strings to Unicode characters (see the section called "Using the socksrv Application," later in this chapter).

The CSockCliDoc class

The CSockCliDoc class (which inherits from CDocument) is responsible for creating the sockets and managing reading and writing through the socket using archives. The CSockCliDoc class has the following member declarations (shown in Code Listing 20-3) for the socket related class objects.

Code Listing 20-3

```
CCliSocket* m_pSocket;
CSocketFile *m_pSocketfile;
CArchive *m_pArcIn, *m_pArcOut;
```

The CSockCliDoc class has a CString member variable called m_Content that holds the contents of the file as it is received from socksrv.

The following member functions implement reading and writing of information through the socket and the manipulation of the file contents being received from socksrv (discussed in "Using the socksrv Application," later in this chapter).

- ✔ GetLine: Reads a line of text from the m_pArcIn archive, which performs a read from the socket.

- ✔ SendString: Sends a line of text to the m_pArcOut archive, which performs a write to the socket.

- ✔ AppendText: Appends a string onto the end of the m_Content string.

- ✔ MoreToRead: Returns TRUE if there are characters to be read from the m_pArchIn archive.

The next six short sections describe the code that I've added to CSockCliDoc. To really appreciate how the code fits together, you should open the sockcli.dsw workspace in Developer Studio — only then can you see the complete picture and understand how the code fits together.

The CSockCliDoc constructor

The CSockCliDoc constructor creates all the objects for managing the socket (Code Listing 20-4). The following arguments are passed to the constructors for these objects:

- ✔ CCliSocket(this): This class (described in the last few sections) is passed a pointer to a CSockCliDoc class object — this refers to the current class object.

- ✔ CSocketFile(m_pSocket): The CSocketFile constructor has an argument that is a pointer to the CCeSocket derived class with which it will be associated.

- ✔ CArchive(m_pSocketfile, CArchive::load): The first CArchive object pointer, m_pArcIn, is passed a pointer to the CSocketFile object that's just been created, and the constant CArchive::load. This constant configures this archive for loading (that is, reading) from the socket.

- ✔ CArchive(m_pSocketfile, CArchive::store): The second CArchive object pointer, m_pArchOut, is passed CSocketFile object, pointed to by m_pSocketfile, and the constant CArchive::store. This constant specifies that the archive is for storing, (that is, writing) to the socket.

Code Listing 20-4 shows all the code for the CSockCliDoc constructor.

Code Listing 20-4

```
CSockCliDoc::CSockCliDoc()
{
  m_pSocket = new CCliSocket(this);
  m_pSocketfile = new CSocketFile(m_pSocket);
  m_pArcIn = new CArchive(m_pSocketfile, CArchive::load);
  m_pArcOut = new CArchive(m_pSocketfile, CArchive::store);
}
```

CSockCliDoc::OnNewDocument

The CSockCliDoc::OnNewDocument member function is called by MFC whenever a new document is created (for example, when the user chooses File➪New).

The code fragments shown in the following bullet list don't include the error checking code that's present in the sample application. You should always check for errors when calling socket functions.

In this application, OnNewDocument is used to

- ✔ **Get the IP address and filename:** The dialog class CSelectFile is used to prompt the user for the IP address and filename to receive from the socksrv application.

- ✔ **Create the Socket:** The following code creates the socket. Note that at this stage, it's not connected.

  ```
  m_pSocket->Create();
  ```

- ✔ **Connect to the socksrv listening socket:** The IP address (which is obtained from the CSelectFile dialog in the member variable) and the port number (I selected 3000) are passed to this function:

  ```
  m_pSocket->Connect(dlg.m_HostName, 3000)
  ```

- ✔ **Send the filename to socksrv:** The filename (obtained from the CSelectFile dialog box) is sent to socksrv (covered in the section "Understanding the socksrv Application") followed by carriage return and linefeed characters. The socksrv application responds by sending the contents of the specified file using the SendString function:

  ```
  SendString(dlg.m_Filename + "\r\n");
  ```

CSockCliDoc::OnNewDocument has no code with which to receive the text sent by socksrv. The CCliSocket::OnReceive function is called by MFC, whenever text is waiting at the socket. The CCliSocket::OnReceive member function reads the text and adds it to the document by calling CSockCliDoc::AppendText.

CString CSockCliDoc::GetLine

This member function reads the next line of text from m_pArchIn using the CArchive::ReadString member function. GetLine returns the string to the caller (see Code Listing 20-5).

Code Listing 20-5

```
CString CSockCliDoc::GetLine()
{
    CString s;
    m_pArcIn->ReadString(s);
    return s;
}
```

CSockCliDoc::SendString

The CSockCliDoc::SendString member function sends through the socket using the m_pArcOut archive object's WriteString member function. This is followed by a call to Flush to ensure that the text is not buffered in the archive and is actually sent out through the socket (see Code Listing 20-6).

Code Listing 20-6

```
void CSockCliDoc::SendString(LPCTSTR lpString)
{
    m_pArcOut->WriteString(lpString);
    m_pArcOut->Flush();
}
```

Always be sure to call the function Flush after writing to an archive. If you don't, the application you're attempting to communicate with doesn't receive the data. In the meantime, your application could be waiting for a response. Eventually, one of the applications will timeout and the communications will fail.

CSockCliDoc::AppendText

The CCliSocket::OnReceive member calls CSockCliDoc::GetLine to get a line of text, and then calls CSockCliDoc::AppendText to append it onto the m_Content variable.

The socksrv application (covered in the section "Using the socksrv Application," later in this chapter) sends a \a character as the first character in a line to mark the end of file. The character is produced by pressing Ctrl+A and has an ASCII value of 1 — this is an arbitrary character that does not occur in ordinary text files.

When a \a character is received, the contents of the variable m_Content must be copied into the view's edit box. This requires a pointer to the application's CEditView class object. (I copied the following code from that written by the AppWizard in CSockCliDoc::OnNewDocument.)

```
CEditView *pEdit =
        ((CEditView*)m_viewList.GetHead());
```

The CDocument class has a list of pointer variables to the view classes associated with the document. In Windows CE applications, you generally only have one view, so the GetHead call always returns a pointer to the one and only view in the application.

After the application has obtained a pointer to the CEditView class object, the application calls the SetWindowText member function to set the contents of m_Content into the edit box. At this point, the entire file has been received, so the socket can be closed by calling the CCeSocket::Close member function (see Code Listing 20-7).

Code Listing 20-7

```
void CSockCliDoc::AppendText(LPCTSTR lpStr)
{
    if(lpStr[0] == '\a')
    {
        CEditView *pEdit =
            ((CEditView*)m_viewList.GetHead());
        pEdit->SetWindowText(m_Content);
        m_Content = "";
        m_pSocket->Close();
        return;
    }
    else
        m_Content += lpStr;
}
```

CSockCliDoc::MoreToRead

The CSockCliDoc class provides the MoreToRead method that allows the CCliSocket class to determine whether it needs more information in order to read from the archive.

The CArchive class provides the IsBufferEmpty method that is used only when an archive is connected to a socket. IsBufferEmpty returns TRUE when there are no more characters waiting to be read, and FALSE if characters are waiting to be read (see Code Listing 20-8).

Code Listing 20-8

```
BOOL CSockCliDoc::MoreToRead()
{
    return !m_pArcOut->IsBufferEmpty();
}
```

Using the socksrv Application

You can copy the source code off the CD-ROM from the \samples\sockscli directory and compile this application using the instructions in the Appendix. This produces a file called sockcli.exe that can be downloaded and run on a Windows CE device.

The sockcli application is an MFC application that uses the CEditView class to display a text edit box in the view. When run, the application displays a dialog box called Socket Server Application that prompts for the IP address to connect to and the filename to download (see Figure 20-4). This filename refers to a file on the machine on which socksrv is running (that is, either a Windows 95 or Windows NT machine).

Figure 20-4:
The sockcli application prompts for an IP address and filename.

Select Filename	OK	X
Host Name:		
Remote filename:		

The sidebar "Connecting to the correct IP address," earlier in this chapter tells you how to find out the IP address of the PC that's running socksrv.

When a valid IP address and filename are entered, the sockcli application connects to socksrv and requests that the file be downloaded. The socket connection is closed when the download is complete. The contents of the file appear in the edit box of sockcli. You can then save this file by choosing File⇨Save As. (Choosing File⇨New repeats the process.)

The socksrv application uses much of the same code and techniques as sockcli. You can find two important differences, however:

✔ The socksrv application creates a listening socket that sockcli connects to.

✔ The socksrv application must convert ANSI characters to Unicode for text that's sent to sockcli, and Unicode to ANSI characters for text that's received from sockcli.

SockSrv is designed to be compiled as an ANSI character application so that it can run both on Windows NT and Windows 95. You could compile for Unicode (by including #define UNICODE in each source file in your application), and then the character conversions would not be required.

You can use the MFC AppWizard to create a Windows CE application that uses sockets. Be sure that the Windows sockets check box is selected in the Step 2 dialog box of the AppWizard.

I describe the code used to create and manage the sockets in the next three sections. You may find it easier to follow the code that I describe if you open the workspace \samples\socksrv\socksrv.dsw on the CD-ROM and review the code in Developer Studio.

You can use the same techniques described here for creating listening sockets on applications that run on Windows CE. You can create listening sockets in Windows CE applications as well as Windows NT and Windows 95 applications. When designing socksrv and sockcli, I implemented the listening socket on the Windows NT/95 application. However, I could have created the listening socket on Windows CE.

The listening socket

The socksrv application declares a new C++ class called CListeningSocket that is inherited from CSocket. This class is used to create a listening socket.

The class CSockSrvDlg contains a CListeningSocket class object, and it uses this object to create a listening socket when the dialog box appears when the application runs.

The following code is the declaration in CSockSrvDlg:

```
CListeningSocket m_listeningSocket;
```

Creating the listening socket

The listening socket is created in `CSockSrvDlg::OnInitDialog`, which is called when the application is first created. The listening socket is destroyed automatically by the `CSocket` destructor when the application terminates.

First, I create the socket and associate it with a port number by calling the member function `Create` (I use 3000 as my chosen port number):

```
m_listeningSocket.Create(3000);
```

The code just shown does not have error checks to ensure that the function calls works. You should always check the values returned from these function calls to ensure that they worked correctly. The code in the socksrv application does have error checking, however.

This function call to the `Create` member function uses the PC's default IP address. You can specify a specific IP address by specifying three parameters to the call to Create. `SOCK_STREAM` must be used to specify that this is a stream socket:

```
m_listeningSocket.Create(3000,
        SOCK_STREAM, _T("192.168.55.99"));
```

After you create the socket, you can set it to listen for a connection attempt by calling the `Listen` member function, as follows:

```
m_listeningSocket.Listen();
```

This function sets the socket into listening mode, and the `CListening Socket::OnAccept` member function is automatically called whenever a socket attempts to connect.

Responding to a connection request

`CListeningSocket::OnAccept` is called whenever Windows CE receives a connection request. In the socksrv application, `OnAccept` performs the following tasks:

- **Declares a CSocket object variable:** This is the socket that actually communicates with the other application. It is declared within the `OnAccept` member function, as follows:

  ```
  CSocket sSocket;
  ```

- **Accepts the connection:** A call is made to `CListening Socket::Accept` to accept the request to connect. The reference to the variable `sSocket` is passed as an argument. On return, `sSocket` connects to the socket in the other application, as follows:

```
Accept(sSocket)
```

- ✔ **Creates** `CSocketFile` **and** `CArchive` **objects:** This application communicates through the sockets by using archives. The code to create these objects, shown in Code Listing 20-9, is the same as the code described in the sockcli application.

Code Listing 20-9

```
CSocketFile *pSocketfile = new CSocketFile(&sSocket);
CArchive *pArcIn = new CArchive(pSocketfile,
        CArchive::load);
CArchive *pArcOut = new CArchive(pSocketfile,
        CArchive::store);
```

- ✔ **Gets the filename to send:** After the socket connection has been made, socksrv can read a string of text from the socket through the archive — this string contains the filename sent by sockcli, and the filename is terminated by the characters `\r\n`. The string is read by calling `CListeningSocket::GetUnicodeStr` (which is described in the section "CListeningSocket::GetUnicodeStr"):

  ```
  CString sFile;
  sFile = GetUnicodeStr(pArcIn);
  ```

- ✔ **Opens the file:** The specified file is opened through a `CStdioFile` class object (Code Listing 20-10). If the file can't be found, an error message is returned to sockcli.

Code Listing 20-10

```
CStdioFile stdFile;
stdFile.Open(sFile,
    CFile::modeRead | CFile::typeText);
```

- ✔ **Sends the file:** The file is read line by line. Each line, terminated with the characters `\r\n`, is sent to sockcli by calling the function `SendUnicodeStr`. Code Listing 20-11 converts the string to Unicode and sends it through the archive to sockcli.

Code Listing 20-11

```
CString sLine;
while(stdFile.ReadString(sLine))
{
    SendUnicodeStr(pArcOut, CString(sLine) + "\r\n");
}
```

✔ **Sends an end of file indicator:** The '\a' end of file indicator is sent to sockcli using the function `SendUnicodeStr`:

```
SendUnicodeStr(pArcOut, "\a\r\n");
```

✔ **Deletes** `CSocketFile` **and** `CArchive` **objects:** Because the variables `pArcIn`, `pArcOut`, and `pSocketFile` were dynamically allocated using the `new` operator, they must be de-allocated using the `delete` operator to free up the memory they occupy (see Code Listing 20-12).

Code Listing 20-12

```
if(pArcIn != NULL)
    delete pArcIn;
if(pArcOut != NULL)
    delete pArcOut;
if(pSocketfile != NULL)
    delete pSocketfile;
```

You should delete the `CSocketFile` object `pSocketFile` and `CArchive` objects `pArcIn` and `pArcOut` in the order shown in Code Listing 20-12. MFC reports an error when you try to delete the `CSocketFile` object first.

✔ **Closes the connection:** After sending the file, the function `OnAccept` returns. The variable `sSocket` goes out of scope and the `CSocket` destructor closes the socket automatically.

The socksrv application can't accept a connection from an application while it is transferring a file to another application. This is because the application only has a single thread. You have to create multiple threads if the socket connections must be kept open for a long period of time. The section "Weaving Threads" in Chapter 13 shows how to create threads.

CListeningSocket::GetUnicodeStr

This function gets a string from a socket through an archive. The function assumes that the string obtained from the socket is Unicode, and it converts it to ANSI characters.

The technique used here for converting Unicode to ANSI does not work for Unicode characters that are not present in the ANSI character set (for example, when using multi-byte character sets). When you work with character sets that use multi-byte characters, use the `wcstombs` function to convert Unicode to multi-byte and `mbtowc` to convert multi-byte to Unicode.

The `CListeningSocket::GetUnicodeStr` function performs the following tasks:

- ✔ **Loops, reading a** `WCHAR` **(Unicode) character one at a time:** Each Unicode character requires two bytes to be read from the archive `pArIn`.

- ✔ **Ignores carriage return characters:** All carriage return characters (\r) are ignored. `WCHAR` is cast to a `CHAR`, which means that this function ignores the second byte in the Unicode (which is a \0 character for ANSI characters stored in a Unicode character).

- ✔ **Terminates the loop on a new line character:** The `while` loop terminates when a new line character '\n' is received. The string `s` is returned to the caller.

- ✔ **Appends other characters to the** `CString` **variables:** All other characters are appended onto the `CString` variable `s`.

Code Listing 20-13 shows the code for `CListeningSocket::GetUnicodeStr`.

Code Listing 20-13

```
CString CListeningSocket::GetUnicodeStr(CArchive* pArIn)
{
  WCHAR wChar;
  CString s;
  while(TRUE)
    {
    pArIn->Read(&wChar, sizeof(WCHAR));
    if((char)wChar == '\r')   // ignore carrage returns
        continue;
    if((char)wChar == '\n')   // end of the line
        return s;
    s = s + (char)wChar;
    }
  return s;
}
```

CListeningSocket::SendUnicodeStr

Use this function to send a string to a connected socket through an archive (which is passed to the function as a parameter). The `CListening Socket::SendUnicodeStr` function (Code Listing 20-14) performs the following tasks:

✔ **Creates a** `for` **loop, looping for each character in the string:** Each character in the string pointed to by `s` is converted to Unicode and then sent to the connected socket.

✔ **Converts a character to Unicode:** Each character is converted from a one-byte ANSI character to a two-byte Unicode character. This is done by using the `MAKEWORD` macro that makes a two-byte value out of two single-byte values.

✔ **Flushes the buffers:** The `CArchive::Flush` method is used to ensure that all the data held in the archive's buffers is sent out through the socket.

Code Listing 20-14

```
void CListeningSocket::SendUnicodeStr(CArchive* pArOut,
          LPCSTR s)
{
  WCHAR wChar;
  for(UINT i = 0; i < strlen(s); i++)
  {
      wChar = MAKEWORD(s[i], 0);
      pArOut->Write(&wChar, sizeof(WCHAR));
  }
  pArOut->Flush();
}
```

Chapter 21

RAS and Network Support

*R*emote Access Services (RAS) is a facility provided by Windows that allows two Windows PCs to connect using serial communications. Windows CE supports RAS, but only as a client. Therefore, Windows CE makes a connection to another computer using RAS, but cannot accept RAS connection requests from other computers. A Windows CE device, therefore, can connect to a Windows 95 or Windows NT PC that's configured to accept RAS connections.

You can use Windows CE devices as network clients on many types of networks, enabling those devices to use shared resources just as Windows 95 and Windows NT PCs can. In this chapter, I show you how to connect to other computers using RAS and then use the WNet API functions to access shared resources.

Managing RAS Connections

You probably use a RAS connection to connect your Windows CE device to a Windows 95 or Windows NT PC. Most Windows CE devices have a preconfigured RAS connection called *Serial Port @ 19200*. You can also add and configure your own RAS connection entries, which you store in the Windows CE registry. (Configuring RAS connection entries is described in Windows CE 2.0 User Guide that is supplied with Windows CE devices.)

You can use RAS functions from within your own applications to make connections to other computers as necessary. Your applications can use the RAS functions to automate connecting to other computers, and I show you how to accomplish this in the next four sections.

The workspace \samples\rasconn\rasconn.dsw contains source code showing you how to find the RAS connection entries in the registry and how to make a connection to another computer by using RAS.

Add the #include statements shown in Code Listing 21-1 to all the .cpp files in your application that use the RAS functions. These two header files contain declarations for the RAS functions.

Code Listing 21-1

```
#include "afdfunc.h"
#include "raserror.h"
```

Using the RAS phone book

Windows CE manages a phone book containing entries that provide information on computers to which you can connect by using RAS. The user typically creates these entries, but applications can also create them too.

Each entry has a unique name and parameter values that specify dialing and connection options, including the following items:

- ✔ Phone number
- ✔ User name to use for connecting to the network
- ✔ Password (This option is valid only if the user elects to save the password)
- ✔ Network domain name to connect to
- ✔ Network options, such as protocols to use and a TCP/IP address to use

Windows NT enables you to store several different phone books in various files. If you're using Windows CE, you always find the phone book stored in the Registry under the registry key HKEY_CURRENT_USER\Comm\RasBook.

Your application may need to give the user the choice of which RAS phone book entry to use for connecting to a particular computer. The application usually accomplishes this task by displaying a list of the phone book entry names (such as Serial Port @ 19200) and enabling the user to select an entry from the list.

The names of the phone book entries are returned to you by Windows CE in a RASENTRYNAME structure. A RASENTRYNAME structure variable contains the name of one entry in the phone book, and has the following members:

▶ dwSize: This member should contain the size of the RASENTRYNAME structure, in bytes.

▶ szEntryName: This member contains the name of the RAS phone book entry. The constant RAS_MaxEntryName gives the maximum length in characters for the name.

You can call the function RasEnumEntries to return the list of RAS phone entry names (Code Listing 21-2). You need to pass the following parameters to the function RasEnumEntries:

▶ **Reserved:** The first parameter is reserved, and you need to pass it as NULL.

▶ **Location of phone book:** The phone book is always located in the registry, so this parameter should be NULL.

▶ **Pointer to array of** RASENTRYNAME **structures:** You need to pass an array of RASENTRYNAME structures and the function RasEnumEntries fills this array with the entry names. RasEnumEntries returns an error if this array isn't large enough to contain all the entries. Code Listing 21-2 dynamically creates an array of 20 RASENTRYNAME structures.

▶ **Pointer to a variable containing the size of** RASENTRYNAME **array:** The DWORD variable this argument points to should contain the size of the RESENTRYNAME array in bytes.

▶ **Pointer to a variable that returns the number of entries:** This DWORD variable contains the actual number of entries that the RASENTRYNAME array returns.

Code Listing 21-2

```
LPRASENTRYNAME lpRasEntry = NULL;
DWORD dwRes, dwSize, dwEntries;
lpRasEntry = new RASENTRYNAME [20];
lpRasEntry[0].dwSize = sizeof(RASENTRYNAME);
dwRes = RasEnumEntries(
        NULL,
        NULL,
        lpRasEntry,
        &dwSize,
        &dwEntries);
```

Don't forget to delete the memory that your application allocated using new for the RASENTRYNAME array. You can use the code in Code Listing 21-3.

Code Listing 21-3

```
if(lpRasEntry != NULL)
{
    delete [] lpRasEntry;
    lpRasEntry = NULL;
}
```

The value that `RasEnumEntries` returns is zero if the function call succeeds or an error value if it fails. The header file `raserror.h` defines the error codes.

The function call that your application makes to `RasEnumEntries` returns the error value `ERROR_BUFFER_TOO_SMALL` if the array pointed to by `lpRasEntry` isn't large enough to store all the RAS phone entries.

Code Listing 21-4 shows how you could add to a list box the entry names that `RasEnumEntries` returns:

Code Listing 21-4

```
for(i = 0; i < dwEntries; i++)
{
    SendMessage(hList, LB_ADDSTRING, 0,
            (LPARAM) lpRasEntry[i].szEntryName);
}
```

The `WM_INITDIALOG` handler in the function `RASDlgProc` that you find in the workspace \samples\rasconn\rasconn.dsw shows the complete code necessary for enumerating the RAS phone book entry names and adding them to a list box in a dialog box.

Making a RAS connection

You make a RAS connection by using the `RasDial` function. This function requires that you initialize a `RASDIALPARAMS` structure with connection information. If the `RASDIALPARAMS` structure doesn't contain sufficient connection information (such as the user name or password), Windows CE prompts the user with a User Logon dialog box.

The entries in this structure that are relevant to Windows CE are as follows:

- `dwSize`: You should initialize the `dwSize` member with the size of the `RASDIALPARAMS` structure in bytes.

- `szEntryName`: The RAS phone book entry name. The maximum length is `RAS_MaxEntryName` characters.

✔ szPhoneNumber: The phone number you want to connect to. The maximum length is RAS_MaxPhoneNumber characters.

✔ szUserName: The user name to use for logging onto the network. The maximum length of the user name is UNLEN characters.

✔ szPassword: The password to use for logging onto the network. Notice that the user may opt *not* to save the password, in which case Windows CE prompts for the password by using the User Login dialog box. The maximum length of the password is PWLEN characters.

✔ szDomain: The Windows NT domain that the program uses to validate the user name and password. The maximum length of the domain name is DNLEN characters.

The easiest way of initializing the RASDIALPARAMS structure is to follow these steps:

1. **Declare a variable of type** RASDIALPARAMS, **as shown in the following example:**

```
RASDIALPARAMS rasDialParams;
```

2. **Initialize the** dwSize **member with the size of the** RASDIALPARAMS **structure, as follows:**

```
rasDialParams.dwSize = sizeof(RASDIALPARAMS);
```

3. **Copy a valid RAS entry name into the** szEntryName **member, as follows:**

```
wcscpy(rasDialParams.szEntryName,
    TEXT("Desktop @ 19200"));
```

You can obtain the RAS entry name from the list box that you display to the user, which is described in the section "Using the RAS phone book."

4. **Call the function** RasGetEntryDialParams **(see Code Listing 21-5).**

The function RasGetEntryDialParams requires the following argument:

• **Location of phone book:** This argument must be NULL, because the phone book is in the registry.

• **Pointer to** RASDIALPARAMS **structure:** You should initialize the structure as I just described in Steps 2 and 3.

• **Pointer to** BOOL **variable:** This BOOL variable contains the value TRUE if you can obtain the password from the phone book; otherwise, the value is FALSE.

The function call to RasGetEntryDialParams results in information being placed in RASDIALPARAMS structure by Windows CE.

Code Listing 21-5

```
dwRes = RasGetEntryDialParams(
    NULL,
    &rasDialParams,
    &bPassword);
```

TIP

If the value in bPassword is FALSE (indicating that Windows CE cannot return the password), you may want to display your own dialog box that prompts the user only for the password and not for the other information that appears in the standard User Login dialog box. The user, therefore, can't change the other values, such as the domain or user name.

After the RASDIALPARAMS structure is initialized by the call to RasGet EntryDialParams, you're ready to make the connection. You need to pass the following arguments to the function RasDial:

- ✓ **RAS Extensions:** Because Windows CE doesn't support RAS extensions, you should pass NULL for this argument.

- ✓ **Location of phone book:** The phone book is always in the registry, so this parameter should be NULL.

- ✓ **Pointer to** RASDIALPARAMS **structure:** You should initialize the structure by calling RasGetEntryDialParams.

- ✓ **Notification Type:** This argument specifies how the application receives notifications about the status of the RAS connection. The only option under Windows CE is for message notification, so you should use the hexadecimal value 0xFFFFFFFF. I show you how to use notifications in the following section.

- ✓ **Notification Window handle:** This argument is the handle of the window that receives the WM_RASDIALEVENT notification messages.

- ✓ **Pointer to a** HRASCONN **variable:** This variable receives a connection handle representing the RAS connection. You should declare it as follows:

```
HRASCONN    hRasConn = NULL;
```

Code Listing 21-6 is an example call to RasDial.

Code Listing 21-6

```
dwRes = RasDial(
    NULL, NULL, &rasDialParams,
    0xFFFFFFFF, hWnd, &hRasConn);
```

The following are a few things to watch out for when making RAS connections:

- ✔ You should close the RAS connection after you finish with the connection by calling the RasHangup function. I describe the RasHangup function in the section entitled "Disconnecting a RAS connection," later in this chapter. Remember that the RAS connection may be using a phone line connection that costs money!

- ✔ If the User Login dialog box appears, Windows CE saves any changes that the user makes to the settings.

- ✔ The call to RasDial returns 0 if the function is successful or an error value if the function call fails. The error codes appear in a list in the header file raserror.h.

- ✔ Don't forget that your call to RasDial fails if another RAS connection or application has already opened the communications port or modem.

- ✔ The IDOK handler in the function RASDlgProc in the workspace \samples\rasconn\rasconn.dsw shows the complete code necessary for initializing a RASDIALPARAMS structure and calling RasDial.

Monitoring a RAS connection

You can monitor the status of a RAS connection by writing a handler for the WM_RASDIALEVENT message. Windows CE sends this message to the window whose handle was passed to RasDial.

The WPARAM value for this message specifies the reason why the notification is sent. The RASCONNSTATE enumeration defines these values. Some of the common values are as follows:

- ✔ RASCS_OpenPort: RAS is about to open the local communications port.

- ✔ RASCS_PortOpened: The local communications port has successfully been opened.

- ✔ RASCS_DeviceConnected: RAS has connected to the remote device.

- ✔ RASCS_Authenticated: The user has been authenticated on the specified network.

- ✔ RASCS_Connected: The RAS connection is now successfully connected.

- ✔ RASCS_Disconnected: The RAS connection is disconnected.

The LPARAM value for the WM_RASDIALEVENT message contains an error code if RAS detects an error in attempting to complete the step being notified or zero if RAS successfully completes the step.

Code Listing 21-7 notifies the user through messages boxes of RAS connects and disconnects.

Code Listing 21-7

```
case WM_RASDIALEVENT:
    if(uParam == RASCS_Connected)
        MessageBox(hWnd, TEXT("Connected!"),
                szTitle, MB_OK);
    else if(uParam == RASCS_Disconnected)
        MessageBox(hWnd, TEXT("Disconnected!"),
                szTitle, MB_OK);
    break;
```

Disconnecting a RAS connection

You should call the function RasHangUp connection after you no longer need the RAS connection. This function takes a single argument, as shown in Code Listing 21-8, which is the connection handle returned from calling RasDial.

Code Listing 21-8

```
if(hRasConn != NULL)
    RasHangUp(hRasConn);
hRasConn = NULL;
```

Network support

Windows CE supports a network stack that enables a Windows CE device to communicate with other computers by using the following protocols:

- ✔ TCP/IP
- ✔ NetBEUI
- ✔ IPX

Windows CE devices typically use a Point to Point Protocol (PPP) connection to a network through a serial connection, although direct network connections are supported with Windows CE, using PCMCIA network adapter cards. The PPP protocol allows network protocols to work across a serial connection.

You can use the WNet API functions to manage network connections. WNet is a set of functions available on Windows 95, Windows NT, and Windows CE that allows network connections to be created, so that files can be shared across a network. Although Windows CE supports many of the same network features through the WNet API as do Windows NT and Windows 95, you find some important differences, as the following list describes:

✔ **Universal Naming Convention (UNC) Support:** Windows CE uses UNC names for accessing network shares with names up to 64 characters in length. UNCs allow network shares to be specified directly, without first mapping to drive letter. For example:

```
\\serverName\shareName\filename.ext
```

✔ **No Drive Letters:** Windows CE doesn't support drive letters at all. Instead, it maps network shares to a subfolder in the \networks folder.

✔ **No Automatic restoring of connections:** Windows CE doesn't automatically restore connections after the user logs in. Instead, it stores information about these connections in the registry.

✔ **Use** GetLastError: Windows 95 and Windows NT use the function WNetGetLastError to retrieve error codes for WNet functions. Under Windows CE, you should call GetLastError instead.

The following list contains a few things to keep in mind when using the WNet functions:

✔ You should include the file Winnetwk.h in your source code whenever using the WNet functions.

✔ To use the WNet functions under Windows CE, you must have the libraries redir.dll and netbios.dll installed on the Windows CE device. If these libraries aren't installed, the WNet functions return the ERROR_NO_NETWORK error.

✔ If you use these functions under emulation, you need to link your application with MPR.LIB. If you're running in the emulation environment, you see the standard Windows NT network dialog boxes and not those that Windows CE uses.

✔ Information on persistent (or remembered) connections is stored in the registry. You can use the WNetOpenEnum function with the RESOURCE_REMEMBERED constant for the dwScope argument to find out information on remembered connections.

Making and Breaking a Connection

You can use the `WNetAddConnection3` function to make a network connection. You need to initialize a `NETRESOURCE` structure variable with all the information on how the connection is to be made (for example, the name the resource is shared as by the remote computer and the name the share will be known as by the Windows CE device).

You can use the `WNetConnectionDialog1` function to open a dialog box that enables the user to browse for network resources to connect to. You don't need to initialize a `NETRESOURCE` when calling the `WNetConnectionDialog1` function because Windows CE requests all the required information from the user.

You can use the `WNetCancelConnection2` function to disconnect a network connection. You can force a disconnection even if applications are currently using the resource.

Part VI
The Part of Tens

The 5th Wave   By Rich Tennant

"ONE OF THEIR BLIMPS BROKE ITS MOORING AND FLOATED IN HERE ABOUT TWO HOURS AGO. THEY HAVEN'T BEEN ABLE TO LOCATE IT YET."

In this part . . .

Using a complex chemical technique — okay, not really — I've condensed all the essential elements of this book into a few short lists. In this, the Part of Tens, I summarize the essential features every good Windows CE application should have. Then, I provide some pointers for helping you migrate an application from Windows NT or Windows 95 to Windows CE. Finally, I list some additional resources for knowledge and information that can get you up to speed quickly.

Chapter 22

Ten Important Features of Windows CE Applications

In This Chapter

▶ Adding great features to your applications
▶ Joining the Windows CE Logo Program

A Windows CE application doesn't have to be complex or large to be good. In fact, the small, lean, and fast applications often end up being the most popular. In this chapter, I list the ten most important features that a Windows CE application should have — in my humble opinion, of course! Include these features in your applications, and you're on your way to producing a great application.

Many of the tips in this chapter come directly from the Windows CE Logo Program. The program is designed to ensure that all Windows CE applications conform to the same standards and that the applications can coexist on the same device. Microsoft set up this program (which is run by Veritest, Inc.) to list, test, and verify a set of requirements and recommendations that your applications should support. Even if you don't want to put your application through the rigors of the Logo Program, you can benefit from adopting its standards and recommendations.

 Refer to the Windows CE Logo Program section in the appendix of the Windows CE SDK online help (not to be confused with the appendix in this book!). You can search for this section by selecting Help⇨Search in Developer Studio, and searching on the keywords Windows CE Logo Program. That section covers the requirements and recommendations that you should follow.

Focusing on Memory Usage

Memory is in short supply on Windows CE devices — both for storing data and for executing applications. Fortunately, many application specifications indicate the amount of memory that they require; this is often the first item that users need to know.

In Chapter 13, I explain how to use memory efficiently and how to determine how much memory your application uses. Chapter 13 provides suggestions and recommendations that help your application use up the smallest possible amount of memory. You should follow these guidelines to make your application memory efficient:

✔ Minimize global memory usage. The global variables in your application use global memory, as does memory that you allocate dynamically using the C++ new operator.

✔ Avoid using global variables or allocating memory for long periods of time.

✔ Implement a `WM_HIBERNATE` message handler to free as much memory and resources as possible.

✔ Look carefully at your file structures and database designs to ensure that memory is not being wasted. Make sure that all the data being stored in files and databases is actually required. You should remove any records from a database that are no longer being used.

Understanding the User Interface

While many of the Windows 95 and Windows NT user-interface principles apply to Windows CE, the small size of the Windows CE devices changes some of the rules. Be sure to check the following items in your application:

✔ Make sure that your application window does not have a caption bar.

Chapter 2 describes how to create windows without caption bars (using the API) and Chapter 3 shows you how to use the AppWizard with the MFC to do the same thing.

✔ Use a command bar in your application window.

Chapter 5 shows how to add a command bar to your application.

✔ Always place the menu on the far left side of the command bar.

In Windows CE, menus must be added to a command bar. Chapter 5 tells you how to do that.

✔ Be sure that menus and command bar buttons follow the standard order.

Chapter 5 shows you the correct order for menus and button bars in Windows CE applications. You should also look at the applications shipped with Windows CE (such as Pocket Word and Pocket Excel) to see how menus and buttons should be implemented.

✔ Design command bar buttons to support tooltips.

Tooltips are added when the command bar buttons are added to the command bar. You should refer to Chapter 5 for instructions and code examples.

✔ Locate the OK and Cancel buttons for dialog boxes in the caption bar.

Dialog boxes need special styles set to display the OK and Cancel buttons in the caption bar. Chapter 6 shows you how to do this.

✔ Design windows so that they don't overlap or aren't resizable.

The code shown throughout Chapter 12 shows the correct way of creating windows for Windows CE applications.

Including a Setup Program

Your application needs to include a setup program that the user runs from a desktop PC running Windows 95 or Windows NT. The setup program must perform the following tasks:

✔ Create a directory for the application

✔ Copy executable and other files to the appropriate locations

✔ Add any Registry entries that are required by the application

Chapter 9 shows you how to create an install (or setup) program for your application with all the required features I list here. An uninstall script, which is automatically created by this process, allows the user to remove the application.

Working with Desktop Communications

Communications in Windows CE applications are essential. For example, a Windows CE application may need to share data with companion programs that run on Windows NT or Windows 95, or communicate with other computers across the Internet. You can use several different communications techniques, depending on what you need to communicate. For example:

✔ **Serial communications:** Used to connect to mini computers and computers running operating systems other than Windows 95 or Windows NT, such as Linux. You can connect to Windows 95 or Windows NT using serial communications, but you normally use Remote Access Services to actually transfer information.

Chapter 19 tells you about serial communications, including instructions and code you can use to add serial communications to your own applications.

✔ **Remote Access Services (RAS) and Point To Point Protocol (PPP):** RAS allows you to connect to Windows NT and Windows 95 machines, and through PPP, transfer information as if you were connected directly to the network using the NetBEUI, TCP/IP, or IPX network protocols. This technique allows you to access files (so that they can be copied to the Windows CE device, or opened as if they were located in the object store). RAS and PPP are also used for connecting to Internet Service Providers (ISPs), so that the Windows CE device becomes part of the Internet.

Code and instructions for using RAS to connect to Windows 95 or Windows NT machines are shown in Chapter 21.

✔ **Windows Sockets:** Windows Sockets allow two applications running on separate computers to transfer data. Windows Sockets are often used across TCP/IP networks. For example, you can connect to HTTP and FTP servers using Windows Sockets.

Chapter 20 shows you how to write applications for Windows 95 and Windows NT that can communicate with applications running on Windows CE using Windows Sockets.

Adding Help Files

Windows CE users often use their devices away from their homes or offices, so they usually don't have access to printed manuals that describe how to use applications. You can alleviate this situation by providing help files that describe how to use your application. Because of memory restrictions, your help files shouldn't be very large, so I recommend that you concentrate on creating how-to items that describe how your application can be used to complete specific tasks.

Chapter 10 describes how to create help files for Windows CE applications using Hypertext Markup Language (HTML).

Saving Data and Settings Information

Your application should save data and settings in either the Registry, files that are in the object store, or in databases. Saving data and settings allows the data to be reloaded back into the application the next time the application is run. The Registry, files, and databases are used to store different types of data:

✔ **The Registry:** Store data relating to settings, preferences, and options that your users want to save in the Registry. This would include data such as the preferred font or color.

Check out Chapter 16 for instructions and sample code showing how to use the Registry.

✔ **Files:** Files are used to save data associated with an application that can't be structured into properties and records.

You can find out how to create, open, read, and write files in Chapter 18.

✔ **Databases:** Many applications use data that is organized into records (for example, address lists) that have well defined fields (for example, street, city, and state). Such data should be stored in databases.

Chapter 18 shows how to create, open, and close databases, together with instructions on how to add, delete, and update records in a database.

Using the Address Book

The Windows CE Logo Program does not allow your application to duplicate information that is held in the address book database. Therefore, you shouldn't maintain your own address information in your application's database or files. Instead, you should always access the address book database to add or retrieve address book information. This is to stop users from having to enter the same information in more than one application. The advantage to you is that you don't need to provide tools for updating the address information, because Windows CE provides the Contacts application to do this.

Chapter 12 describes the Windows CE functions that you can use to access the address book database.

Including Shell Support

The Windows CE shell provides the desktop user interface and related functions. Your application should use the following user interface shell features:

✔ **A shortcut to your application in the Programs folder:** Your users can choose Start➪Programs from the taskbar and run your application directly from the Programs folder.

✔ **The document name in the taskbar buttons:** Users can run more than one copy of your application with different documents open. Users can click the correct button on the taskbar for the document they want to work with.

✔ **Common dialog boxes where appropriate:** Users know how to use the command dialog boxes (for example, the file open and file save dialog boxes). Using the common dialog boxes also saves you development time!

Chapter 16 shows you how to add these shell features in your application.

Supporting Long Filenames

Windows CE fully supports long filenames — in fact, Windows CE does not differentiate between long and short filenames. A problem can arise, though, if your code makes invalid assumptions about which characters can be used in a filename. To avoid this, adhere to the following rules:

✔ Permit the user to enter filenames of up to 255 characters in length, including all uppercase and lowercase standard characters, embedded spaces, embedded periods, and so on.

✔ Strip leading and trailing spaces with the Save As command. If you're using MFC, you can use the `CString` class `TrimLeft` and `TrimRight` member functions to remove leading and trailing blanks. When programming using the API, use the C standard library string functions to manipulate character arrays.

✔ Design your application so that question marks anywhere in the filename prevent the user from saving the file. Your application does not need to display an error message.

✔ Make sure that your application allows the following characters in a filename: period (.), plus sign (+), comma (,), semicolon (;), equal sign (=), and brackets ([]). Your application should not display error messages when the user puts these characters in a filename.

Using the Windows CE Logo Program

To display the Windows CE Logo Program, your application must be verified by an independent laboratory run by VeriTest, Inc. You can find more details about this program by visiting `www.veritest.com` or by sending e-mail to `wcelogo@veritest.com`.

Chapter 23

Ten (or so) Tips for Porting Existing Windows 95/NT Applications

. . . .

In This Chapter

▶ Adapting a Windows NT or Windows 95 application for Windows CE

▶ Sharing code between applications

▶ Watching out for differences between Windows CE and Windows 95/NT

. . . .

*U*sers who have a Windows 95 or Windows NT application probably want to have a Windows CE version too. Windows CE programmers can use two approaches, depending on the type of application and how it's used:

✔ **Create a *companion* program:** In this case, you create a small application that has a sub-set of the Windows 95 or Windows NT desktop application's functionality. The application shares data (either as files or database records) with the desktop application, and allows this data to be synchronized. Pocket Word is a companion to Word For Windows.

✔ **Create a *mini* program:** Suppose your desktop application provides functionality such as Web browsing, but it doesn't have data that it needs to share with a Windows CE version. In this case, create a cut-down (or mini) version of your desktop application, carefully selecting the essential functionality that your users require. A mini program doesn't need to share or synchronize data between the desktop, Windows 95, or Windows NT version and the Windows CE version of your application. Pocket Internet Explorer is a mini version of Internet Explorer.

In either case, you need to make sure that you minimize the amount of reprogramming by sharing code between the Windows NT and Windows 95 version and the Windows CE version of your application. However, you must still ensure that you write a good Windows CE application.

Select Appropriate Features

Users typically only utilize 10 to 20 percent of an application's capabilities, which leaves you lots of opportunities to cut out features and still make an application fit onto a Windows CE device. Of course, the difficulty is selecting the proper 10 to 20 percent of the functionality that the users *do* use!

Following are some tips that may help you select the appropriate features:

- ✔ Revisit the prime task that the application is used for and select the functionality required to complete only that task.
- ✔ Limit the configuration options and preferences.
- ✔ When writing a companion program, rely on the desktop application to implement more advanced features. (Take, as an example, Pocket Word. This word-processing application allows you to type in text, but you really need Word for Windows to format a document.)
- ✔ Omit functionality that requires a complex user interface, such as fast keyboard input or precise mouse control. For example, drawing applications require the user to select and move drawing objects using the mouse to precisely position the objects. Such precise manipulation of drawing objects with the stylus in Windows CE is difficult.

Design the User Interface

Look carefully at your Windows NT/95 application's user interface and think about what you can cut out. For example:

- ✔ **Simplify Menus:** Look at all the menu commands and choose a subset of these commands that represents the essence of your application's features.
- ✔ **Reduce the number of toolbar buttons:** Review the toolbar buttons in your Windows NT/95 application. As a general rule, your Windows CE application should have no more than six buttons on the command bar.
- ✔ **Remove the status bar:** Windows CE applications don't generally use status bars, because there is too little screen space to display them.
- ✔ **Display data with care:** Look carefully at how data in your application appears. You don't have room for complex diagrams, detailed bitmaps, or large diagrams that don't scroll. The physical size of Windows CE device screens is much smaller than standard screens, and the screen resolution (the number of pixels that can appear across and down the screen) is much lower (the most popular resolution is 480 pixels x 240 pixels).

> ✔ **Don't rely on color:** At present, most Windows CE devices only support grayscale displays.
>
> ✔ **Simplify Dialog boxes:** Dialog boxes in Windows CE applications should be smaller and have fewer controls than in Windows NT/95 applications. You need to decide which controls are really important, and include only those.

In Chapters 3 and 4, I show you how to build a Windows CE application that has a standard interface. Chapter 5 looks at adding a command bar to your application, while Chapter 6 explains how to design and code dialog boxes.

Sharing Code

Windows 95, Windows NT, and Windows CE all share a similar Applications Programming Interface (API), but with important differences. You probably won't be able to maintain a single set of source files for all three platforms, but certain key source files should be sharable.

You can use #ifdef statements with _WIN32_WCE to compile different code for the Windows CE version. The C/C++ compiler defines the constant _WIN32_WCE for every source file that is compiled in a Windows CE application. In Code Listing 23-1, the hCursor member of the WNDCLASS structure is initialized differently for the Windows CE version of the application:

Code Listing 23-1

```
#ifdef _WIN32_WCE
    wc.hCursor = NULL;
#else
    wc.hCursor - LoadCursor(NULL, IDC_ARROW);
#endif
```

Adding Communications

When writing a companion program, you must have some mechanism for transferring data from the Windows CE application to the desktop. The most popular communications techniques are described in Part V:

> ✔ Serial communications (Chapter 19)
>
> ✔ Windows sockets (Chapter 20)
>
> ✔ Remote Access Services (RAS), Point to Point Protocol (PPP), and network support (Chapter 21)

Unicode Issues

If your desktop application is written for the ANSI (8-bit character) set, you need to ensure that the code that you share with the Windows CE application supports the Unicode character set. See the guidelines below for supporting both character sets:

- ✔ Use data types that are character-size neutral. For example, TCHAR and LPTSTR have the appropriate declarations whether they are used in an ANSI or Unicode application.

- ✔ Use #ifdef statements to conditionally compile code that is dependent on a particular character size. For example, code that calls string functions like strlen and wcslen requires #ifdef statements.

- ✔ Take care when transferring data from a Windows 95 or Windows NT application using the ANSI character set to a Windows CE application that uses Unicode.

The section "Changing to Unicode Strings" in Chapter 3 shows the techniques you need to use Unicode strings in your applications.

Missing Functions

The biggest problem that you will probably encounter when adapting Windows 95 or Windows NT applications to Windows CE is the number of API functions that are entirely missing, or have modified or limited functionality. Unfortunately, you have to encounter a lot of these through trial and error!

The Appendices in the Windows CE Reference in the on-line help (not to be confused with the Appendix in this book!), provide a list of functions that are either not supported in Windows CE, or have different or more limited functionality. The on-line help can be viewed from Developer Studio by clicking the InfoView tab.

Limiting Emulation Differences

The biggest mistake you can make is relying too much on emulation for testing your application. Emulation does not always faithfully emulate the differences between Windows NT and Windows CE function calls. Testing regularly on a true Windows CE device is essential. (See Chapter 2 for more on emulation.)

Chapter 24

Ten (or so) Important Windows CE Resources

. . . .

In This Chapter

▶ Visiting Web sites and newsgroups relating to Windows CE

▶ Locating books and other sources of information

. . . .

*K*nowing where to find the solution to a problem can save you much development time. In this chapter, I list various Windows CE resources that I find particularly useful.

Newsgroups are a particularly good source of information, as they allow you to converse with peers who can help you solve specific problems and answer difficult questions. After all, a problem shared can be a problem solved!

Microsoft Windows CE Web Site

Because you're now a full-fledged Windows CE developer, you want to keep up-to-date with the latest breaking news. The site, www.microsoft.com/windowsce, is the starting point for finding out what's happening with Windows CE and how people are using it.

For pure development news, go straight to www.microsoft.com/windowsce/developer, and don't worry about that commercial stuff! At this site, you can find developer information (such as white papers describing different Windows CE technologies) and software downloads. For example, running up to the release of Windows CE 2.0, Microsoft posted a beta version of the Windows CE Toolkit for Visual C++ and the Windows CE Toolkit for Visual Basic. However, because these packages were about 80MB *each,* you had to find a friend with a high-speed Internet link or dial-up over a weekend and say goodbye to your social life.

Look carefully at what you're downloading. Sometimes this software has an expiration date after which you're required to purchase a copy of the software!

You can also search the Microsoft knowledge base (www.microsoft.com/kb) for a list of common Windows CE problems.

As you would expect, the Microsoft Windows CE site is optimized for the Windows CE Pocket Internet Explorer (PIE). This means that the site detects that you're connecting with PIE and adjusts the width of the Web pages accordingly. Pretty cool, huh?

The Windows CE Webring

The Windows CE Webring is one-stop shopping for finding sites relating to all topics to do with Windows CE. The site is located at www.jimmy.com/morency/webring.html, and contains a growing list of links to Windows CE sites. The site's background is interesting too — it seems to encapsulate the essence of college life in the sixties.

You can even add your own site to the list of Windows CE sites through a registration form — instant fame and fortune (but I'm not promising either).

Software Paths Web Site

Being biased, I'm bound to mention the site www.softpath.ie/windowsce (because the site is run by the company I work for in Ireland). It's worth a visit, because you can find articles, code, and samples that relate to Windows CE development — hey, you'll also be visiting another country (electronically, of course).

Handheld PC Web Site

This site has some really great cartoon characters to guide you through the pages, but I suppose the main reason for visiting the site (at www.windowsce.com), is to find information about Windows CE. The site includes:

- ✔ News about new hardware and software, along with other stories that are important to Windows CE.
- ✔ Sources of shareware and freeware, with links to sites where shareware and freeware can be downloaded.

✔ Advertisements for second-hand equipment.

This equipment is useful for getting together a collection of Windows CE devices for testing.

✔ Links to other Windows CE-related Web sites.

Newsgroups

Web sites are great for browsing through information, and perhaps finding the answer to your problems (I'm talking *computer* problems here). However, what you may need sometimes is someone to call up and ask "Have you ever seen this problem before?" Well, I have some good news — that's what newsgroups are about. I frequently visit the newsgroup `microsoft.public.win32.programmer.wince` on the NNTP server `msnews.microsoft.com`. This newsgroup contains many postings by real live developers asking questions or posting replies. You can start by asking questions and before long, you'll probably see a question that you can answer. Go ahead, post the answer — you'll be repaying your debt to society!

Sample Applications

The Microsoft samples shipped with the Windows CE Toolkit for Visual C++ provide an invaluable source of ideas, inspiration, and (of course) source code! All of this stuff is located, by default, in \programfiles\devstudio\ wce\samples. You can find two directories — Win32 for API applications and MFC for Microsoft Foundation Class examples.

Other ...For Dummies Books

One of the really great things about Windows CE is that it shares so much in common with Windows NT and Windows 95. In this book, I show you lots of features that are specific to Windows CE, but many tips and techniques apply equally to Windows NT or Windows 95. So, if you like, you can now add Windows CE, *and* Windows 95, and Windows NT programming to your résumé!

However, if you're new to Windows API or MFC programming, you may want to take a look at *Visual C++ 5.0 For Dummies,* by Michael Hyman and Robert Arnson, and *Windows 95 Programming For Dummies,* by Steven R. Davis (both by IDG Books Worldwide, Inc.). Both of these books concentrate on Windows NT and Windows 95 programming specifics, and provide good, all around information that is also applicable to Windows CE development.

Microsoft Developers Network CD

Why reinvent the wheel — there's no fun or satisfaction in that. You'll probably be amazed how often the problem you grapple with has already been solved and the solution is on the Microsoft Developers Network CD (MSDN CD). Just a few minutes searching can save hours of frustration. (Mind you, it's no substitution for the latest Tom Clancy novel, but the CD does have its charm.)

All copies of Visual C++ and Visual Studio come with a copy of the MSDN CD. You'll need to subscribe in order to keep up-to-date with new copies of the MSDN CD.

Appendix

About the CD

In This Chapter

▶ Figuring out the system requirements

▶ Finding out what's on the CD

▶ Using sample applications

*T*he CD that comes with this book contains all the source code described throughout this book and two software package demos: CE Install and The Expense Tracker. The code examples are all contained in working Windows CE applications that you can compile and test on any Windows CE device — you can also copy the relevant code sections from the source code files directly into your own applications.

System Requirements

To use the CD, you need:

✔ A CD-ROM drive.

✔ Microsoft Windows NT 4.0.

You can always compile Windows CE applications on a PC running Windows 95, but you cannot run the emulation environment on Windows 95 because Windows 95 does not have full Unicode support — only Windows NT does.

✔ At least 24MB of RAM.

✔ Microsoft Visual C++ 5.0.

✔ Microsoft Visual C++ for Windows CE 2.0.

✔ Ideally, a Windows CE device with a working connection to your PC.

You can browse the source files without the Visual C++ development environment. You can open the .CPP and .H source files by using any text editor (such as Notepad) or word processor (such as Microsoft Word for Windows).

CE Install Demo

CE Install (from Applian Technologies, Inc.) is the fastest way to write installation programs for your Windows CE 2.0 applications. Just edit seven lines of text and that's it — you're done. (Check out the Applian Web site at www.applian.com/products/CEInstall/ceinstall.htm.)

The CD that comes with this book includes a free demo that comes in a game called Blox (itself, a cool arcade-type game), which gives you an example of how CE Install can work with your own applications. To install Blox, open the ceinstall folder on the CD and run bloxzip.exe.

Be sure that your H/PC is connected to your desktop (and if it is, just press OK in any dialog boxes that prompt you to connect it).

The Expense Tracker Sample Form

Expense Tracker is a sample form that was created in less than 30 minutes, using Visual CE, a visual development environment for Windows CE (from SYWARE, Inc.). Although you can't modify the form itself, the Expense Tracker gives you a good idea of the power of Visual CE. (Check out more information on Visual CE and SYWARE at www.syware.com.)

To install Expense Tracker, open the expsform folder on the CD and run expsform.exe. This is a self-extractor that copies the program's setup files to your Windows\Temp folder, and then runs the setup program.

Make sure that your H/PC is connected to your desktop when setup runs.

Sample Source Code

The sample Windows CE application source code is located in directories off the \samples directory. Each directory contains a Visual C++ workspace. Table A-1 lists the workspaces, together with the chapters in which they are described and the major features that they demonstrate.

Table A-1	List of Sample Projects on the CD-ROM		
Project Title	*Chapter*	*Topic*	*MFC/API*
Cardfile	N/A	Example of a complete Windows CE application using databases	API

Project Title	*Chapter*	*Topic*	*MFC/API*
CBar	5	Command bar with menu, buttons, and combo box	API
ConDB	12	Accessing the contacts database	API
dbMFC	11	Using MFC database classes for Authors database	MFC
DlgDisplay	6	Programming dialog boxes	API
DlgMFC	6	Programming dialog boxes with MFC classes	MFC
dllapp	15	Using DLL's. Contains the project TestDll that implements a DLL	API
DrawAPI	7	Drawing using API functions	API
FileIO	18	File I/O and serialization with Archives	MFC
FirstApp	3	Your first API application. The file mincode.txt contains the minimum code required to build an API application	API
GenSetup	9	Generic setup program for Windows 95 or Windows NT	API
MemMan	13	Memory management functions, processes, and threads	API
MFCFirst	4	First MFC Application	MFC
ObjStr	17	Object store and registry samples	API
pmgmt	14	Power management sample application	API
RASConn	22	Connecting using Remote Access Services (RAS)	API
SamHelp	10	Sample help files	MFC
SerCom	20	Serial communications	API
shelleg	16	Shell, common dialog boxes, and notification functions	API
SockCli	21	Socket client application	MFC

(continued)

Table A-1 *(continued)*

Project Title	Chapter	Topic	MFC/API
SockSrv	21	Socket server application (for Windows 95 or Windows NT)	MFC
start	1	Small application to test development environment	MFC

The Cardfile application is a fully working card file application for Windows CE which uses Windows CE databases. You should look at this source code to see how to structure a Windows CE application using the API. You can view the source files directly from the CD, but if you want to build and run the applications, just follow these steps.

1. **Copy the files.**

   Try using the self-extractor, called samples.exe, to copy all of the files to the C:\samples folder on your hard drive.

2. **Run Developer Studio and select File⇨Open Workspace.**

   The Open Workspace dialog box appears, where you can locate the folder that contains your newly copied workspace files.

3. **Click on the file with a .dsw extension and choose Open.**

   The workspace opens and loads all the project information. You can now use Developer Studio to browse through the source files.

4. **Choose Build⇨Set Active Configuration.**

   By choosing this command before building the application, you ensure that the correct target device is selected. This command displays the Set Active Project Configuration dialog box. You can select either Win 86em for emulation on the desktop PC or MIPS or SH3, depending on which chip your Windows CE device has.

   You can find out what type of chip your Windows CE device has by clicking the System icon in the Control Panel on your Windows CE device. The name of the chip (for example, SH3 or MIPS) appears in the System Properties dialog box.

5. **Choose Build⇨Execute to build and run the application.**

   This builds and executes the application on the specified target device.

After you explore the source code and run the application, you can copy the appropriate source code directly into your application.

Index

• ♪ •

(continued)

(continued)

(continued)

• W •

• X •

IDG Books Worldwide, Inc., End-User License Agreement

READ THIS. You should carefully read these terms and conditions before opening the software packet(s) included with this book ("Book"). This is a license agreement ("Agreement") between you and IDG Books Worldwide, Inc. ("IDGB"). By opening the accompanying software packet(s), you acknowledge that you have read and accept the following terms and conditions. If you do not agree and do not want to be bound by such terms and conditions, promptly return the Book and the unopened software packet(s) to the place you obtained them for a full refund.

1. **License Grant.** IDGB grants to you (either an individual or entity) a nonexclusive license to use one copy of the enclosed software program(s) (collectively, the "Software") solely for your own personal or business purposes on a single computer (whether a standard computer or a workstation component of a multiuser network). The Software is in use on a computer when it is loaded into temporary memory (RAM) or installed into permanent memory (hard disk, CD-ROM, or other storage device). IDGB reserves all rights not expressly granted herein.

2. **Ownership.** IDGB is the owner of all right, title, and interest, including copyright, in and to the compilation of the Software recorded on the disk(s) or CD-ROM ("Software Media"). Copyright to the individual programs recorded on the Software Media is owned by the author or other authorized copyright owner of each program. Ownership of the Software and all proprietary rights relating thereto remain with IDGB and its licensers.

3. **Restrictions on Use and Transfer.**

    (a) You may only (i) make one copy of the Software for backup or archival purposes, or (ii) transfer the Software to a single hard disk, provided that you keep the original for backup or archival purposes. You may not (i) rent or lease the Software, (ii) copy or reproduce the Software through a LAN or other network system or through any computer subscriber system or bulletin-board system, or (iii) modify, adapt, or create derivative works based on the Software.

    (b) You may not reverse engineer, decompile, or disassemble the Software. You may transfer the Software and user documentation on a permanent basis, provided that the transferee agrees to accept the terms and conditions of this Agreement and you retain no copies. If the Software is an update or has been updated, any transfer must include the most recent update and all prior versions.

4. **Restrictions on Use of Individual Programs.** You must follow the individual requirements and restrictions detailed for each individual program in the "About the CD" Appendix of this Book. These limitations are also contained in the individual license agreements recorded on the Software Media. These limitations may include a requirement that after using the program for a specified period of time, the user must pay a registration fee or discontinue use. By opening the Software packet(s), you will be agreeing to abide by the licenses and restrictions for these individual programs that are detailed in the "About the CD" Appendix and on the Software Media. None of the material on this Software Media or listed in this Book may ever be redistributed, in original or modified form, for commercial purposes.

5. **Limited Warranty.**

   (a) IDGB warrants that the Software and Software Media are free from defects in materials and workmanship under normal use for a period of sixty (60) days from the date of purchase of this Book. If IDGB receives notification within the warranty period of defects in materials or workmanship, IDGB will replace the defective Software Media.

   (b) **IDGB AND THE AUTHOR OF THE BOOK DISCLAIM ALL OTHER WARRANTIES, EXPRESS OR IMPLIED, INCLUDING WITHOUT LIMITATION IMPLIED WARRANTIES OF MER-CHANTABILITY AND FITNESS FOR A PARTICULAR PURPOSE, WITH RESPECT TO THE SOFTWARE, THE PROGRAMS, THE SOURCE CODE CONTAINED THEREIN, AND/OR THE TECHNIQUES DESCRIBED IN THIS BOOK. IDGB DOES NOT WARRANT THAT THE FUNCTIONS CONTAINED IN THE SOFTWARE WILL MEET YOUR REQUIREMENTS OR THAT THE OPERATION OF THE SOFTWARE WILL BE ERROR FREE.**

   (c) This limited warranty gives you specific legal rights, and you may have other rights that vary from jurisdiction to jurisdiction.

6. **Remedies.**

   (a) IDGB's entire liability and your exclusive remedy for defects in materials and workmanship shall be limited to replacement of the Software Media, which may be returned to IDGB with a copy of your receipt at the following address: Software Media Fulfillment Department, Attn.: *Windows® CE 2 Programming For Dummies,* IDG Books Worldwide, Inc., 7260 Shadeland Station, Ste. 100, Indianapolis, IN 46256, or call 800-762-2974. Please allow three to four weeks for delivery. This Limited Warranty is void if failure of the Software Media has resulted from accident, abuse, or misapplication. Any replacement Software Media will be warranted for the remainder of the original warranty period or thirty (30) days, whichever is longer.

   (b) In no event shall IDGB or the author be liable for any damages whatsoever (including without limitation damages for loss of business profits, business interruption, loss of business information, or any other pecuniary loss) arising from the use of or inability to use the Book or the Software, even if IDGB has been advised of the possibility of such damages.

   (c) Because some jurisdictions do not allow the exclusion or limitation of liability for conse-quential or incidental damages, the above limitation or exclusion may not apply to you.

7. **U.S. Government Restricted Rights.** Use, duplication, or disclosure of the Software by the U.S. Government is subject to restrictions stated in paragraph (c)(1)(ii) of the Rights in Technical Data and Computer Software clause of DFARS 252.227-7013, and in subparagraphs (a) through (d) of the Commercial Computer–Restricted Rights clause at FAR 52.227-19, and in similar clauses in the NASA FAR supplement, when applicable.

8. **General.** This Agreement constitutes the entire understanding of the parties and revokes and supersedes all prior agreements, oral or written, between them and may not be modified or amended except in a writing signed by both parties hereto that specifically refers to this Agreement. This Agreement shall take precedence over any other documents that may be in conflict herewith. If any one or more provisions contained in this Agreement are held by any court or tribunal to be invalid, illegal, or otherwise unenforceable, each and every other provision shall remain in full force and effect.

Installation Instructions

For a detailed listing of the wonderful treats and surprises on this CD-ROM, check out the Appendix at the back of this book.

Step 1: Insert the *Windows CE 2 Programming For Dummies* CD-ROM into your computer's CD-ROM drive.

Step 2: Double-click the My Computer icon located on your desktop.

Step 3: Double-click the icon for your CD-ROM drive (usually the D: drive).

Step 4: Double-click the license.txt file to take a look at the end-user license agreement.

Step 5: Double-click the file called readme.txt to read further instructions about the contents of the CD.

You may find it helpful to leave this text file open while you use the CD.

Step 6: Double-click the folder for the demo or sample file that you're interested in.

The About the CD Appendix has descriptions of these programs and detailed instructions on how to access them.

IDG BOOKS WORLDWIDE
BOOK REGISTRATION

Register This Book and Win!

We want to hear from you!

Visit **http://my2cents.dummies.com** to register this book and tell us how you liked it!

- ✔ Get entered in our monthly prize giveaway.

- ✔ Give us feedback about this book — tell us what you like best, what you like least, or maybe what you'd like to ask the author and us to change!

- ✔ Let us know any other ...*For Dummies*® topics that interest you.

Your feedback helps us determine what books to publish, tells us what coverage to add as we revise our books, and lets us know whether we're meeting your needs as a ...*For Dummies* reader. You're our most valuable resource, and what you have to say is important to us!

Not on the Web yet? It's easy to get started with *Dummies 101*®: *The Internet For Windows*® *95* or *The Internet For Dummies*®, 4th Edition, at local retailers everywhere.

Or let us know what you think by sending us a letter at the following address:

...*For Dummies* Book Registration
Dummies Press
7260 Shadeland Station, Suite 100
Indianapolis, IN 46256-3945
Fax 317-596-5498

BUSINESS AND
GENERAL
REFERENCE
BOOK SERIES
FROM IDG

COMPUTER
BOOK SERIES
FROM IDG